Democracy, Aristocracy, Theocracy and the Rule of Law in the New England Colonies, 1620-1686

Democracy, Aristocracy, Theocracy and the Rule of Law in the New England Colonies, 1620–1686

LIEVIN KAMBAMBA MBOMA

NASHVILLE, TN

COPYRIGHT Registration Number TXu 2-336-469

Copyright @ 2022 Lievin Kambamba Mboma. All rights reserved. No part of this book may be reproduced, stored in a retrieval system, or transcribed, in any form or by any means without the prior written permission of the publisher. Lievin K. Mboma Press, P.O. Box, 24424 Nashville, TN 37202.

ISBN: 978-1-7373384-2-0 (hardcover)/ 978-1-7373384-3-7 (paperback)/ 978-1-7373384-4-4 (ebook)

Cover image credit:
The landing of the Pilgrims at Plymouth, Mass. Dec. 22nd 1620
- G4811 U.S. Copyright Office.
- Title from item.
- Caption: The Mayflower left Delft Haven in Holland Sept. 6th 1620, and after a boisterous passage of sixty-three days, anchored within Cape Cod. In her cabin the first Republican government in America was solemnly inaugurated. That vessel thus became truly the "Cradle of Liberty" rocked on the free waves of the ocean.
- Copyright 1876, by Currier & Ives N.Y.
- Copyright stamp on lower left corner.
- Gale, 3705
- Conningham, 2826

Medium
1 print : lithograph ; 22.7 x 32.5 cm (image), 33.3 x 44.5 cm (sheet)

Call Number/Physical Location
PGA - Currier & Ives—Landing of the Pilgrims ... (A size) [P&P]

Repository
Library of Congress Prints and Photographs Division Washington, D.C. 20540 USA http://hdl.loc.gov/loc.pnp/pp.print

Digital ID
pga 09270 //hdl.loc.gov/loc.pnp/pga.09270
cph 3a06959 //hdl.loc.gov/loc.pnp/cph.3a06959

Library of Congress Control Number
2002707741

Reproduction Number
LC-DIG-pga-09270 (digital file from original item) LC-USZ62-3461 (b&w film copy neg.)

Rights Advisory
No known restrictions on publication.

Online Format
Image

LCCN Permalink
https://lccn.loc.gov/2002707741

Contents

	Acknowledgements	ix
	Preface	xi
	Introduction	1
Chapter 1	Forms of Government in Plymouth and the Massachusetts Bay Colony	5

    Democratic Form of Government in the Plymouth Colony

    Representative System

    Advocacy for Better Governance

    Franchise and Rights to Hold Offices

    Master of Families and Servants' Right to Vote

    The Observance of Rule of Law in the Plymouth Colony

    Mixed Forms of Government in the Massachusetts Bay Colony

    Democratic Form of Government under Governor John Endicott

    Democratic Principles in the Massachusetts Bay Colony

    Pacific Resistance against Arbitrary Government Policies in Massachusetts

    Civil Dialogues

    Power of Electors

    Democratic Elections

    Decriminalization of Election Crimes by the Massachusetts Bay Government

    Liberal Approach for the Union of New Hampshire with Massachusetts Bay

    Representative Government in Massachusetts Bay

        The Perceptions of Massachusetts' Officials on the Forms of their Government
        Theocratic Governance in Massachusetts Bay
        Aristocracy in Massachusetts Bay

Chapter 2 Democracy in Rhode Island and Connecticut, and the New Haven Aristocracy   36
        Democracy in Rhode Island
        Democratic Principles in Rhode Island
        Inhabitants' Engagement
        Franchise System
        Election in the Rhode Island Colony
        Consensual System in Rhode Island
        Democratic Form of Government in Connecticut
        Evidence of Democratic Norms and Principles in Connecticut
        The Connecticut Fundamental Orders
        The Clerical Address of Rev. Thomas Hooker
        Principles Advocated by Rev. Thomas Hooker for the Formation of the Government
        Theocracy, Aristocracy and Democracy in New Haven
        Democratic Principles in New Haven

Chapter 3 Mixed Forms of Government in New Hampshire and Maine   60
        Government under Proprietors in New Hampshire
        New Hampshire Settlements under the Massachusetts Bay Government
        The New Hampshire Government under the Royal Province
        Democratic Principles in New Hampshire
        Early Government in Maine
        The First Municipal Government in Maine
        The Government of Thomas Gorges
        Maine under the Administration of Richard Vines
        Western Maine under Edward Godfrey's Governance

Contents vii

          Alexander Rigby and George Cleeves' Governments
          Maine under the Massachusetts Bay Government
          Pemaquid under the New York Government
          Maine under the Royal Government

Chapter 4 Freemen Liberties in the New England Colonies   74
          The Massachusetts Bay Body of Liberties
          Personal Security
          Similar Articles to the Body of Liberties
            in the United States
          Personal Liberties
          Judicial Proceeding Liberties

Chapter 5 Principle of Equality in New England   96
          Equality under Codified Laws in the New England
            Colonies
          Impartiality and Equal Justice in New Hampshire
          Equality and Impartiality Beyond the Judiciary System
          Equality in Business
          Equality in the Establishment of Schools and the
            Treatment of Students
          Equality and Impartiality in Dorchester Schools

Chapter 6 Liberty of Conscience in the
          New England Colonies   115
          Freedom of Worship in Providence
          Protection of Quakers from the United Colonies
            and the Massachusetts Bay Colony
          Religious Freedom in Newport and Portsmouth
          Religious Freedom Granted to the Rhode Island
            Freemen in the 1663 Charter
          Religious Freedom in New Hampshire and Maine

Chapter 7 Town Liberties and Self-Governing
          in the New England Colonies   130
          The Emergence of Self-Government in New England
          The Mayflower Compact

The Massachusetts Bay Company Letters Patent

The Expansion of Self-Government by New England Freemen in New York and New Jersey

Self-Governing under Puritans in New York and New Jersey

Dorchester, Massachusetts Freemen in South Carolina and Georgia

Early Town Orders, Power, and Liberties

Orders for the Regulation of Towns

The Emergence of Municipal Government in New England

Towns' Statutory Powers in the New England Colonies

Chapter 8   Representative Democracy in the New England Colonies   150

Representative System in the Massachusetts Bay Colony

The Impact of Deputies on the General Court of Massachusetts Bay

Introduction of the Representative System in the Plymouth Colony

Representative System in Connecticut and New Haven

The Development of a Representative System in Rhode Island

Representative System in New Hampshire under the Royal Province

Chapter 9   Summary and Conclusion   170

Endnotes   173

Bibliography   203

Index   211

Acknowledgments

From the first draft of this book to the completion of it, I received support and guidance from Dr. John Vile, Dean of the Honors School at Middle Tennessee State University. He proofread and edited the first draft. With his expertise on the topic, he was able to point out the areas that needed improvement. I would like to thank Motlow State Community College instructors William Parker and Samuel Short for editing the final draft of this manuscript. Dr. Raymond Kinzounza, Nashville Public Library Manager, also deserves credit for editing this book. I further credit the Editor in Chief of Elevated Editing Services, Dr. Amani Ani, for proofreading the final draft of this book manuscript. Among the reviewers, I credit Dan Hinchen, a reference librarian at the Massachusetts Historical Society. In like manner, I acknowledge the input of Tom Hardiman, Keeper and Executive Director of the Portsmouth Athenaeum for his review of this book. Moreover, I acknowledge Nicole Luongo Cloutier, Supervisor of Reference Services at the Portsmouth Public Library for her recommendation of my reviewer. She advised me to select Hardiman due to his intensive knowledge on the subject under analysis. Additionally, I credit Rachel Hinson for also proofreading this book. She completed excellent work, and her contributions are also worth noting. I also acknowledge Charles M. May, Librarian of the Learning Resource center at Nashville State Community College, for proofreading a draft of the book manuscript. Finally, I am indebted to Keata Brewer of E.T. Lowe Publishing Company for typesetting this book.

Preface

Scholars and historians in the United States and England have devoted considerable attention to the history of the New England Colonies. Moreover, in the region under examination, local historians have examined the organization of town governments and town meetings. Yet, the emergence of democratic and mixed governments are less explored. There are also limited studies on the observance of rule of law in the New England Colonies. For these reasons, I decided to investigate the emergence and implementation of both democratic principles and rule of law in this region. Furthermore, I examined the forms of government instituted in the New England Colonies. For a better understanding of the forms of government in the New England Colonies, I asked a several questions.

For instance, did the founders of the New England Colonies establish authoritarian, oligarchic, democratic, monarchic, aristocratic, or theocratic governments? The answer to this question will help us understand which form of government each colony established for the governing of their freemen. The term freemen in the New England Colonies had a special importance. Each colony had its own procedural laws regarding the admissions of a person to the status of "free." In Plymouth, the signers of the Mayflower Compact were freemen. In Massachusetts, honest and good men admitted to some churches within the limits of that colony were deemed freemen. In Connecticut and Rhode Island, freemen in each town had the power to admit new residents as freemen. Similarly, in New Hampshire and Maine, this status was also obtained in accordance with the orders made by the freemen of each town.

Other important questions can be raised about the New England Colonies. Did residents observe the rule of law? Was there a colony where government officials instituted a mixed form of government? If so, in a mixed form of government, did the officials observe the rule of law? Furthermore, was there a colony where officials instituted a pure form of democratic government? The answers to these questions will be based on critical analysis of the literature from the region under study.

Regarding the implementation of rule of law in the New England Colonies, a multitude of books cover the enactments and codifications of laws for the better governing of the colonies. In Massachusetts, *The Charters and the Laws of the Colony and Province of Massachusetts Bay in New England* contains important data covering laws of this colony. This document has authoritative data on the laws of the Massachusetts Bay colony. It is an important document for scholars and historians who are interested in the laws and legal history of Massachusetts Bay. During my research, I consulted this document various times. In addition to *The Charters and the Laws of the Colony and Province of Massachusetts Bay*, I used *The Compact, Charter and Laws of the Colony of New Plymouth* for the same purpose. Moreover, the work of Governor John Winthrop, the *History of New England*, received the same attention as the previously mentioned documents.

The book of Governor Winthrop is an important piece of work for scholars and historians interested in New England history. Governor Winthrop is one of the architects of the government of the Massachusetts Bay colony. As a governor, he was one of the framers of laws and policy makers. In addition to Governor Winthrop, various authors focused on the laws of the New England Colonies. Emory Washburn is among them. In his book, *Sketches of the Judicial History of Massachusetts from 1630 to the Revolution in 1775*, he recorded salient information on that topic. As a result, I consulted his book with keen attention. Like the work of Washburn, the book of William H. Whitmore, *A Bibliographical Sketch of the Laws of the Massachusetts Bay Colony from 1630 to 1686*, gathered important laws of the colony of Massachusetts Bay. In his book, he discussed the Body of Liberties of the Massachusetts Bay colony. Finally, Francis C. Gray's book, *Remarks on the Early Laws of Massachusetts Bay*, also included records on the Massachusetts Body of Liberties which was composed of 100 laws. From this book, I collected laws covering the liberties of the freemen in Massachusetts Bay.

In the colonies under investigation, government officials had a culture of recording laws, judicial proceedings, and the organizations of their government. In Connecticut, Rhode Island, New Haven, and Plymouth such records contain various data on the laws, the people, and the government of the period under examination. Even though these documents exist, the implementation of rule of law in the New England Colonies is less examined. Evidence from public records and legal documents indicate the observance of rule of law by the freemen and government officials. Furthermore, government officials enforced laws for the control officers, judiciary, and elected officials in each colony. It appears that local and colonial officials had the same liberties and legal privileges as other inhabitants and foreigners.

In this work, I recorded various biographical data on the architects of rule of law and democratic principals in the New England Colonies. The rule of law instituted in the colonies was based on the colonists' religious beliefs as well as the environments where they resided. In this region, religious leaders had the power to regulate freemen and servants' behaviors. Religion and laws were inseparable. Religious authorities such as Rev. Nathaniel Ward of Ipswich composed the laws of the Massachusetts Body of Liberties with the assistance of government officials and freemen. In addition to the founders' belief in rule of law, the inhabitants of these colonies were advocates of personal liberties, personal security, right to own property, and equality before the law. They thought that these principles were inviolable and valued them as did their brethren in England.

Introduction

Studies on the rule of law and the forms of government in the New England Colonies are limited. From the various books that I consulted, I discovered that scholars were prone to discuss the development of laws in the New England Colonies but put less emphasis on the enforcement of the rule of law. In addition to the laws, historians have studied the incorporation of religion into the judiciary system. Public records of the New England Colonies contain pertinent data on the administration of justice and the forms of government instituted by the founders of the colonies. In books authored by early historians, local and international, the forms of government implemented in each colony are described.

For example, Charles Borgeaud, a German scholar, examined the forms of government which the founders of Connecticut, Massachusetts, and Rhode Island established in their respective colonies. In his book, *The Rise of Modern Democracy in Old and New England*, he revealed the existence of the democratic principles in the New England Colonies. In the same book, he also mentioned the founders' advocacy for theocratic and aristocratic principles in Massachusetts. Professor Borgeaud noted authoritatively that democratic principles and norms incorporated in political institutions in the colonies began in England before their arrival in North America. Contrary to Borgeaud's study, however, John Fiske wrote of the theocratic system of government in New England. In his book, *The Beginnings of New England* or the *Puritan Theocracy in Its Relations to Civil and Religious Liberty*, Fiske documents the forms of government and relationship between law and religion in the New England Colonies.

Still, in addition to theocratic principles, Fiske also documented the existence of democratic principles in colonies such as Connecticut and

Rhode Island. Furthermore, while he discussed the forms of government in the New England Colonies, he did not incorporate the principles of rule of law in his work. Consequently, it is ambiguous to discuss democratic norms without recourse to the rule of law. Democratic principles and rule of law are inseparable. This book accordingly examines both principles and rule with the same magnitude and interests.

In the same spirit as Fiske, H.F. Uhden in his book, *The New England Theocracy: A History of the Congregationalists in New England to the Revivals of 1740*, discussed theocratic principles in the New England Colonies. He focused on the historical development of theocratic norms and principles in the Massachusetts Bay Colony. He stressed the political culture of the leaders of the Massachusetts Bay Colony and pointed out democratic principles such as freedom of liberty advocated by Roger Williams in Rhode Island. He also credited the founders of the colony of Connecticut for their adoption of a democratic constitution.

Like the previously mentioned authors, Alexander Johnston authored an important book on the emergence of democratic norms and principles in Connecticut. In his book, *Connecticut: A Study of a Commonwealth-Democracy*, Johnston detailed with passion the advocacy and implementation of a modern democratic system of government in Connecticut. His book gives us a clear look at the political culture of Connecticut's founders. However, Johnston, like Fiske, failed to incorporate the rule of law in his study. Specifically, he did not explore Connecticut's liberties for freemen. He also omitted discussion of the established laws for the enforcement of democratic principles. Contrary to his work, the present study connects democratic, theocratic, and aristocratic principles with the rule of law within the same sphere of existence.

I also consulted Alan F. Hattersley's *A Short History of Democracy*. Hattersley mentioned the development of democratic principles and norms in Plymouth. He also stressed the existence of mixed forms of government in Massachusetts Bay. Nahum Capen in his book, *The History of Democracy; Or, Political Progress, Historically Illustrated from the Earliest to the Latest Periods: With Portraits of Distinguished Men, Vol. 1*, documents the emergence of a democratic form of government in Rhode Island. Similarly, in the *Records of the Colony of Rhode Island and*

Providence Plantations in New England, 1636 to 1663, the editor recorded data on democratic principles in town governments.

Regarding the principles of rule of law in Massachusetts, I consulted the books written by William H. Whitmore, William Chauncey Fowler, Emory Washburn, and Francis C. Gray. Whitmore and Gray's books contain laws from the Massachusetts Body of Liberties. From these documents, I was able to collect laws and orders that covered the rule of law and the liberties of the inhabitants of the colony. I also incorporated the work of English legal writers such as Sir Edward Coke, Chief Justice of England, and that of Sir William Blackstone. These English legal scholars recorded data on English liberties. Additionally, they gave convincing interpretations and analyses of the charters of English liberties. Both analyzed, for example, the articles of the Magna Carta and gave clear explanation of the true intent of those articles.

As the Massachusetts Body of Liberties had the same legal language as the Magna Carta, these works served as reference books in this research. In addition to the work of Sirs Coke and Blackstone, the book of Sir Matthew Hale, *The History of the Common Law of England*, was also one of the reference books used for this study. Furthermore, the work of Henry Care, *English Liberties; Or, the Free-Born Subject's Inheritance, Containing 1. Magna Carta, The petition of Right, the Habeas Corpus Act, and Divers other Most Useful Statutes: With Large Comments Upon Each of Them*, served as a reference book in this study. Likewise, the work of Sir John Fortescue, *The Governance of England*, offered documentation on the forms of government in England and France. From his book, I discovered that the founders of Massachusetts Bay instituted a mixed government as that of England. Moreover, the book of E.S. Creasy, *The Textbook of the Constitution: Magna Carta, the Petition of Right and the Bill of Rights*, served the same purpose.

The Constitution of the United States and the constitutions of the States of Massachusetts, Connecticut, Rhode Island, New Hampshire, Maine, and Vermont were also reference documents in this study. The U.S. Constitution has limited articles akin to the Massachusetts Body of Liberties, Magna Carta, Connecticut Code of 1650, and Rhode Island Code of 1647. As such, these documents were indivisible. Therefore, their use was imperative in this examination. These documents had factual data on freemen liberties in England and the colonies. Like the constitutions of the states noted above, the charters granted to the Rhode Island freemen and those of Connecticut by King Charles II emphasized the same liberties as those discussed in the U.S. Constitution and the Massachusetts Body of Liberties.

With the assistance of the previously noted documents and my academic knowledge in criminal justice, I was able to create this book examining the forms of government in the colonies, the presence of English liberties in the New England Colonies, and the implementations of rule of law, religious liberties, town liberties, and representative systems.

Chapter 1

Forms of Goverment in Plymouth and the Massachusetts Bay Colony

The form of government advocated by the founding fathers of the Plymouth and Massachusetts Bay colonies is of interest to various legal and political science scholars. Data from various historical documents indicate that the colonies did not have the same forms of government. In his book, *The Pilgrims in their Three Homes England, Holland, America*, William Elliot Griffis noted that Pilgrims in Plymouth founded their government with democratic principles. Like Griffis, Charles Borgeaud recorded the same information on the Plymouth government. Borgeaud, the author of *The Rise of Modern Democracy in Old and New England*, authoritatively detailed the democratic principles in the Plymouth colony. On the other hand, he articulated that Massachusetts Bay officials governed their colony through a mixed form of government. Like the authors noted above, George Bancroft, an American historian, wrote about forms of government in the New England colonies, and in his address delivered to the participants in Springfield and young men of Connecticut said that New England inhabitants had democratic principles which they brought from England. He also stressed that the New England towns were democratic.

In his address in both orations, he elucidated the relationship between democratic principles and rule of law. He described democracy as eternal justice, ruled through the people, being characterized by equal laws for the general good, and the rejection of monopolies. He went on to articulate that in a democratic nation, judges plead cases through the existing laws, but not laws made by themselves. Moreover, he noted that judges do not have the power to alter the criminal code. He documented the power of the jury system in a nation governed through democratic principles and norms.¹ In the same address in Springfield, Bancroft admitted that "the principles of democracy were brought to our shores by the breezes that wafted the Mayflower across the Atlantic."² From his work, I conclude that the Plymouth Colony was a democratic one. Democratic principles enumerated in Bancroft's orations were the same as those observed by the freemen in Plymouth. Like Bancroft, Oliver Gray Hall, the author of the *Mayflower Democracy* asserted that the Pilgrims in Plymouth established a pure democracy where people governed themselves. He went on to stress that Plymouth Pilgrims deserve credit for being the architects of the fundamental principles of a true democracy.³

Like the authors previously mentioned, Paul E. Lauer, in his book *Church and State in New England*, examined the form of government established in the New England Colonies and concluded that the colony of New Plymouth was democratic. In 1901, Viola A. Conklin, in his book *American Political History to the Death of Lincoln Popularly Told*, draws a correlation between theocratic and democratic forms of governments in the New England Colonies. H.F. Uhden also recorded important information on theocracy in the New England Colonies. While examining theocratic principles in the colonies, Uhden did tackle democratic principles advocated by the colonists in Massachusetts, Connecticut, and Rhode Island.

In New England, devoted religious leaders and the founders of Plymouth and Massachusetts Bay colonies advocated civil liberties according to their convictions and perceptions. As a result, each colony formed a government based on their religious beliefs. In the case of Plymouth, the founders were separatists who rejected the methods of the Church of England's sermonizing. On the other hand, those of the Massachusetts colony were of the same views with the Church of England in various facets, though they rejected the corrupt and abusive methods observed by religious ministers in England. Those two entities did not have the same vision on the administration of the affairs of government. Another point of difference was the framework of their governments. The founders of Plymouth colony envisioned a government with features of religious freedom, while the originators of Massachusetts Bay were more capitalistic and resolved to restrict religious liberties. Moreover, the Massachusetts Bay government was formed in accordance with the charter which they received from the crown of England. On March 4, 1629, the crown granted them a charter of civil constitution with mercantile and territorial privileges.[4] Resultantly, they established a government with mixed features. On the other hand, the Plymouth colonists formed a simple government with democratic norms.

Democratic Form of Government in the Plymouth Colony

Based on the accounts of various authors and historians, the government of Plymouth was democratic. From a multitude of documents, I discovered that freemen in this colony were participants in the management of the colony, not mere observers. In the earliest years of the colony, the whole body of freemen were lawmakers. They assembled in town meetings where they enacted and repealed laws. The freemen further enacted equal laws for common good. They held annual elections for the selection of officials for their government. Furthermore, the freemen believed in the notion of rule of law. Thus, in 1623, Pilgrims introduced trial by jury. That year, "the court held that all criminal facts, and also all matters of trespasses and debts between man and man should be tried by the verdict of twelve honest men to be impaneled by authority in form of a jury upon their oath."[5]

Regarding the official government, there is a consensus among authors that democratic principles existed in the Plymouth colony. Notably, Bancroft writes that a form of democratic government emerged in New England with the arrival of the Pilgrims in the colony of Plymouth.[6] He went on to point out that the compact made by the Pilgrims aboard the Mayflower gave birth to popular constitutional liberty. In his view, the Pilgrims put forth their right in the cabin of the Mayflower and instituted a government with equal laws for the general good.[7] His analysis was based on the language of the Mayflower Compact, signed by the Pilgrims in 1620. In the same vein, Griffis recorded that the compact made by the Pilgrims advocated democratic principles. He wrote that "the compact of the people, for the people, and by the people was expressed in a truly democratic document and furnished the basis of one of the best governments that could be advised."[8] He further stated that the "Pilgrim republic was a true prototype of the United States of America, cosmopolitan tolerant, Christian. Pilgrims made no form of words to bind the conscience."[9] Griffis' perception and view on the Pilgrim's democracy is the same as the previously named authors: Plymouth's democratic principles are parallel to the United States government.

Regarding the notion of tolerance, the case of Roger Williams is proof of its observance in Plymouth. When Williams was under the pressure of the Puritan clerics in Massachusetts Bay, he took refuge in the Plymouth Colony. The inhabitants and officials were tolerant toward his beliefs. In this colony, they welcomed him as one of their religious members. They did not discriminate against him. Upon his arrival, Governor Bradford in his book, *History of Plymouth Plantation*, stated that,

> Roger Williams, a man godly and zealous, having many precious parts, but very unsettled in judgement, came over first to the Massachusetts but upon the same discontent left the place, and came hither (where he was friendly entertained, according to their poor ability) and exercised his gifts among them and after time was admitted a member of the church; and his teaching well approved, for the benefit where of I still bless God. And a thankful to him, even for his sharpest admonitions and reproofs, so far as they agreed with truth. He this year before to fall into some strong opinion to practice, which caused some controversy between the church and him, and in the end some discontent on his part, by occasion on whereof he left them. I shall leave the matter, and desire the Lord to show him his errors, and reduce him into the way of truth, and give him a settled judgement and constancy in the same; for I hope he belongs to the Lord, and he will show him mercy.[10]

Governor Bradford's remarks reveal the depth of the Pilgrims' tolerance. From this quote there is an argument to be made for drawing a correlation between the Pilgrim's tolerance and that of the United States at large. In the United States, tolerance is the foundation of the government. This is the pillar of a democratic form of government. Without tolerance, injustice and violence would infect the notion of the rule of law. With respect to tolerance, it is logical to discern that the foundation of the principle emerged in the Plymouth colony of New England. This principle was indubitably part of the Pilgrims' culture. They either internalized this principle while in exile in Holland or it was part of their religious beliefs.

Paul E. Lauer, in his book *Church and State in New England*, argued that the Pilgrims mastered the notion of tolerance in Holland. While there, they learned to value the conscience of those who did not belong to their religious creed.[11] As such, they brought this culture with them to Plymouth. According to Lauer, "a liberal, charitable policy toward those of other beliefs always prevailed at Plymouth."[12] Even though Plymouth government officials maintained a policy of tolerance, there are data on the mistreatments of Quakers in the colony for their religion. It is unknown whether the colonists in Plymouth acted in this manner to please their brethren in Massachusetts Bay, where religious intolerance was prevalent. For instance, and it is important to note that, in 1643, the colonies of Massachusetts, Plymouth, Connecticut, and New Haven formed a confederation, which they termed the "United Colonies." In this confederation, colonists supported each other in matters of internal and external security. Quakers then received the same treatments in Connecticut as they did in Plymouth.

In addition to the principle of tolerance, the colonists in Plymouth governed their affairs through consensus. The colonists were not under any obligations to foreign nations regarding the management of their affairs and there is no evidence indicating the imposition of laws on them. Instead, they agreed that "law shall be made or imposed by consent according to the free liberties of the state and kingdom of England and not otherwise."[13] The language of this act was customary, for as the Pilgrims in Plymouth, the English kings did not recognize any foreign authority as his superior or impose laws from them. It is certain that English subjects, wherever they founded a colony, would follow the same political culture as their king. They did not introduce foreign legal systems in their domains. This is the case with the United States of America, where no foreign power is superior to them or can impose laws on them. The U.S. only obeys laws made by the consent of its citizens through Congress. In addition to the rejection of foreign laws, in the Kingdom of England, John Fortescue wrote:

> The king can not by himself, or his ministry, lay taxes, subsidies, or any imposition, of what kind soever upon his subject; he can not alter the laws, or make new one, without the express consent of the whole kingdom in parliament assembled.[14]

I discovered the same law in the contemporary state of Massachusetts. In this state, Article XXIII of the Constitution declared that "no subsidy, charge, tax, impost, or duties, ought to be established, fixed, laid, or levied, under any pretext whatsoever, without the consent of the people, or their representatives in the legislature."[15]

In the Plymouth colony, Pilgrims obeyed laws freely without intimidations. Each one observed the laws enacted for the welfare of the colony in accordance with the Mayflower Compact. According to historians, the Compact was the first document that described the duties of government officials and their limitation of power, and the duties of freemen to their government. From 1620 to 1632, the Plymouth colony organized a patriarchal government, and there is no evidence indicating that a formal government existed before this period.

As early as 1632, freemen had legal power to make laws for the management of the colony. That year, Pilgrims made acts for the elaboration of laws for the colony. Namely, the Act of 1632 prohibited the enactment of laws in the colony without the consent of the freemen. The same act stipulated that no power should make laws for them or impose laws onto them.[16] The Pilgrims were English citizens even though their religious views were different from those of the Church of England. Politically, they had the same legal culture as that of England.

The design of a democratic government in Plymouth was consented to by the Pilgrims on the Mayflower in 1620. Their compact indicates that the Pilgrims planned to form a government based on the will of the people. In the Mayflower Compact, the Pilgrims inserted language that revealed their desire to establish a colony based on the rule of law. In the same context, they established a judiciary system with features that protected individual, property, and institutional rights, establishing laws for the protections of the same. Furthermore, they established a representative system through the election process. Thus, as early as 1632, they prescribed by law the duties of the governor, deputy governor, and local officials. In the *Compact and Charter of the Laws of the Plymouth Colony*, I further discovered that freemen consented to the punishment of elected officials who refused to serve in the government after a free election. In the same year, Plymouth became the seat of the government with the consent of the freemen.

By involving freemen in decision-making, the colony observed democratic principles. When the freemen made Plymouth the seat of the government, no single person objected to that plan. As the principles of tolerance and inclusion of the freemen in the management of government held true, the principle of equality received equal value. The Act that settled the seat of the government reads as follows: "It was by full consent agreed upon and enacted that the chief government be tied to the town of Plymouth, and that the Governor for time being be tied there to keep his residence and dwelling. And there also to hold such courts as concern the whole."[17] The agreement made by the Plymouth freemen for the settling of the seat of the government was purely democratic. Their full consent is a strong indication of the establishment of a democratic government in Plymouth.

Representative system

Regarding the legislature, Lauer wrote that the entire body of freemen participated.[18] In 1638, a representative government in Plymouth emerged. That year, the General Court ordered the election of four representatives from New Plymouth and two from each of the towns to represent the freemen in the Court. Deputies or representatives of the freemen had the power of enacting, repealing, and revising laws.[19] The emergence of a representative system indicates the existence of a democratic form of government. In this colony, freemen had the power to choose their own town representative to represent them in the General Court.

Advocacy for Better Governance

The Pilgrims formed a body politic for the welfare of their association. For the maintenance of this government, the founders of the colony advocated for better governance and preservation. In addition to better governance, government authorities consented to the establishment of just and equal laws for the observance of laws and improved administration, including the protections of rights and the institutionalization of impartial judiciary systems.[20] The signers of the Mayflower Compact had aimed for the protections of liberties, rule of law, religious liberties, and tolerance. For instance, the covenant signed in the Mayflower at Cape Cod reads as follows:

> Having undertaken for the glory of God, and advancement of the Christian faith, and the honor of our king and country, a voyage to plan the first colony in the Northern parts of Virginia; do by these present solemnly and mutually, in the presence of God and one another, Covenant and combine ourselves together into a civil body politick, for our better ordering and preservation, and furtherance of the ends aforesaid: And by virtue hereof, do enact, constitute and frame such just and equal laws, ordinances, acts, constitutions, and officers, from time to time, as shall be though most meet and convenient for the general good of the colony; into which one promise all due submission and hereunto subscribed our names, at Cape Cod, the eleventh of November, in the reign of our Sovereign Lord, King James, of France and Ireland, the Eighteenth, and of Scotland the Fifty-fourth, Anno. Dom. 1620.[21]

The submission to colonial laws was a crucial factor for the preservation of law and order in Plymouth. In a society where citizens do not submit to the laws framed for the better governing therein, it is more likely that the entire territory becomes lawless. When citizens obey laws, peace and order prevail. Regarding the Pilgrims, it is certain that the signers of the Mayflower Compact desired that each freeman abide by the established laws and believe in them. In this case, freemen accepted the judiciary system of the colony. In like manner, they supported colonial institutions.

Franchise and Right to Hold Offices

Another piece of convincing evidence for the existence of democratic principles in Plymouth is the franchise system. In Plymouth, government officials did not limit enfranchisement to religious members only. Religious affiliation was neither a prerequisite for the admission to the status of freemen. Though a religious test was not a requirement, freemen took an oath of fidelity to the government and the institutions in the colony, and in 1632, the government ordered a penalty for freemen who refused to serve in the government. A fine for failure to serve as governor, for instance, was twenty pounds. Those who refused to serve as a counsellor after elections paid a fine of ten pounds. There were exceptions for officials who served a year in a previous term, however.[22] Such laws indicate that freemen in Plymouth valued the voice of the electors. Furthermore, the law of 1636 imposed a three shilling fine for election delinquency. This act reveals that the participation of every freeman in the election process was valued. As they did in towns, democratic principles emerged in the newly founded plantations.

Master of Families and Servants' Right to Vote

Regarding the franchise system, every freeman had the right to vote and serve in office. In general, every freeman was franchised. According to the *Massachusetts Law Quarterly*, servants and foreigners inhabiting Plymouth voted for deputies in accordance with the act of the general court. At the local level, settlers who were not freemen did not hold the position of selectmen, except being jurors, constables, and more likely other minor officers.[23] In the Scituate village of Plymouth, members of the servant class had the same voting privileges as the freemen. In 1638, the colony permitted servants and foreigners to participate in Scituate town affairs. The same year, large numbers of Englishmen in Scituate were not freemen. With such demography, it was justifiable for them to engage in the management of their town, including voting. Further, from the work of Samuel Deane, data indicates that the founders of Scituate were of different religious and cultural backgrounds. The *History of Scituate, Massachusetts* showed that the merchant adventurers of London, the Men of Kent, and followers of Rev. John Lothrop of Boston inhabited the town of Scituate.[24] Notably, Rev. Lothrop served as a pastor in London, England.

The Observance of Rule of Law in Plymouth Colony

As noted by the aforementioned principles, the Pilgrims cemented the system of the rule of law in the Plymouth colony. From *The Compact with Charter and Laws of the Colony of New Plymouth*, I discovered the components of the criminal justice system instituted by the freemen such as court, police, and correctional institutions. In Plymouth, the constable had police power and maintained law and order. For better administration of justice, elected magistrates held court and judged cases brought before them. On December 17, 1623, twelve honest men selected by authority in the form of a jury after taking an oath tried all criminal and civil cases.[25] This was the emergence of the jury system in the Plymouth colony. In addition to jury trials, government officials punished offenders who violated laws. Judiciary officers tried cases in accordance with the established laws.

Mixed Forms of Government in the Massachusetts Bay Colony

Historically, Massachusetts Bay was under a mixed form of government as the founders of this colony did not have the same political and religious visions. Among them, I found religious ministers, traders, lawyers, and adventurers. According to John Barry, the founders of Massachusetts Bay were nevertheless experienced leaders and skillful diplomats.[26] Regarding the organization of government, for example, the elections of the Massachusetts Bay Company officials were in England, where it developed. According to historical data, the elections of the company's officials happened in London. Such election of the governor and of assistants represent the observance of democratic norms, and the transfer of the company's charter also democratic. A majority of the company's leaders approved its transfer to the colony.

During the period under investigation, data indicate freemen founded settlements, plantations, and towns in the colony of Massachusetts with full consent from each member of the organization. As early as 1632, there were eight towns in Massachusetts Bay. As a result, the increase in population and towns impacted the policy of government as well as the formation of it. Freemen engaged in the affairs of the colony at that time. Data also shows that colonial officials included freemen in the assessment of taxes.

Moreover, each individual governor played a role in the formation of policy during the development of the government. In this colony, Governor John Winthrop's policy regarding form of government was different from that of Governors Thomas Dudley, John Haynes, Henry Vane, and Richard Bellingham. According to information from various sources, Winthrop favored an aristocratic form of government, and he espoused liberal policies during his administration.[27] In 1635, during a reconciliation meeting held in Boston between Governors Winthrop and Dudley, Governor John Haynes stated that Winthrop was remiss in point of justice. In answer to this criticism, Winthrop responded to Haynes and ministers that,

> In the infancy of plantations, justice should be administered with more lenity than in a settled state, because people were then more apt to transgress, partly of ignorance of new laws and orders, partly through oppression of business and other straits; but if it might be made clear to him, that it was an errour, he would be ready to take up a stricter course.[28]

At the conclusion of the meeting, ministers determined that "strict discipline both in criminal offences and in martial affairs, was more needful in plantations than in a settled state, as tending to the honour and safety of the gospel."[29] Governor Winthrop's response to the participants in the meeting indicates that he cherished a liberal approach in dealing with the inhabitants of the Bay colony during his terms as governor.

Contrary to Winthrop, Governor Dudley was strict in his policy. He believed in the principle of the rule of law and democracy. From his own statements, I conclude that he believed in freedom of expression and thought. He was against the abuse of power by any government officials. For instance, he held Governor Winthrop accountable for his abuse of power when he moved the capital of the colony from Cambridge to Boston at will without the consent of the company's members.[30] In addition to his resistance to abuses of power, during his administration as governor, and with the consent of the freemen, Dudley ordered the emergence of a representative form of government. In 1634, under his administration, the entire body of freemen were present at the court of election for the selections of their officials.[31] From his own statement, I can speculate that Governor Dudley championed the principle of free speech. Furthermore, in 1632, when he threatened to resign from his deputyship, one of his reasons was to keep public peace and the advocacy of free speech and conscience.[32] During his administration in 1634, the inhabitants of Boston excluded the principal men during the election of a seven-man body for the division of land. It is certain that the Boston freemen acted freely based on their own conscience.[33] Further noteworthy, the exclusion of the Boston principal men through election did not displease former Governor John Winthrop. He accepted the result of the election while Rev. John Cotton objected to it.[34]

Data shows that Governor John Haynes exempted freemen from paying taxes for one year following his election in 1635. He believed that former administrations pressed freemen with charges, harshly affecting poor people. Furthermore, deputies were free to oppose judiciary proceedings administered by the magistrates. As a result, they declared openly that the procedural law under the magistrates was a danger for the colony. The magistrates, it was further declared, administered justice according to their discretion because the colony did not have positive laws. Due to their complaints, the General Court ordered the selection of fit officials to frame a body of the ground laws resembling the Magna Carta.[35] Thus, there is reason to believe that Governor Haynes believed in democratic principles. The invocation of the Magna Carta by deputies as a reference for better laws is palpable proof that they advocated the same liberties as their brethren in England.

In 1636, under the governorship of Henry Vane, democratic principles such as individual rights, freedom of religion, and human rights prevailed. In fact, during his administration, Governor Vane observed tolerance toward believers and ministers of different religious persuasions. This was the case of Anne Hutchinson, John Wheelwright, and others. In addition to his contributions in the colony, Governor Vane, while a member of Parliament in England, helped to create a liberal charter for the Rhode Island freemen in 1643, and for those in Connecticut in 1662. Finally, like Governor Vane, Richard Bellingham contributed to the rule of law in the colonies when in 1641, the deputies and freemen under his governorship codified 100 laws which they called Body of Liberties. As a magistrate, deputy governor, and governor, Bellingham contributed enormously to the framing, revising, and repealing of colonial laws. He was a member of the committee charged with the revision of laws for many years. Thus, did data from the work of Francis C. Gray, author of *Remarks on the Early Laws of Massachusetts Bay*, posit that in 1635, Richard Bellingham was among the officials deputed with the framing of drafting laws for the colony. Governors John Haynes, John Winthrop, and Thomas Dudley were such delegated alongside Bellingham, whose framing responsibilities continued in 1636.[36]

In addition to the governors, assistants had an impact in the forming of the Massachusetts Bay government. The governor, deputy governor, and assistants formed a court which they named the Court of Assistants. In the early years of the colony, this court had executive, legislative, and judicial power. Magistrates or assistants were also members of the General Court. They had the power to make laws, appoint officers, and revoke them. Regarding the form of government, it is plausible that the assistants agreed on the introduction of theocratic principles. Consider, for instance, that a former Massachusetts Governor and historian, Thomas Hutchinson, wrote that the Massachusetts Bay Company organized its government in 1630, and at the first Court of Assistants on August 23rd of that year was appointed a beadle, or ceremonial officer, and decided the power of the governor, deputy governor, and assistants. The assistants also limited the power of the governor and deputy governor.

According to an order convened on this date, the governor and deputy governor had the power of the justices of the peace, like those of England. The four assistants present at the court had the same power as the governor and deputy governor. They had also the power to punish criminals.[37] Furthermore, in May 1631, the governor, deputy governor, and ministers enacted an order for the admission of freemen in the body politic with their support. The order of 1631 declared that "no man shall be admitted to the freedom of this commonwealth, but such as are members of some of the churches within the limits of this jurisdiction."[38] Franchised freemen had the right to hold offices such as governor, deputy governor, secretary, representative, assistant, selectmen, constable, and more. This was the first time that a theocratic government had legal acceptance in Massachusetts Bay.

Furthermore, religious leaders such as Rev. John Cotton had an influence on the policy of the government. This minister championed the aristocratic form of government for the colony. On the other hand, ministers such as Nathaniel Ward, Thomas Hooker, and Roger Williams were advocates of a democratic form of government. These ministers were against the aristocratic, theocratic, *and* oligarchical forms of government. Among the named ministers, Williams was the most outspoken against both the church and civil governments. He opposed injustice, the interference of government officials in matters of religion, and abuses of power by government officials. Along with the aforementioned ministers, freemen revolted against the interference of government officials in matters of religion. Further, Rev. John Wheelwright was among the ministers who worked against the aristocratic church government in the Bay, though Rev. Cotton had more influence on the colony's religious and governmental policies.[39]

Like the facts mentioned above, the political spirits of the freemen shaped the policy of the officials. In Massachusetts, the advocates of democratic principles had revolutionary spirits. They insisted upon all having the same liberties as Englishmen. As a result, they had to struggle to maintain the same. The insistence of those rights began early. In the Massachusetts Bay colony, freemen revolted against the aristocratic and oligarchic forms of government more than expected. Though they did not have fame, money, or power, they were unafraid to confront the policies of ministers and government officials who favored arbitrary methods of governing.

The perceptions and visions of the freemen regarding their liberties had significant impacts on the policies and regulations of the government. Freemen were of strong political and religious spirits. They advocated democratic principles as well as religious liberties. In towns such as Boston, Salem, and Marblehead, freemen were antagonistic toward aristocracy. For example, the inhabitants of Marblehead disobeyed the laws of the Puritans in Massachusetts. In this settlement, settlers were not believers of Puritanism. In fact, Samuel Roads, Jr. wrote that the inhabitants of Marblehead were far from being a religious people. As such, they did not have freemen in this settlement. In accordance with the laws of the colony, colonial officials disenfranchised them from the election process. In like manner, they excluded them from the government and as a result, this settlement did not have a local government.[40]

Like the Marblehead inhabitants, the freemen in Watertown were against unjust levying of taxes in the colony. They believed that the government did not have the power to collect taxes. Surely after this revolt, the General Court in Massachusetts entrusted the freemen and colonial officials with the levying of taxes. Consequently, it is sound to note that democratic principles in the colony of Massachusetts Bay resulted from the struggle of the freemen and the growth of democratic principles was progressive.

Historically, the colony was a corporate body assigned to a certain number of people. Stockholders of the Massachusetts Bay colony formed this body in accordance with the charter granted to them by the crown of England. We must ask ourselves, was this document permanently observed? And further, were the officials of Massachusetts Bay consistent in their observance of the charter? The responses to these questions should be based on an analysis of the forms of government instituted in the colony. Data indicates that the founders of the Massachusetts Bay Company were wealthy English nobles and religious ministers. Additionally, in the *Records of the Company of the Massachusetts Bay in New England*, the Massachusetts Bay Company was a private government.[41]

According to New England historians as well as leaders who served in the colony, it had mixed forms of government—democratic, theocratic, and aristocratic. The founders of Massachusetts Bay governed freemen with the principles of those in England until the reign of King Charles II. The supports of each form of government in the colony consisted of ministers, assistants, or freemen. However, the majority of the freemen advocated the democratic form of government. It was a minority of leaders who advocated for the theocracy and aristocracy in the Massachusetts Bay colony. In their native country, the government was both democratic and aristocratic. To wit, from the work of John Fortescue, I discovered that England was a mix of republican government and regal or absolute.[42] According to Fortescue, England was a constitutional monarchy. The power of the representatives came from the people. Contrary to this system, in a regal or absolute form of government, the king is the lawmaker and enforcer. He appoints agents to enforce the same and imposes his laws without the people's consent.

Democratic Form of Government under Governor John Endicott

In 1629, the Massachusetts Bay Company in New England under Governor John Endicott observed a democratic form of government. Here, Governor Endicott received the instructions on how to form his government applying democratic principles. The Company's officials in England also ordered him to be inclusive in his government. For instance, from the letter which company officials sent to him came strong advice to include the old planters in his government. Additionally, officials ordered him to be impartial in his administration of justice. The inclusion of freemen in government was not based on religion or other rules in the letter. Therefore, it appears in this example, under Governor Endicott, that the planters agreed on the Massachusetts Bay form of the government for the management of company affairs.

Data in historical records reveal the existence of free elections in the selection of Salem town officers. As in Salem, Charlestown planters consented to plantation building sites. In Charlestown and other towns in Massachusetts Bay, free elections were common. Each town elected its own town officers free from impositions or interference from colonial officials. Also in Salem, church officials were democratically elected. Historically, democratic principles began in the church government in

Massachusetts. For example, the elections of Samuel Skelton and Francis Higginson were democratic in 1629. After the free election of the people's choice, Skelton was the pastor of the Church of Salem. On the other hand, Higginson was the teacher. According to Governor Bradford of Plymouth, Higginson had three votes and Skelton had four.[43] These were the first democratically elected church officials in Salem because planters had the right to choose church officials freely.

Regarding the management of company affairs, Governor Endicott governed the colony in accordance with Company leaders in England. In the first letter of the Company in England, stockholders directed Endicott to apply the same justice to freemen and servants as to principal men. In his oath, he agreed to appoint impartial officers. Moreover, Company leaders prohibited him from making laws without the consent of the government formed in New England. Endicott was also instructed to form an inclusive government of 13 officials including himself. Among the officials, he further had to appoint two members among the old planters. According to the letter, the council formed in Salem had the power to make laws and regulations for the management of the Company.[44]

In the second letter, I discovered that the Company entrusted Governor Endicott with the power to establish the components of the criminal justice system—including a court and house of correction. Regarding the administration of punishment, the Company's officials in England told him to inflict punishment impartially to all. The house of correction had the same mandate as our modern era. That is, the government under Governor Endicott established a house of correction for specific and general deterrence for law violators.[45] In Salem, he formed a consensual government with the servants and old planters. The process of electing local officials was undeniably democratic. However, the government of Governor Endicott was short lived. In 1630, with the arrival of Governor Winthrop, it saw its end. The Massachusetts Bay Company was no longer a private company but a colonial entity.

Democratic Principles in the Massachusetts Bay Colony

As noted above, with the arrival of Governor John Winthrop under the royal crown, the Massachusetts Bay Company became a colonial entity.

As such, his government had the power of managing all the existing and future plantations and settlements. When Winthrop first assumed his role, settlers had few settlements in the region. Under his governorship, freemen established towns and plantations. These plantations or towns were democratically governed. The process of building those towns was in accordance with democratic principles. The foundations of plantations and towns were by mutual consent of the principal men of those entities. In a free society, the decision-making through a consensual practice is purely democratic. In the United States, for instance, local, state, and federal government officials govern with the same mutual decision-making approach.

In addition to the establishment of towns, Massachusetts Bay government officials made rules and orders with the consent of the freemen or a major part of them. Yet, although local governments were democratic, residents who were not freemen did not participate in the management of town affairs. Like the excluded English, other freemen in the colony objected to the arbitrary policy used against them. As a result, the freemen used peaceful resistance for the remediation of their plights. Like the freemen, Deputy Governor Thomas Dudley also used untroubled resistance against the abuse of power by Governor John Winthrop. I will discuss the examples of pacific resistance in the following section. Regarding Governor Dudley, he was against the abuse of power by Governor Winthrop during his first years in executive office. With the exclusion of part of the society in the decision making of town affairs, the government system became semi-democratic. In villages or towns where the populace was of the approved churches in the colony, those entities were purely democratic.

Like the freemen in Massachusetts Bay, citizens in the United States stand against the abuse of power by government officials. In this country, citizens observe the policies of their government officials, however, constituents also challenge government officials who deviate from the established American standards. The Constitution of the United States and those of states prohibit police abuses of power, for example. In Massachusetts Bay and other New England Colonies, abuse of power was sanctionable.

Pacific Resistance against Arbitrary Government Policies in Massachusetts

Throughout history, societies where inhabitants have overlooked government's authoritarian or arbitrary policies have precluded the success of democratic principles. It is useless to overlook malfeasances from government officials due to fear of punishments or sanctions. It is unproductive to support a dictator or an authoritarian official because he or she belongs to your tribe or political party. In the colony of Massachusetts Bay, the inhabitants were aware of such negligence and passivity, and they utilized non-violent procedures to challenge the arbitrary policies used against them by government officials. As early as 1632, the inhabitants of Watertown, for instance, refused to pay taxes requested of them because they believed that the process was illegal. According to church leaders and other freemen of that town, colonial officials did not have the power to collect taxes without the consent of the people. According to the Watertown freemen, the government in Massachusetts Bay was like that of the Aldermen and Mayor of London and was not a parliamentary form of government.[46] These freemen wisely went on to voice that they feared establishing a precedent that would have made their posterity slaves.

Watertown freemen and colonial officials solved this issue peacefully. Government officials explained to them that the colony of Massachusetts Bay was a parliamentary form of government. This is the first time the use of democratic resistance occurred in the colony. It is important to note that in any democratic country or a free state, citizens often use non-violent or pacific methods against injustice or arbitrary legal procedures directed at minorities. This is the best action that citizens of free societies use for the remediation of their rights and plights. In Watertown, individuals challenged the policy of colonial officials openly or by sending letters to England. In 1630 or 1631, colonial officials punished Philip Ratcliff, a servant of Matthew Cradock, for criticizing church leaders and the government of the Massachusetts Bay. As a form of peaceful resistance, officials used civil dialogue to solve their differences. In Massachusetts, magistrates, deputies, the governor, his deputy, and church ministers preferred solving their difference through a civil dialogue as much as the people preferred non-violent resistance.

Civil Dialogues

In Massachusetts Bay, colonial officials solved their differences through civil dialogues. From John Winthrop's book, I discovered that he was in a power struggle with Thomas Dudley, his deputy governor. At any given time when they were in conflict, the governor and his deputy met with ministers and assistants for a peaceful resolution to their personal conflicts. Like Winthrop and Dudley, various church ministers, assistants, and deputies utilized the same approach in managing their differences. Colonial officials did not use violent methods for political, social, and religious solutions. They engaged in peaceful resolutions or sought the judiciary system for that end. For example, in 1632, colonial officials in Massachusetts opposed the resignation attempt of Deputy Governor Thomas Dudley rationally. When he presented his resignation letter, colonial officials rejected his request. At the General Court, they told him that he could not resign from his deputyship and assistantship at whim but only by the power which put him in these positions.[47] When Governor Winthrop moved the colonial capital from Cambridge to Boston without the consent of other officials, his deputy, Dudley, denounced him. Another disagreement ended civilly happened when Governor Winthrop and Deputy Governor Dudley were in conflict over government policy. During a meeting convened by Rev. John Wilson, Henry Vane, John Cotton, and their assistants, they criticized Winthrop's policy. Each party had to openly explain his position on Winthrop's policy without recourse to violence.[48]

In the United States, politicians as well as government authorities advocate sincere civil dialogue where each party expresses his concerns freely without imposition or fear of the other party. This culture can be traced to the colonial era in Massachusetts Bay colony. Under the leadership of Vane, ministers convened a meeting for the mediation of their conflict. This issue involved various people in the colony. Governor Winthrop and Deputy Governor Dudley each had supporters, for instance. According to Winthrop, persons of quality and magistrates sided either with him or Dudley. Under the care of ministers, they nevertheless resolved their differences peacefully.[49] Jealousy did not cause disruption of the government nor their friendship. They convened together before church leaders and managed their conflict calmly.

Massachusetts colonial officials further used political dialogue and peaceful resolutions with neighboring colonies such as Connecticut and Plymouth. Governor Winthrop wrote that when they had differences with their brethren in Connecticut, they solved those differences without recourse to weapons or wars. In his book, *The History of New England*, he wrote as follows:

> ... differences between us and those of Connecticut were divers; but the ground of all was their shyness of coming under our government which, though we never intended to make them subordinate to us, yet they were very jealous, and therefore, in the articles of confederation, which we propounded to them, and whereby order was taken, that all differences, which might fall out, should be ended by a way of peace, and never to come to a necessity or danger of force—they did so alter the chief article, as all would have come to nothing. For whereas the article was, that, upon any matter of differences two, three, or more commissioners of every of the confederate colonies should assemble, and have absolute power (the greater number of them) to determine the matter—they would have them only to meet, and if they could agree, so; if not, then to report to their several colonies, and to return with their advice, and so to go on till the matter might be agreed; which beside that it would have been infinitely tedious and extreme chargeable, it would never have attained the end; for it was very unlikely, that all the churches in all the plantations would ever have accorded upon the same propositions."[50]

In addition to peaceful resolutions, freemen in Massachusetts used the elections to punish arbitrary and unfit colonial officials. Freemen did not re-elect Deputy William Coddington in 1637. Like Coddington, Vane lost his re-election because his supporters, the Boston freemen, did not vote. Those county towns supported the candidacy of Governor

Winthrop. During this election, Thomas Hutchinson noted that "there was great danger of a violent tumult that day. The speeches on both sides were fierce, and they began to lay hands on one another, but the manifest majority on one side was a restraint to the other."[51] Similarly, Roger Ludlow lost his re-election because freemen disavowed his political culture. John Endecott received a similar punishment after he defaced the cross in the king's ensign.[52]

Power of Electors

In a constitutional democracy, electoral power observed by citizens enables them to express discontent against government officials. In the New England colonies, freemen exercised this power to punish officials they believed to be unfit to serve their interests. Inversely, they rewarded those who worked for the common good. Through the democratic process, freemen had the power to sanction officials whom they deemed incapable of performing the government duties entrusted to them. As in the United States, in the colony of Massachusetts, freemen were protective of their rights. As a result, they sanctioned officials who deviated from political norms. For example, in 1635, Roger Ludlow lost his election because he argued against the successful election of the governor, which was fair and democratic as agreed by the freemen and Massachusetts Bay representatives. Like Ludlow, Endecott lost his election because freemen sanctioned him due not to his religious views, but his behavior concerning them. He defaced the king's cross without the consent of the freemen or magistrates. He acted with more authority than the patent allowed him.[53] According to Governor Winthrop, the people voted Endecott out because they had absolute power.

In the current constitution of the Commonwealth of Massachusetts, the legislature established a law indicating the power of electors. Namely, in Article V of the Massachusetts constitution of 1780, the legislature established a law which reads as follows:

> All power residing originally in the people, and being derived from them, the several magistrates, and officers of government, vested with authority, whether legislative, executive, or judicial,

are their substitutes and agents, and are at all times accountable to them."[54]

Now and during the colonial era, freemen had the power to sanction those in power. They had the power to elect their elected officials, including local representatives. During dialogues with the freeman, Governor Winthrop said that according to the charter, the freemen had the power to choose the assistant and remove him from office and put in others of their choice. The statement of Governor Winthrop to the Watertown freemen reflects Article V of the Massachusetts Bay adopted in 1780. Furthermore, as in Article V, Article VIII of the same constitution empowered the freemen of Massachusetts with the same power as stated by Governor Winthrop to the Watertown freemen. Article VIII of the Massachusetts constitution ordered that,

> In order to prevent those, who are vested with authority, from becoming oppressors, the people have right, at such period, and in such manner, as they shall establish by their frame of government, to cause their public officers to return to private life; and to fill up vacant places, by certain and regular elections and appointments.[55]

Keeping with the language of Article VIII of the Massachusetts constitution, in 1641, the freemen of the Massachusetts Bay colony elected Richard Bellingham as governor in opposition to Governor Winthrop. According to Jacob B. Moore, members of the General Court favored Winthrop for that position, but Bellingham was the candidate of the people.[56] Governor Elect Bellingham won by a majority vote during the election.[57] It is important to note that Massachusetts Bay freemen disapproved of lifetime appointments. Governor Winthrop held the post for years. Church ministers and elders opposed his re-election in 1641.

Democratic Elections

In the Massachusetts Bay, freemen elected their local to colonial officials through free and fair elections. Eligible voters and candidates were members of an approved church with the exception of settlements in New Hampshire and Maine. Under the jurisdiction of Massachusetts, religious tests did not apply to the freemen of Portsmouth, Dover, or Exeter. In Connecticut, every freeman was an eligible voter. Free elections emerged in Massachusetts with the selection of Governor Winthrop in 1630, the same year the freemen elected him to that position. Like politics, religious elections for pastors and elders started in the same way; by the imposition of hands. On the election of religious ministers, Governor Winthrop in *The History of New England from 1630 to 1649, Vol. 1*, wrote that "we used imposition of hands, but with this was protection by all, that it was only as a sign of election and confirmation, not of any intent that Mr. Wilson should renounce his ministry he received in England."[58] In 1630, at this election, Wilson was elected teacher, and Increase Nowell an elder.

Regarding the election process, electors voted for their chosen candidates via paper ballots. Governor Winthrop reported that voters received a paper ballot with the names of the men bidding for governor and deputy positions. In the same process, election officials gave voters blank papers without a name of the candidates for the election of the assistants. Each elector had figures or scrolls representing a candidate.[59] Richard Frothingham, Jr. in his book *The History of Charlestown, Massachusetts*, noted that after the election, "the ballots were to be put into the box, open or once folded (not twisted or rolled up)." He went on to point out that the freemen elected the assistants or magistrates.

Also, according to Frothingham, the election of assistants and magistrates was by corns and beans. Corns indicated election and beans were the contrary.[60] This process was for election by proxy only. Constables or deputies from each town sealed up the ballots and carried them to Boston after the election.[61] In Newbury, Edward Woodman, John Woodbridge, Henry Short, Christopher Hussey, Richard Kent, Richard Brown, and Richard Knight were elected as selectmen by paper ballots.[62] From this account, it is clear that election by paper ballot was also used in the local elections for minor offices. In Massachusetts, illegal voting was punishable by law. On May 25, 1635, voters were fined sixpence a piece for electing a deputy who was not a freeman.[63] However, officials sometimes decriminalized election crimes in consideration of public interests.

Decriminalization of Election Crimes by the Massachusetts Bay Government

Massachusetts colonial officials took a progressive approach when enacting their laws. They valued the notion of public interests or good in their election laws. This was the case of the franchise law. According to the law, only freemen belonging to an approved church in the colony were eligible to vote and hold a government office. Charles H. Bell, the author of *History of the Town of Exeter, New Hampshire*, called this law "a cardinal doctrine in Massachusetts."[64] He went on to point out that the New Hampshire towns were allowed elective franchise in the colony of Massachusetts without reference to the qualification of the church membership test.[65] In the case of New Hampshire, this law was decriminalized as a price for the extension of the jurisdiction of the colony. On the other hand, in Marblehead, colonial officials repealed this law for the common good. As the colonial officials believed in law and order, it was unproductive to overlook all types of disorders that happened in the plantation without taking workable measures.

Liberal Approach for the Union of New Hampshire with Massachusetts Bay

Data from various sources indicate that the residents in the settlements of Dover and Portsmouth were not religious. These residents came to New England as employees of certain proprietors, such as John Mason or Sir Ferdinando Gorges. As such, they maintained their industrious culture without being involved deeply in religious affairs. In 1641, when the plantations of Dover and Portsmouth united with the Massachusetts Bay colony, they retained that approach. Resultantly, the officials of Massachusetts Bay overlooked the franchise law enacted in the colony in 1631. Furthermore, in 1642, Massachusetts Bay officials authorized the residents of New Hampshire to form their own local governments and send deputies to the General Court. J. B. Clarke thus noted that in 1642, "it was ordered that all the present inhabitants of Piscataqua who formerly were free there shall have liberty of freemen in their several towns to manage all their town affairs, and shall each town send a deputy to the General Court, though they be not at present church members."⁶⁶ Clarke further noted that the prerequisite of church membership was surrendered when New Hampshire's settlements entered into union with Massachusetts Bay.⁶⁷ Even though such policies were overlooked in New Hampshire and Marblehead, voters in Newbury were punished for violating the franchise law previously mentioned.

In Marblehead, violations of colonial laws were prevalent. Namely, settlers in this plantation neglected laws often. Samuel Roads, Jr. wrote that settlers in Marblehead treated unspecified laws with contempt.⁶⁸ As the entire population neglected laws, the government was unable to punish them. Settlers were not church members of an approved congregation in the colony. Even though they supported a religious teacher, they did not have Sunday church ordinances. Consequently, they did not have a local government. Roads, Jr. further wrote that this plantation did not have magistrates or officers to govern them. Thus, as Salem was far from Marblehead, the General Court made an order that authorized the governing of this plantation by inhabitants who were not freemen. The Order of the General Court for the formation of a local government in Marblehead reads as follows:

> That in defect of freemen at Marblehead, the inhabitants of Salem shall have liberty to command some honest and able man, though he be not a freeman, and the deputy Governor shall have power (if he think fit) to give him the oath for constable of that place till this court shall take further order.⁶⁹

After the passage of this order, David Curwithin was elected Constable by the inhabitants of Salem for one year. Regarding the violation of colonial law, it is also important to note that the inhabitants of Marblehead did not obey liquor laws. Roads, Jr. stated that any vessel in Marblehead had large quantities of liquors, indicating that the custom of drinking liquor in Marblehead was universal. According to him, in town meetings freemen served liquors to those who were present. As a result, there were often quarrels between them.⁷⁰

Representative Government in Massachusetts Bay

The emergence of a representative government in the colony of Massachusetts Bay is another strong indication of democracy in the colonies. Even though this system was in a mixed form, freemen indeed voted for their representative. Colonial officials did not impose any candidate on them. By law, freemen in each town had the power to elect two candidates by choice. In the Massachusetts Bay colony, freemen firmly rejected arbitrary features in governance. They were against a system where the officials would have held their positions for life. They challenged colonial officials' exclusive policies. And as early as 1634, freemen wanted to know the privileges granted to them in the colony's company charter. When they discovered they had the power to make their own laws by charter stipulation, they discussed their will to Governor Winthrop. During the discussion, he told them that when the charter was issued, the number of the freemen was small. However, by 1634, the number of freemen in the colony had increased. Due to the numerical augmentation of the freemen, each town had to send its representatives to the General Court to assist with the revision and reform of laws which they found amiss.[71] As the plantations were established at great distances from each other, the freemen could not come to the General Court all the time and an order was passed ordering the elections of two or three representatives from each town to assist the governor, deputy governor, and assistants with enacting and repealing laws at the General Court. From thereon, assistants and deputies voted together at the General Court. In 1634, the colony had 24 deputies from the eight towns of the colony. At the General Court of May 13, 1634, these 24 deputies sat together with the governor, deputy governor, and six assistants at the court.

In 1644, the General Court formed two houses of representatives, the House of Deputies, and the House of Assistants. Unfortunately, the division of the assistants and deputies did not happen peacefully. Jealousy was the main reason why these two bodies fell apart from each other. The increase of deputies in the colony threatened the power of the assistants who were in the minority. Hoping to retain their power, the assistants separated themselves from the deputies. After examining democratic principles in Massachusetts, it is pertinent to investigate the perceptions of Massachusetts Bay colonial officials on the form of their government.

The Perceptions of Massachusetts' Officials on the Forms of their Government

In Massachusetts, colonial officials openly declared the forms of government that existed in their colony. In *the Records of Massachusetts, 1642-1649*, I discovered that the colony had a mixed form of government. The Board of Trade asked the elders whether their government was a pure aristocracy, or a mixed for including democracy? If mixed, they asked, should it not be unmixed in all administration of government? The answer from ministers was that the Massachusetts Bay government was not a pure aristocracy or democracy in respect of the General Court. They went on to note that the Court of Assistants was aristocratic, but the selection of jurors was democratic.[72] Like the elders, John Cotton gave his views on the type of government which was feasible in the Massachusetts Bay colony.

In a letter to Lord Say, Rev. Cotton wrote that God did not direct democracy as a fit government for the church or the commonwealth. He posed the question of who should be governed if the people are governors? As for monarchy and aristocracy, he believed that God ordained the best form of government for the church and the commonwealth in the scripture. He went on to state that God set up a theocracy for both.[73] Rev. Cotton supported the principles of a theocratic government because in this type of government, magistrates are men who fear God. He supported his reasoning by quoting the book of Exodus XVIII.21. He further declared that those magistrates are the chosen of their brethren. He took this quote from Deut. XVII.15.[74] Justin Winsor similarly purported that Massachusetts theocratic officials advocated a government ruled by God's chosen in a church covenant. Rev. Cotton is important because in his time, he was the most influential man in the colony. Thomas Hutchinson noted that he was instrumental in the settlement of their civil as well as ecclesiastical policy over any other religious and political leader.[75] Like Rev. Cotton, Governor Winthrop was also in favor of an aristocratic government. His governing approach leaned towards aristocracy and theocracy. He did not believe that democracy was the best form of government in the colony.

Theocratic Governance in Massachusetts Bay

Theocratic government emerged during the first term of Governor Winthrop. With Governor Endicott, there is no evidence that such a system was in use. In 1631, Massachusetts passed an order which created a theocratic government. In this year, the election, as well as the inclusion in the colony body politic, was based on a religious test. As discussed above, according to various sources, only inhabitants who belonged to an approved church in the colony became freemen. Once approved, they had the right to elect officers at each level of government. They further had the privilege to serve as government officials at local and colonial levels. In his book, *The New England Theocracy: A History of the Congregationalists in New England to the Revivals of 1740*, H.F. Uhden showed that, in May 1631, Massachusetts colonial officials passed an act for the obtention of the freemen status. The law reads as follows: "for the future no one shall be admitted to the freedom of this body politic; unless he be a member of some church within the limits of the same."[76] The word in the "future" indicates the existence of planters or English who were not church members. John Maverick, William Blackstone, and old planters joined the Massachusetts Bay body politic even though they were not church members.[77] Those previously listed as freemen were old planters who resided in the region before the arrival of Governors Endicott and Winthrop.

More evidence of theocratic advocacy is found in 1634 in Boston. When the freemen of Boston excluded principal leaders from the committee for the division of land, Rev. Cotton invoked scripture to convince them that they were in error of judgement. According to Governor Winthrop, in 1634, freemen of Boston met to choose seven men who should divide parcels of land. They chose by papers and in their choice left out Mr. Winthrop, Coddington, and other chief men; they instead chose one of the elders and a deacon, and the rest of the inferior sort (i.e., normal people). Some of the chief men disapproved of the election. They were surprised that Boston should be the first town to challenge the authority of chief men, especially Coddington, who had been an advocate of their plight. While the rest of the men did not challenge the result, Rev. Cotton expressed to the Boston selectmen that "it was the Lord's order among the Israelites to have all such business committed to the elders, and that it had been nearer the rule to have chosen some of each sort, &c."[78] They all agreed to go to a new election, which was referred to the next lecture day. This was a clear example of advocacy for a theocratic government. In addition to theocratic elements, the colony had aristocratic features.

Aristocracy in Massachusetts Bay

Charles Borgeaud, in his book, *The Rise of Modern Democracy in Old and New England*, emphasized the existence of an aristocratic form of government in Massachusetts. From his records, the colony had a mixed form of government, namely democratic, aristocratic, and theocratic. Like Borgeaud, Willis Mason West noted that the early Massachusetts government was aristocratic. He believed that the aristocracy's authority in Massachusetts Bay resulted from the language of the charter. He noted that the charter had democratic and aristocratic features. For years, Massachusetts Bay Company's members governed the colony. Newly elected freemen did not hold executive office positions.

For example, Governor Winthrop served as an executive officer for almost twenty years with few interruptions. Similarly, Governor Dudley, also a member of the Company, served in the same capacity. Moreover, Richard Bellingham, another Company member, also served as a governor in Massachusetts Bay. These elections indicate that certain groups of people were privileged with higher positions in the government. Furthermore, like the position of governor, assistants were aristocratic. Although freemen elected the governor, they did not select the *candidates* for this position. Joseph Story writes that close members of the Company formed the government of the Massachusetts Bay colony.[79]

Like the authors previously noted, Charles M. Andrews, in his book, *The River Towns of Connecticut: A Study of Wethersfield, Hartford, and Windsor*, indicated that the colonists in Massachusetts Bay did not value equality in men; instead, they established a privileged class of assistants.[80] Religious ministers refused to accept that they were aristocratic. When the board of trade pressed them on the form of the government in the colony, they responded that they had a mixed form of aristocracy and democracy in respect to the General Court. Ministers went on to say that they had a mixed system in the General Court because men formed the government. Therefore, it was free for them to make it mixed and simple. Furthermore, they articulated that in other areas of the General Court, the government was unmixed and the form of government in the courts was in accordance with the pleasure of the ordained. Meanwhile, this meant that powerful officials made a set of rules for the protection of their interests, but not for the common good. The form of government instituted in Massachusetts was in accordance with the patent. Religious ministers asserted that the patent permitted a mixed government. But the subordinate administrators of justice were aristocratic by the patent.

On the other hand, the impaneling of jurors was a democratic process.[81] Scholars believe also that Rev. John Cotton supported aristocratic government. Proof of his support for the aristocratic government comes for a 1634 sermon. At the General Court of this year, Rev. Cotton "preach[ed] and delivered this doctrine, that a magistrate ought not be turned into the condition of a private man without just cause, and to be publicly convict[ed], no man than the magistrates may not turn a private man out of his freehold, &c. without like public trial, &c."[82]

Chapter 2

Democracy in Rhode Island and Connecticut, and the New Haven Theocracy

Historians, scholars, political scientists, and legal scholars, identify Rhode Island and Connecticut freemen as the architects of pure democracy in the New England colonies.[1] Historically, these colonies had leaders with strong spirits for advocating for freedom and challenging authoritarian political policies. Moreover, they opposed the arbitrary judicial system enforced by the assistants in Massachusetts Bay. They opposed the aristocratic and theocratic systems of government established there. Willis Mason West said that the founders of Rhode Island were against theocratic government in Massachusetts, and that Connecticut's founders were against the aristocracy there. West goes on to describe Thomas Hooker as the apostle of modern democracy.[2]

In Rhode Island, Roger Williams established the principle of religious liberty as a means of opposing the Massachusetts theocracy. Like Williams and Hooker, Coddington was also a supporter of democratic principles. Moreover, the inhabitants of Watertown in Massachusetts Bay were advocates of democratic principles. The result was that such principles flourished in their settlement in Connecticut. Additionally, officials, religious leaders, and the freemen of Dorchester and Cambridge, including Roxbury, had the same spirit. These are people who established settlements or plantations with those of Watertown in the Connecticut Valley. The freemen of Watertown were the first settlers to reject paying taxes without their consent. Those of Boston were the first to oppose aristocratic governance in that town. They instead espoused religious liberties. In Boston, an unspecified number of the inhabitants supported the religious views of Rev. John Wheelwright and Mrs. Anne

Hutchinson. During the Antinomian controversy, the freemen of Boston sided with the previously named religious free leaders.

Democracy in Rhode Island

The founders of Rhode Island were dissatisfied officials and banished Puritans from Massachusetts Bay. Few among them served in their former colony as ministers or magistrates. Good examples of those who did serve include Williams and Coddington. In Massachusetts, Williams was a pastor in Salem, while Coddington served as an assistant and magistrate. Both were antagonistic to the shift towards theocracy and aristocracy championed by Governor Winthrop and Rev. Cotton. As was the case with Williams and Coddington, Samuel Gorton was also of the same political and religious spirit. He was a fearless political advocate of liberties. In Rhode Island, when each of these officials founded their towns, they advocated the observance of democratic principles and rule of law. In this colony, an agreement consented to by the founders of the towns of Portsmouth and Newport indicate their advocacy for the principle of a democratic form of government. The founders of these settlements agreed as follows:

> It is ordered and unanimously agreed upon, that the Government which this Body politick do attend unto in this land, and the jurisdiction thereof, in favor of our prince is a Democracy or popular Government that is to say, it is in the power of the body of freemen orderly assembled, or the major part of them, to make or constitute just laws, by which they will be regulated, and to depute among themselves such ministers as shall see them faithfully executed between man and man."[3]

Between 1641–1642, William G. Goddard revealed that the Portsmouth and Newport freemen formed a democratic government after their union. He reported that freemen in Rhode Island established a democratic government. To support his narrative regarding democracy in colonial Rhode Island, he quoted the language used by the founders during the Court of Election. The views of the founders at the Court reads as follows:

> It was ordered and unanimously agreed upon, the Government which this Bodie [sic] Politick doth attend unto in this island, and the jurisdiction thereof, in favor of our prince, is a Democracie [sic], or popular government,' that is to say, it is the power of the Body of Freemen orderly assembled, or the major part of them, to make or constitute just law, by which they will be regulated and to dispose from among themselves and to depute from among themselves such ministers as should see them faithfully executed between Man and Man.[4]

In 1647, when the four towns of Rhode Island—Providence, Portsmouth, Newport, and Warwick—unified under the Parliamentary Patent of 1643, they envisioned the formation of a democratic form of government. The *Records of the Colony of Rhode Island and Providence Plantations, in New England* records the agreement made by the freemen for the organization of the government which reads as follows:

> It is agreed, by this present Assembly thus incorporate, and by this present act declare, that the form of Government established in Providence Plantation is Democratical; that is to say, a Government held by the free and voluntary consent of all, or the greater part of the free inhabitants."[5]

The government thus formed in 1647 was done voluntarily by the inhabitants of this town. Before the formation of that government, the committee from Providence received instructions from Roger Williams for that purpose.

Williams, the founder of Providence, ordered the committee to advocate democratic principles for the government. One of his instructions regarded the jurisdictional power of local officers. Williams instructed that,

> We desire to have full power and authority to choose, ordain, authorize, and confirm all our particular town officers, and also,

that the said officers, shall be responsible unto our particular town, and that there may be no intermixture of general and particular officers, but that all may know their bounds and limits.[6]

Williams' orders indicate that he championed the notion of decentralization. Additionally, he and many of his fellow Rhode Islanders were firm believers in limiting the power of elected officers. Moreover, colonial officials championed the division of power as in our modern era.

In the charter or patent of 1643, the King of England identified the freemen of Rhode Island as industrious English subjects. As such, they had the same liberties and privileges as Englishmen. Williams received the Parliamentary Patent of 1643 with the advocacy of Sir Henry Van, a champion of democratic principles, such as freedom of religion. As English subjects, a free charter of civil incorporation and government was also issued for Rhode Island. This free and absolute charter was known as the Incorporation of Providence Plantations, in the Narragansett-Bay, in New England.[7] The 1643 charter is the first constitution ever issued in Rhode Island. The policy of Rhode Island was in accordance with it. According to the charter, the freemen had the power and authority to govern themselves. Additionally, they had the power to elect, order, and appoint their own government officials. Again, the establishment of a representative government indicates the institutionalization of democratic principles.

Democratic Principles in Rhode Island

Documents on the emergence of democratic principles in colonial Rhode Island are abundant. Before the charter of 1643, each town in the colony was democratic. In 1636, when Williams and his associates formed Providence, they administered town affairs collectively. They made orders by the consent of the freemen. The agreement signed by Providence freemen is an excellent example of the advocacy of the rule of law and democratic principles. The compact signed in 1636 reads as follows:

> We whose names are hereunder, desirous to inhabit in the town of Providence, do promise to subject ourselves in active and

> passive obedience to all such orders or agreements as shall be made for public good of the body in an orderly way, by the major consent of the present inhabitants, master of families, incorporated together in the town fellowship, and others whom they shall admit unto them only in civil things.[8]

The compact reveals the form of government envisioned by the founders of Providence. Here, they stressed the observance of the rule of law by all. They emphasized the enactment of laws by the freemen. In this case, the town government was purely democratic because the power of the government resided in the hands of the people. Furthermore, the notion of equality between the freemen in Providence is also another indication that democratic principles existed in that town. The phrase "incorporated together in a town fellowship" is the same as the ideal of equality. Surely, the freemen in Providence established a governmental system where the inhabitants had an equal voice in the administration of town affairs.

The engagements written for the officers and the freemen in Rhode Island in 1647 is further evidence of democratic principles in the colony. Consider the following engagement reserved for officers:

> You, A.B., being called and chosen into public employment, and the office of, by the free vote and consent of the inhabitants of the province of Providence Plantation (now orderly met, do, in the present assembly, engage yourself faithfully and truly to the utmost of your power to execute the commission committed unto you: and do hereby promise to do neither more nor less in that respect than that which the colony [authorized] you to do according to the best of your understanding.[9]

This engagement was purely democratic in its form as well as in its content. Elected officers had to obey the law and work for the common good of the colony. Moreover, the discretionary powers of officers were within the limits of the power granted to them by the charter. The abuse of this power was against the law.

Inhabitants' Engagement

For the better ordering of law and order by officers, the inhabitants were expected to treat public officials with civility and conform to the laws established by them. The agreement for the Rhode Island inhabitants, therefore, reads as follows:

> We, the inhabitants of the province of Providence Plantations being here orderly met, and having by free vote chosen you, to public office and officers for the due administration of justice and the execution thereof throughout the whole colony, do hereby engage ourselves to the utmost of our power to support and uphold you in your faithful performance thereof."[10]

There is no question that the engagement of the inhabitants of Rhode Island is an expression used in contemporary free countries such as the United States. In their engagement, government officials in Rhode Island educate us about how law enforcement officers received unconditional support from freemen in the colonial era. Officers were tasked with enforcing only those laws within their power.

Franchise System

In Rhode Island, every freeman had the right to vote. In the four towns of the colony, colonial and town officers did not require religious identification for election purposes. In Portsmouth, town officials authorized newcomers to become part of the body politic by the consent of the freemen. Moreover, they had to accept the form of government instituted in that town. The founders of Portsmouth formed a government according to the word of God. This was a mixed form of government—democratic and theocratic. Yet in this settlement, a theocratic government did not stand. Yet, the vision of forming a government according to the word of God was unrealistic in Portsmouth because most of the founders advocated democratic principles. In Providence, residents who observed public orders or engagements were franchised. It is sound to note that government officials in Portsmouth and Newport had a liberal policy.¹¹ A religious test was not one of the requirements for the obtainment of the status of freemen.

Among the freemen of these towns, inhabitants from Salem followed their brethren in Providence or Newport. It is certain that they enjoyed the same voting privilege as those who arrived before them. Like those of Salem, Quakers were freemen in the colony in later years. There is evidence indicating the election of Quakers to executive offices in Rhode Island. Nicholas Eaton, a Quaker, served as deputy governor and governor in Rhode Island, for instance. Rayner Wickersham Kelsey writes that from 1675–1676, the government of Rhode Island was in the hands of Quakers. He goes on to note that "in latter part of the seventeenth century, several Friends [Quakers] were elected to the governorship and other high offices in the colony."¹² The data indicates that Quakers were not excluded from the body politic in Rhode Island. Such organization of free and fair elections indicates the existence democracy.

Election in the Rhode Island Colony

From the early years of the formation of plantations, freemen settled affairs in town through a vote. Freemen also had the right to elect both their town's officers and representatives to the General Assembly. Regarding the voting system, they agreed to use paper ballots electing government officials.¹³ In addition to the voting system, a date for the election was set with the consent of the freemen gathered in a meeting. Furthermore, colonial officials established a Court of Election for that purpose. The *Records of the Colony of Rhode Island and Providence Plantations, in Rhode Island*, show the following:

> It is ordered, that the Court of Election shall always be held upon the first Tuesday after the 15th of May, annually if wind or weather hinder not. General Court of Election shall be held at Providence town. Furthermore, it is agreed, that forasmuch as many may be necessarily detained, that they cannot come to the General Court of Election, that then they should send their votes sealed up unto the said court, which shall be effectual as their personal appearance.¹⁴

Vote by proxy was common in the New England Colonies. The elections were free and fair. Election officers counted votes. This system existed in New Plymouth, Massachusetts Bay, Connecticut, New Haven, New Hampshire, and Maine. Moreover, the consensual system of governance was an indication of the democratic form of government in Rhode Island.

Consensual System in Rhode Island

Throughout New England, governing by consensus was a settled policy. This method, which included resolving problems, deciding on legal cases, dividing lands, and the settling of government policy by consensus, emerged first in New Plymouth. There, freemen established law and order with the general consent of the freemen. In all the other colonies, the management of town governments was by consensus. In Rhode Island, officials did not pass laws or orders without the consent of all the freemen or a majority of them. Similarly, the appointments or elections of local officials was by the consent of the freemen. Newcomers received the status of freemen with the consent of town's current freemen.

Courts, prisons, and other agencies were also formed in this manner. In town meetings, freemen made laws, elected officials, and settled differences. Those who failed to attend the meeting were punished. In 1663, when the inhabitants of Rhode Island formed a government in accordance with the charter of King Charles II, democratic norms continued to flourish in the colony. Also in 1663, this body corporate took the name of The Governor and Company of the English Colony of Rhode Island and Providence Plantations, in New England, in America. The 1663 charter identified the freemen of Rhode Island as "English." With such status, they enjoyed the same liberties as the English in England. The observance of the freedom of conscience as well as the rule of law were in the charter of 1663.[15]

Democratic Form of Government in Connecticut

The history of Connecticut starts with the migration of the inhabitants of Watertown, Newtown, Dorchester, and Roxbury in the Connecticut

Valley. As former residents of the Massachusetts Bay, local institutions established in Connecticut were the same as that colony. At town meetings, freemen managed their local affairs in the same manner as Massachusetts Bay as well. In the beginning of the newer settlements, the Massachusetts Bay colony granted them commissions for managing local affairs. After discovering that they were out of the jurisdiction of Massachusetts Bay, freemen in Connecticut wrote a constitution to serve as an instrument for the formation of a democratic government. Moreover, the charter of 1662 of King Charles II assured the continuations of democratic principles written in the constitution of 1639. King Charles II, for the continuance of liberties and privileges for the freemen, was liberal and democratically oriented.

With the unification of the New Haven and Connecticut colonies in 1665, the Fundamental Orders and 1662 were directed both territories. More specifically, the charter of 1662 made the colony of Connecticut a body politic and corporate by the name of Governor and Company of the English Colony of Connecticut, in New England, in America.[16] The charter was liberal with democratic principles embedded. On March 14, 1661, the General Court of Connecticut petitioned the King of England for the continuance and confirmation of privileges and liberties elaborated by the freemen in that colony in 1639. In the same year, John Winthrop, Jr. went to England as the colony agent to request a charter for the freemen of Connecticut. In 1662, King Charles II issued it.[17]

Hammond Trumbull, Henry R. Stiles, George Brinley, and Frances Manwaring Caulkins have recorded important data on the formation of town government in the Connecticut settlements. In addition to these authors, Judge Dwight Loomis and Gilbert J. Calhoun contributed the same. They discussed the history of the early form of government in Connecticut in their book, *The Judiciary and Civil History of Connecticut*. Their work is important for those who want to investigate further the type of government instituted in the towns of Hartford, Windsor, and Wethersfield. In addition to the early government, the judiciary system of these towns have received the same attention. Like other writers, Alexander Johnston, a former professor of jurisprudence and political economy at Princeton University, examined the development of democratic principles in the Commonwealth of Connecticut. His book contains pertinent information regarding the constitution of Connecticut written in 1639.

On March 3, 1636, the inhabitants of Hartford, Windsor, and Wethersfield received a commission to form a government in Connecticut.[18] Isaac William Stuart writes that, before June 1636, the inhabitants of Hartford held town meetings before the formal organization of the government. Additionally, in 1635, the freemen held their meeting in Hartford. It is certain that when the emigrants from Massachusetts reached Hartford, they joined together at the site of the plantation and blessed the name of their God. Regarding the town government, Stuart documented that "the organization of the town was democratic."[19] From 1636 to 1639, Hartford, Windsor, and Wethersfield were under the jurisdiction Massachusetts. In 1639, these three towns, or little colonies, voluntarily separated from the government of the Massachusetts Bay. Massachusetts colonial officials did not oppose their separation. Upon disassociating themselves from the former colony, they formed a confederation which they termed a public state. Hamond J. Trumbull in his book, *The Memorial History of Hartford County Connecticut* noted the formation of the government by the inhabitants of Hartford, Windsor, and Wethersfield on the 14th day of January 1639.

Trumbull went on to elucidate that they "adopted by their votes a form of government and associated and conjoined themselves to be as one public state or commonwealth."[20] When the adoption of the government was concluded, the inhabitants of the previously mentioned towns voluntarily wrote the Fundamental Orders, the instrument which they utilized for the governing of the confederation for the present and future towns in the colony. The language of the Fundamental Orders was as follows:

> Forasmuch as it has pleased the Almighty God by the wise disposition of his divine providence so to order and dispose of things that we, the inhabitants and residents of Windsor, Hartford and Wethersfield are now cohabiting and dwelling in and upon the River of Connecticut and the lands thereunto adjoining; and well knowing where a people are gathered together the word of God requires that to maintain the peace and union

of such a people, there should be an orderly and decent government established according to God, to order and dispose of the affairs of the people at all seasons as occasion shall require; do therefore associate and conjoin ourselves to be as one public state or commonwealth, and such as shall be adjoining to us at any time hereafter, enter into combination and confederation together, to maintain and preserve the liberty and purity of the gospel of our Lord Jesus, which we now profess, as also the discipline of the churches, which according to the truth of the said gospel is now practiced amongst us, as also in our civil affairs to be guided and governed according to such laws, rules, orders, and decrees, as shall be made, ordered and decreed, as follows:

It is ordered, sentenced and decreed, that there shall be yearly two General Assemblies or Courts, [one] on the Second Thursday, in April, the other the Second Thursday in September, following; the first shall be called the Court of Election, wherein shall be yearly chosen from time to time so many magistrates and other public officers as shall be found requisite: whereof one to be chosen Governor for the year ensuing until another be chosen, and no other magistrate to be chosen for more than one year; provided always there be six chosen beside the Governor; which being chosen and sworn according to an oath recorded for that purpose shall have power to administer justice according to the laws here established, and for want thereof according to the rule of the word of God; which choice shall be made by all that are admitted freemen and have taken the oath of fidelity, and do cohabite [sic] within this jurisdiction (having been admitted inhabitants by the major part of the town wherein they live), or the major part of such as shall be then present.[21]

In addition to the previous article, other acts or orders discussed election laws, selection of officials, the enactment of laws, selection of deputies from each town, and the jurisdictions of the General Court. The Fundamental Orders outlined what every inhabitant and government official had to observe. The oath of both the governor and the inhabitants were in accordance with the Fundamental Orders or constitution. This document ordered the governor to administer justice in accordance with the law enacted by the General Court. Pursuant to the Fundamental Orders, the administration of justice by the governor had to be according to the rule of the word of God. The oath indicates the founders valued the principle of the rule of law.

After the founders of Connecticut agreed to the Fundamental Orders, they formed a government unifying the three towns—Hartford, Windsor, and Wethersfield. Trumbull writes that the formalizing of the government happened on the 14th of January 1639.[22]

Judge Loomis and Attorney Calhoun also attested that the founders of Connecticut formed the government after the popular assembly held in Hartford on January 14, 1639. They stated that the Connecticut Fundamental Orders was the constitution of these three towns.[23] After 15 years, Connecticut colonial officials did amend the Fundamental Orders. *The Public Records of the Colony of Connecticut* indicates that on May 18, 1654, members of the General Court added an article empowering them to hold a General Court in the absence of the governor and his deputy. To be certain, they added this amendment to avoid the intermission of the affairs of the government while the executive officials were absent or unable to perform their duties as prescribed by the laws of the colony. The Fundamental Orders guided the duties of the governor, deputy governor, and deputies. It is possible that without this amendment, convening a General Court in the absence of the governor would have been unconstitutional. Therefore, to avoid the same, an amendment was written.

The amendment of the Fundamental Orders in 1654 reads as follows:

> The freemen voted [and] ordered to be added to the Fundamental. That the major part of the magistrates, in the absence of the Governor [and] Deputy, shall have power to call on General Court; and that any General Court being legally called and met, the major part of the magistrates and deputies then met (in the absence of the Governor and Deputy) shall have power to choose into two from among themselves, a Moderator; which being done, they shall be deemed as legal a General Court to all intent and purpose as if the Governor or Deputy were present.[24]

The amendment of the Fundamental Orders indicates that colonial officials abided by democratic principles in the Connecticut colony.

Evidence of Democratic Norms and Principles in Connecticut

Connecticut takes credit for pioneering the first written constitution in the New England colonies. Experts believe that the constitution written in the Connecticut colony was unique and previously unknown to the world. Authors such as Leonard Bacon and John Fiske have documented this accolade. In his book, *The Beginnings of New England; Or the Puritan Theocracy in its Relations to the Civil and Religious Liberty*, Fiske writes that,

> [The constitution of Connecticut] was the first written constitution known to history, that created a government, and it marked the beginnings of American democracy, of which Thomas Hooker deserves more than any other man to be called the father. The government of the United States today is in lineal descent more nearly related to that of Connecticut than to that of any of the other thirteen colonies.[25]

A similar view regarding the exceptionality of the Connecticut constitution was noted by Bacon. In his book, *A Discourse on the Early Constitutional History of Connecticut, Delivered before the Connecticut Historical Society, Hartford, May, 17, 1843*, he writes that,

> This [constitution], if I mistake not, is the first example in history of a written Constitution, a distinct organic law; constituting a government, and defining its powers. The middle age had abounded in charters, but they were of the nature of treaties between people in arms, and the sovereign whom they acknowledged; or of grants from the sovereign to a particular community.[26]

Like the aforementioned authors, Trumbull concluded that Connecticut was the first Republican colony in the world. In his book *Historical Notes on the Constitutions of Connecticut, 1639–1818*, he writes that,

Connecticut exhibits the only instance in the history of nations of a government purely Republican, which has stood the test of experience for more than a century and a half, which firmness enough to withstand the shocks of factions, and revolution.[27]

By this written constitution, I can conclude that the colony of Connecticut was free and democratic. First, the Connecticut colonial officials wrote and promulgated this constitution with the approval of the freemen. There is no evidence indicating that a foreign nation or officials forced them to write it. It was a freely written constitution for the self-government. In the preface of his book, Johnston writes that,

> The first conscious and deliberate effort on this continent to establish the democratic principle in the control of government was the settlement of Connecticut, the first written and democratic constitution on record, was the starting point for the democratic development which has since gained control of all our commonwealths, and now makes the essential feature of our commonwealth government.[28]

He goes on to articulate that "the government of the people, by the people, for the people, first took shape in Connecticut, and that the American form of government of commonwealth originated there, and not in Massachusetts, Virginia, or any other colony might well stop."[29]

The analysis of Professor Johnston has merit because the constitution of Connecticut was framed with the approval of the freemen. The preamble of the constitution reveals pertinent information on the nature of the Connecticut government and the framing of this document by the freemen. Throughout the history of the English colonies in North America, there is no prior evidence indicating the formation of a constitutional government by freemen. Massachusetts, Virginia, and Maryland had patents from the crown of England. However, colonial officials in these colonies governed the people in accordance with those patents.

Alan F. Hattersley is of the same views as Johnston on Connecticut democracy. In his book, *A Short History of Democracy*, he writes that the Fundamental Orders of Connecticut was the "first written constitution of modern democracy."[30] Hattersley utilized the same language as Johnston. Additionally, a clear and objective interpretation of the Connecticut colony's constitution was that of Henry R. Stiles, author of *The History of Ancient Windsor, Connecticut*. In his book, Stiles describes the Connecticut constitution as the first written constitution that defined the power of the government in the colony. In this constitution, he writes, the authority of the people was supreme. They recognized no other power except that of God.[31]

The Connecticut Fundamental Orders

The Orders were formatted constitutionally. The founders of the colony framed the preamble before articulating the orders or articles which each officer or freemen were expected to observe. According to the *Records of the Colony of Connecticut*, the Fundamental Orders was composed of eleven articles. Among them, the term of the governor, magistrates and other public officers was decidedly for one year.[32] Furthermore, the election of the governor and his deputy was to be by paper ballots cast by qualified freemen in each town. Like the governor and his deputy, magistrates and other officers were elected. The Orders limited the power of the government and established democracy. Connecticut's thus government met the description noted by George Sidney Camp in his book, *Democracy*. Camp wrote that "in a democratic government, people have the right to govern themselves."[33] In Connecticut, solid data indicates that the freemen were sovereign. They had the power to make laws through their deputies as the Fundamental Orders required, and each town had to send deputies to the General Court as their representatives.

Another indication of the existence of democratic principles in Connecticut is the franchise system. Every freeman was an elector and a member of the body politic. Colonial officials did not use religious affiliation as a prerequisite for becoming a freeman, being an elector, or holding a government office. Election officials administered the election in accordance with the language of the Fundamental orders. According to the constitution, the election of governor, deputy governor, and other officers was by paper ballots. Deputies also had the power to investigate the election process. When they discovered illegalities in the process, they could nullify the election in part or the entire process and re-start de novo. Furthermore, they could punish violators of the election process.[34] A sermon delivered by Rev. Thomas Hooker in 1638 before the writing of the constitution is another indication that Connecticut officials had a vision for a democratic government in the colony.

The Clerical Address of Rev. Thomas Hooker

Historians such as Trumbull, Johnson, and Fiske link a sermon of Rev. Hooker to the writing of the Connecticut constitution. They believe that he played a significant role in its formation. Namely, his sermon of May 31, 1638, at Hartford is considered the germ of the constitution. The Connecticut Historical Society wrote that the sermon of 1638 "was apparently designated to lead the way to the general recognition of the great truths which were soon to be successfully incorporated in the Fundamental laws."[35] Hooker gave a second notable sermon on April 11, 1639, the day of the first election under the constitution of that year.[36]

In Connecticut, democracy was not biased towards wealth, power, or class. The power of the government rested in the hands of all the freemen. A good example of Connecticut's democracy happened in Ancient Greece. In Ancient Greece, such as Sparta or Dorians, the people had the legislative power. In popular assemblies, the people elected their magistrates.[37]

Rev. Hooker believed in a government which worked according to the will of God but was against that of men. His political experience in Massachusetts and Holland instructed him on how to form a freedom-based constitution: He lived in Massachusetts where aristocratic principles were from time to time observed, but in Holland, he witnessed the force of democracy in the management of government affairs. All things considered, Rev. Hooker was well-equipped to assist Connecticut's leaders in the formation of a pure democratic form of government. Wethersfield freemen were the first opponents of taxation without representation of the freemen while in Watertown, Massachusetts Bay. Newtown [Cambridge] freemen were also against excess power of government officials. They were present when in 1632 the Deputy Governor charged Governor Winthrop with abuse of power.[38]

Principles Advocated by Rev. Thomas Hooker for the Formation of the Government

It has now been established that Rev. Hooker was the father of Connecticut democracy. Walter Seth Logan in his address delivered before the New York Historical Society characterized Hooker as the "First American Democrat."[39] In 1891, George Leon Walker referred to Rev. Hooker as a preacher, founder, and democrat.[40] Trumbull and Johnston stressed the importance of the sermon preached by Rev. Hooker in 1638 before the writing of the Fundamental Orders. As there is no earlier evidence pointing to another figure so strongly associated with the Orders, Hooker's sermon is an authoritative reference in connection with the document. In terms of scholarship, the record of Rev. Hooker's sermon is cited in various works written by authors, such as the aforementioned. All believe that Rev. Hooker made an impact in the framing process of the Fundamentals. His sermon reads as follows:

> Text: Deut. I. 13. Take you wise men, and understanding, and known among your tribes, and I will make them rulers over you; captains over thousands, and captains over hundreds, over fifties, over tens, etc.
>
> Doctrine I. That the choice of public magistrates belongs unto the people, by God's own allowance.
>
> II. The privilege of election, which belongs to the people, therefore, must not be exercised according to their [humors], but according to the bless will and law of God.
>
> III. They who have power to appoint officers and magistrates, it is in their power also, to set the bounds place unto which they call them.
>
> Reasons
>
> 1. Because the foundation of authority is laid, firstly, in the free consent of the people.

2. Because, by a free choice, the hearts of the people will be more inclined to the love of the persons chosen and more ready to yield obedience.

3. Because of the duty and engagement of the people.[41]

Democracy is prominent in Rev. Hooker's language. His reasoning was the same as those of other writers concerning the rule of law and democracy. Baron De Montesquieu stressed in his book, *The Spirit of Law*, that in a democratic society, the supreme power is in the hands of the people. He went on to stipulate that the people are sovereign. He also noted that suffrage is the will of the people.[42] Henry Stiles noted that Roger Ludlow, John Haynes, Henry Wolcott, and Edward Hopkins were also among the architects of the Connecticut Fundamental Orders.[43]

Ludlow was a colonial lawyer and a jurist by training. As a lawyer, he made an important contribution to the framing and adoption of the constitution. He codified the laws as the General Court ordered him to. Before his emigration to Connecticut, he was an assistant or magistrate in Massachusetts. In that colony, he lost his election for magistracy due to his criticism of the election process. Regarding the franchise system, the founders of Connecticut did not want to antagonize the people. Like Ludlow, John Haynes was a magistrate as well as governor in Massachusetts Bay. He served as governor in 1635 by popular vote. In his address to the inhabitants of the colony, he showed his appreciation for his election. He also spared them from taxes during his term of service. He believed that the poor were burdened due to excess taxes.[44] It is plausible to say that he was a modest leader and cared for the impoverished.

During his inaugural address in 1635 as governor of Massachusetts Bay, Haynes did not accept his salary which the freemen tried to reward him because they were burdened with excessive taxation.[45] The refusal of collecting his salary is an indication that Governor Haynes was against excess taxes. As such, it is safe to note that he, too, made a plausible contribution in the framing and adoption of the Fundamental Orders. Moreover, due to his experience as assistant and governor in the Massachusetts Bay colony, it is reasonable to speculate that other leaders present during the convention paid attention to his comments and suggestions. Among them, Haynes was the only leader who held the position of governor. Consequently, freemen re-elected him as governor after the election of 1639.

Theocracy, Aristocracy and Democracy in New Haven

The founders of New Haven observed a mixed system of government as did their brethren in Massachusetts Bay, with extreme measures concerning enfranchisement and inclusion in the body politic. From the colony's inception, government officials observed theocratic, aristocratic, and democratic principles. To some extent, aristocratic principles were also supported by the leading or prominent men in the colony. In New Haven, Rev. John Davenport and Theophilus Eaton, for instance, were in favor of an aristocratic form of government in addition to theocracy supported by the free burgesses.

The language used in the formation of the New Haven civil government is an ample illustration of the advocacy of a mixed form of government. During the initial formation of the civil entity in the colony, the founders advocated the establishment of a government where the word of God was supreme. In 1639, before the establishment of the government, planters assembled in a meeting discussing the same. During the assembly, planters and their ministers' opinions on how the government should operate showed similarities to the management style of the plantation. After some discussion, all agreed that their government would be based on the word of God. In the same assembly, officials decided that only church members were eligible for elections and the holding of offices.[46]

Moreover, freemen in the meeting prescribed the duties of magistrates. They ordered that "magistrates and officers, making and repealing of laws, dividing allotment of inheritance and all things like nature had to rule in accordance with the scripture of God.[47] To distinguish their government from a church institution, their decree was termed a "Plantation Covenant."[48] In New Haven, Rev. Davenport had much influence on the formation of the policy for the government. For example, he proposed the qualifications for those who would govern the freemen. Moreover, he decided that free burgesses must be members of the church because such persons feared God.⁴⁹ For the safety of the colony, the General Court made an order styled as "Free Mans Charge" for freemen to observe."⁵⁰

The Free Mans Charge reads as follows:

> You shall neither plot, practice nor consent to any evil or hurt against this jurisdiction, or any part of it, or against the civil government here established. And if you shall know any person, or persons which intend, plot, or conspire anything which tends to the hurt or prejudice of the same, you shall timely discover the same to lawful authority here established and you shall assist and be helpful in all the affairs of the jurisdiction, and by all means shall [promote] the public welfare of the same, according to your place, ability, and opportunity, you shall give due honor to the lawful magistrates, and shall be obedient and subject to all the wholesome laws and orders, always made, or which shall be hereafter made, by lawful authority aforesaid. And that both in your person and estate; and when you shall be [duly] called to give your vote or suffrage in any election, or touching any other matter, which concern this commonwealth, you shall give it as in your conscience you judge may conduce to the best good of the same.⁵¹

On October 25, 1639, the court in New Haven worked in accordance with the Fundamental Agreement concluded from June 4, 1639. As a result, freemen selected seven officials for the management of the affairs of the church. The names of the seven persons listed in the *Records of the New Haven Plantation* were as follows: "Theophilus Eaton, John Davenport, Robert Newman, Mathew [Matthew] Gilbert, Thomas Fuggill, John Ponderson, and Jerimy [Jeremy] Dixon."⁵² Among these named officials, Eaton was selected the magistrate of the colony, and four others were entrusted with assisting the magistrates in the public affairs of the plantation.

The magistrate worked with the assistance of the associates. According to historical records, Robert Newton, Mathew Gilbert, Nathaniel Turner, and Thomas Fugill were associates of the magistrates. In addition to being a magistrate, Fugill was also a public notary officer in the plantation. Keeping court records and other decisions were also part of his duties.[53] In addition to the officials previously listed, Robert Seely was marshal in the plantation. Furthermore, on November 25, 1639, freemen built a meeting house for the management of town and religious affairs in New Haven.[54] With the formation of a government, each free burgess abided by the New Haven Fundamentals consented to by all. In this colony, like others, freemen, or some part of them, agreed on orders and fundamentals. Freemen generally did not approve laws passed without their consent.

The Fundamental Agreement of New Haven reads as follows:

> ... that as in matters that concerns the gathers and ordering a church, so also in all public offices which concern civil order, as choice of magistrates and officers, making and repealing laws, dividing allotment of inheritance, and all things of a like nature they would all of them be ordered by the rules which the scriptures to hold forth.[55]

This was the first pure theocratic government established in New England colonies. Other plantations under New Haven's jurisdiction governed their entities in accordance with the New Haven Fundamentals. This was the case with the planters at Stanford. In 1642 or earlier, data indicate that the planters joined the New Haven government. The officials at New Haven approved their request because the Stanford inhabitants supported the New Haven fundamentals. It appears that in 1643, the magistrates and deputy for Stanford approved the Fundamentals and declared its inviolability.[56] Like Stanford, the planters at Manunkatuck or Guilford did the same. They joined into a union with New Haven by accepting the Fundamentals set forth by that plantation.

Even though suffrage and holding offices in New Haven were for church members only, this was not the case in Milford. Before the union of Milford with New Haven, six non-church members were freemen. Upon unionizing, the town of Milford thus had six non-church members. Even though they were members of the Milford body politic, they did not have the right to serve as deputies to the General Court. However, they had the privilege to vote in the election of deputies.[57] Regarding the election process, the authority in New Haven established an order for that purpose. The order for the election reads as follows:

> It was agreed and concluded as a fundamental order not to be disputed or questioned hereafter that none shall be admitted to the free Burgess in any of the plantations within this jurisdiction for the future, but such planters as are members of some or other of the approved churches in New England; nor shall any but such free Burgesses have any vote in any election; (the six present freemen at Milford enjoying the liberty with the cautious agreed) Nor shall any power or trust in the ordering of any civil Affairs be at any time put into the hands of any other than such church members; though as free planters all have right to their inheritance and to commerce according to such grants, orders, and laws as shall be made concerning the same.
>
> All such free Burgesses shall have power in each town and plantation within this jurisdiction to choose fit and able men from among themselves (being church members as expressed before) to be the ordinary judges to hear and determine all inferior causes, whether civil or criminal; provided that no civil cause to be tried in any of the plantation courts in value exceed 20. S: and that the punishment of such criminals according to the mind of God revealed in his word touching such offences do not exceed stocking and whipping, or if the fine be pecuniary that it exceed not five pounds, in which the magistrates, if any be chosen by the free Burgesses of the jurisdiction for that plantation, shall set and assist with due respect to their place, and sentence shall pass according to the vote of the major part of each such court only if the parties or any of them be not satisfied with the justice of such sentence or executions, appeals or complaints may be made from and against these courts to the courts of magistrates for the whole jurisdiction.
>
> All free Burgesses in the jurisdiction shall have a vote in the election of magistrates, whether governor, deputy-governor

or other magistrates, with a vote for the treasurer, secretary and marshal, &c. for the jurisdiction, and for the case of such Burgesses, and especially in remote plantations they may vote by proxy by sending in their votes, which votes shall be sealed in the presence of the free Burgesses, and the free Burgesses may choose for each plantation as many magistrates as the situation of affairs may require, and no plantation shall be left destitute of magistrates if they desire one chosen out of those in church fellowship with them.[58]

These selected articles of the Fundamental Agreement reveal important data on the vision of the government established in New Haven. Government officials championed theocratic principles like in Massachusetts Bay. From these articles, I discovered that the New Haven government had a mixed form of theocracy, aristocracy, and democracy like Massachusetts Bay. In addition to the observance of the above democratic principles, New Haven's government further advocated for the implementation of the rule of law. When the plantations of New Haven, Milford, Guilford, Branford, Stamford, and Southold on Long Island united under a commonwealth, the Fundamental Agreement became a constitutional instrument for all.

Edward R. Lamber wrote that the first settlements were independent from each other. The unification of these plantations into a colony was likely due to a spirit of self-preservation. Namely, given attacks from Native Americans, it was beneficial for planters to unite into a body politic. On April 5, 1643, freemen from the New Haven colony towns framed the first colonial laws as well as introduced the representative system.[59]

Democratic Principles in New Haven

The first evidence supportive of democratic principles in New Haven is that of the election. Additionally, liberties and powers of the towns' government in this colony were based on democratic principles. According to the Fundamental Agreement, free burgesses in each town elected fit or able judges for the administration of justice. Free burgesses elected the governor, deputy governor, secretary of the colony, and other officers. Furthermore, an election by proxy was in accordance with the Fundamentals Orders. In such elections, each voter sealed his paper ballot in the presence of the free burgesses.[60]

In 1665, with the unification of New Haven and Connecticut into one body politic, the freemen in New Haven continued to observe theocratic principles in their government as before. As the officials of the Connecticut colony governed their region in accordance with the letter patent of King Charles II and the Fundamental Orders of 1639, the entire colony including New Haven observed democratic principles in accordance with the charter.

Chapter 3

Mixed Forms of Governments in New Hamphsire and Maine

The establishment of the settlements in New Hampshire and Maine was unlike New Plymouth, Massachusetts Bay, Rhode Island, and Connecticut. Compared to the other colonies, New Hampshire and Maine were only provinces. The planters in these regions did not form colonies like their brethren in the previously noted colonies. Historically, the settlements in New Hampshire and Maine were under proprietary administration or government. The proprietors governed these settlements in accordance with the letters patent issued for them. The territory of Maine was under the control of Sir Ferdinando Gorges and New Hampshire was under Sir John Mason. They made laws and orders for the administration of the settlements. The proprietors appointed government officials. J. B. Clarke, in his book *The Government and Laws of New Hampshire before the Establishment of the Province, 1623-1679*, noted that settlers did not attempt to organize a government in Maine. He went on to point out that in practice, no form of government existed in Maine except the orders enacted by the proprietors for the general administration of their businesses.[1] Like Clarke, Charles H. Bell, the author of the *History of the Town of Exeter, New Hampshire*, noted the nonexistence of municipal regulations or any sort of civil government in New Hampshire before the formation of the voluntary association consented by the freemen.[2] This was the case in the settlements of Portsmouth and Dover. According to Bell, these two settlements were weak as there was no government in New Hampshire.[3]

After the death of the proprietors, the freemen in these settlements formed a voluntary community government, or combination, each for the management of their own affairs. Freemen in each community government observed democratic principles. Like during the proprietary and communal governments, under the colony of Massachusetts, the settlements enjoyed the same liberties and immunities as the inhabitants of Massachusetts Bay. Democratic principles instituted in the Massachusetts Bay colony were the same as in New Hampshire and Maine. In New Hampshire, when the settlements came under the royal government, data shows that the administration was of mixed form.

Government under Proprietors in New Hampshire

In the settlements of Northam and Strawberry Bank, wrote James Phinney Baxter, Capt. Walter Neal was Governor of Piscataqua appointed by Sir. Ferdinando Gorges and John Mason.[4] Governor John Winthrop also identified Capt. Neale as governor. In his book, *The History of New England from 1630 to 1649*, Winthrop records that Capt. Neale, as Governor of Piscataqua, sent him a package directed to Sir Christopher Gardiner.[5] Like Capt. Neale, Governor Winthrop further noted that Capt. Thomas Wiggin was the governor of the upper plantation. He worked for Lord Say and Brooke in that plantation.[6] The upper plantation was the first settlement planted by the Hilton families.

The *Provincial Papers, Documents and Records relating to the Province of New Hampshire*, recorded that Capt. Wiggin was the chief authority in Dover. He was among the magistrates listed in this document. According to the *Provincial Papers*, he was the chief authority from 1634 to 1637. From 1637 to 1638, Rev. George Burdett was the governor of this colony. Burdett was a clergyman who emigrated from England to Salem, Massachusetts in 1634. He was a freeman and served for a year as a preacher. Due to his religious views, Massachusetts authorities disenfranchised him. After losing his voting right, he went to Dover where he became governor. Like Burdett, Massachusetts authorities disenfranchised Capt. John Underhill and banished him from the colony due to his religious opinions. He went to Dover where freemen enjoyed freedom of conscience. In Dover, he preceded Rev. Burdett as governor, serving from 1639 to 1640. In April 1640, Thomas Roberts was the chief authority of this colony.[7] In 1634, more settlers, especially Puritans, joined their brethren in Dover Neck. According to Scales, women and children were among those who migrated to Dover in 1634. Capt. Wiggin served as governor until 1637. Scales recorded that in 1637, the freemen elected George Burnett as governor of that town. They elected him by popular vote.

Captain Underhill was a deputy to the General Court from Boston in 1634. In 1638, the freemen in Dover elected him governor. Due to his religious views, Massachusetts Bay officials contested his election. After two years of serving as governor, in 1640, Thomas Roberts succeeded him. Scales stated that Governor Roberts held that position until the plantation of Dover came under the control of the Massachusetts Bay.[8]

Like Dover, the settlement of Strawberry Bank, sometimes called the lower plantation, was under the control of the agents of Capt. Mason. Emigrants from London inhabited this settlement. Records indicated that Capt. Walter Neal managed Strawberry Bank for Capt. John Mason.[9] Years after, the inhabitants of Strawberry Bank named this settlement Portsmouth. Stackpole noted that Capt. Neal came to the Piscataqua around June of 1630. He arrived at the Little Harbor under the account of Capt. Mason as the proprietor of that settlement, and Ambrose Gibbons was a general manager for the plantation.[10] In the book, *An Old Mountaineer*, Capt. Neal was identified as the first superintendent of the lower plantation at Portsmouth.[11] Scales referred to him as the boss at "Strawberry Bank", which was later called Portsmouth.[12] In addition to Capt. Neal, Francis William served as governor of Strawberry Bank. Rev. Jeremy Belknap wrote that during his administration, the inhabitants of Strawberry Bank formed a body politic.[13] He continued to serve in this capacity until 1641 when this plantation came under the administration of Massachusetts Bay. From *Calender of State Papers*, I discovered that Capt. Neal served in various king's expeditions for almost 20 years. According to this document, he perfected the company of Artillery Garden. He spent three years in New England where he discovered unexplored territories. Due to his accomplishments, the king recommended to the Lord Mayor of London to elect him as a captain of the Artillery Garden.[14]

In addition to Dover and Portsmouth, the inhabitants of Massachusetts Bay settled in Hampton in 1638. Contrary to the first named settlement, Hampton was under the government of Massachusetts Bay colony. The government and the judiciary system were the same as in other Massachusetts towns and settlements. Governor Winthrop recorded that in 1638, the inhabitants of Massachusetts Bay established a plantation at Winnacunnet.[15] In 1639, this plantation became a town by the order of the General Court of Massachusetts Bay. Joseph Dow recorded that, in 1639, the Court ordered that "Winnacunnet is allowed to be a town and have power to choose a constable and other officers and make orders for the well ordering of their town, and to send a deputy to the court." In the same order, Christopher Hussey, Willi Palmer, and Richard Swain were entrusted with judiciary power to settle cases under 20 shillings. In the same year, the Court ordered that Winnacunnet shall become Hampton.[16] Winnacunnet being a town in Massachusetts Bay, John Moulton could behave like deputies of other towns in the disposal of land. William Wakefield served as town clerk,[17] and Hampton was independent like others. As in the case of Hampton, John Wheelwright, a banished minister from Massachusetts, founded the town of Exeter.

In 1638, Governor Winthrop recorded that Rev. John Wheelwright, after his banishment from Massachusetts, went to the Piscataqua region where he founded his settlement which he named Exeter.[18] In this plantation, in 1639, settlers voluntarily formed a government for the management of the affairs of the plantation. The government instituted in Exeter was different from that of the colonies of New Plymouth, Massachusetts, Rhode Island, and Connecticut. In Exeter, a ruler along with magistrates governed the freemen. According to Charles Henry Bell, a board composed of three magistrates had executive and judiciary power. Also in Exeter, freemen made laws with the approval of the ruler, who was always an elder. Historians thus believe that the government in the settlement of Exeter was a pure democracy. Charles Bell discovered that in 1639, Isaac Gross was the first ruler of Exeter. Nicholas Needham succeeded Gross and served as ruler from 1639 to 1643. After serving for three years, Thomas Wilson succeeded Needham. He served from 1642 to 1643. These rulers had a deputy or assistant who aided them in the management of the settlement. Augustine Stone and Anthony Stanyan were two individuals who filled that role.[19]

New Hampshire Settlements under Massachusetts Bay Government

New Hampshire settlements were unpopulated and weak. Additionally, the freemen in New Hampshire were of independent spirits. Due to a misunderstanding between them in forming a government, the plantations of Dover and Portsmouth voluntarily decided to join into union with Massachusetts Bay. The union of these two plantations occurred in 1641. As part of this colony, the administration of justice as well as the government was like that of Massachusetts' towns.

By contrast, the plantation of Exeter became a part of Massachusetts Bay after the petition of its inhabitants in 1643. On September 7, 1643, the government of Massachusetts declared as follows: "Whereas Exeter is found to be within our patent, upon their petition they were received under our government and Mr. William Paine, Mathew [Matthew] Boyse or Boyes, and John Saunders are appointed to settle the bonds between Hampton and Exeter on two month."[20] As a plantation, the inhabitants of Northam or Hampton petitioned the General Court to have a status of a town. The General Court approved their petition, and Hampton exercised the same privileges and immunities as other towns in Massachusetts.[21]

In creating a local government, in 1642, the settlements of Dover and Portsmouth had the power to self-govern as other towns in Massachusetts Bay. The order of the Court reads as follows: "It is ordered, that all the present inhabitants of Piscataqua who formerly were free there shall have liberty of freemen in their several towns to manage all their own town affairs, and shall each town send a deputy to the General Court, though they not at present church members."[22] In this case, Massachusetts Bay officials had a liberal view pertaining to religion in New Hampshire. The settlements listed above were not under a central government prior to their union with the colony of Massachusetts Bay.[23] The freemen of Dover and Portsmouth had the privilege of sending their representative to the General Court. As part of Massachusetts Bay, officials introduced the title of "Selectman" in New Hampshire. In Massachusetts Bay, selectmen had the power to administer their respective towns. Being under Massachusetts Bay, Dover and Portsmouth observed the same local government principles.

In 1642, the same year of the General Court order empowering the Dover and Portsmouth settlements to self-govern in Massachusetts Bay, freemen commissioned Capt. Thomas Wiggin, Edward Hilton, and William Walderne to assist the magistrates in Piscataqua.[24] In 1643, New Hampshire settlements were under the county government in Massachusetts Bay. According to the *Records of the Governor and Company of the Massachusetts Bay in New England, 1642-1649*, the General Court partitioned the colony of Massachusetts Bay into four counties—Essex, Middlesex, Suffolk, and Norfolk. In this year, Hampton, Exeter, Dover, and Strawberry Bank were under the authority of Norfolk County, like Salisbury and Haverhill.[25] Exeter, Dover, and Portsmouth were under the authority of the county court at Ipswich and Essex.[26] In 1679, the plantations or towns noted above became a separate and royal province from the Massachusetts Bay colony.

The New Hampshire Government under the Royal Province

As a royal province, a president, deputy, and five councilors governed the province of New Hampshire. In this province, the founding charter favored the mixed system of government combining the aristocracy and democracy. Regarding the aristocratic form of government, the king in England appointed the governor, deputy governor, and the assistants. The charter made the observance of the rule of law imperative in the oath sworn by the governor. The English crown ordered the governor to administer justice impartially and with equity. Like in the charter, democratic principles were in the code of the colony enacted by Governor John Cutt. In this code, in each town, freemen had the privilege to elect deputies to the General Court. Freemen elected their government officials in March. Portsmouth, Hampton, and Dover each sent three representatives to the General Court, and the town of Exeter sent two deputies.[27]

Democratic Principles in New Hampshire

During the proprietary government, freemen in New Hampshire observed democratic principles and self-rule the same way as their peers in

Massachusetts Bay. They continued to enjoy the same privileges during the royal administration. In the beginning of the settlements, freemen formed a consensual government. In Portsmouth, Dover, and Exeter, the elections of officers were free and fair. As evidence, in Dover, freemen elected George Burdett by popular vote. From 1641 to 1679, the laws of the colony of Massachusetts Bay were in force in the four towns in New Hampshire. They had the same privileges and immunities as the inhabitants of Massachusetts Bay. In 1641, Massachusetts Bay colony authorities approved the Body of Liberties in Dover and Portsmouth.

Early Government in Maine

The province of Maine was under various governments, such as that of Sir Ferdinando Gorges, the government of Massachusetts Bay, New York, and Plymouth. In addition to the agents of Sir Gorges, George Cleeves and Edward Godfrey governed settlements in this province. Furthermore, this province was also under the protection of the crown of England. Regarding the sort of government in the settlements of Maine, William Willis believed that the inhabitants in this region formed combination governments as their brethren in the settlements of New Hampshire did. He went on to note that each plantation may have regulated their own police without any assistance from other plantations.[28] In 1636, George Folsom discovered that Thomas Lewis was ordered to report to the court held at the house of Thomas Williams for refusing to deliver up to the combination which the planters signed for the formation of a government.[29] This information produces evidence that combination government was in existence in the territory which became known as Maine. John Josselyn, an English traveler, recorded the names of various towns and settlements in Maine, and according to his recollection, Winter Harbor, Cape Porpus, Saco, Black Point, and Casco were towns and settlements in the colony. Saco was the largest town in Maine. Kenebeck and Sagadebock were also towns in Maine. Josselyn documents that the town of Kittery was very populous. In his view, Gorgeana was the metropolitan of the province. English planters also settled in the settlements of Wells and Cape Porpus. Even though Josselyn recorded the settlements, plantations, and towns in Maine, he did not comment on the form of the governments established in these areas. On the other hand, he revealed salient data on the government established by the agents of Sir Ferdinando Gorges.[30] Regarding the administration of justice, William D. Williamson writes that Thomas Elbridge, a son of a proprietor, had a court at Pemaquid where he judged cases and imposed fines and penalties. Abraham was an agent and magistrate when Elbridge was absent from the settlement.[31]

The First Municipal Government in Maine

The territory of Maine belonged to Sir Ferdinando Gorges, one of the members of the Council of Plymouth. In 1635, when the Council of Plymouth resigned their charter to the crown of England, Gorges received his own grant from the king. At the time, he named his territory New Somersetshire when Capt. William Gorges was deputy governor of the province. According to William Willis, Gorges arrived in Maine in 1636 and held a court at Saco. Willis wrote that the court held by Gorges was the first of that kind held in Maine. At this court, Capt. Richard Bonighton, Capt. Thomas Cammock, Henry Jocelyn, Capt. Thomas Purchase, Edward Godfrey, and Thomas Lewis were commissioners.[32] On March 21, 1636, Capt. Gorges held the first court at the house of Bonighton in Saco.[33] This government lasted for less than two years. On April 3, 1639, King Charles I issued Sir Gorges a charter for the province or colony of Maine. In 1640, Sir Gorges received a new charter. For the administration of the province of Maine, he appointed Thomas Gorges, a cousin, to governor.

The Government of Thomas Gorges

Under Governor Gorges, Agamenticus was the seat of the government. In 1641, Gorges changed the name of Agamenticus to Gorgeana. Here, a mayor and eight Aldermen had executive, judicial, and legislative powers. Government officials for Gorgeana were as follows: Edward Godfrey, Roger Garde, George Puddington, Bartholomen Barnett, Edward Johnson, Arthur Bragdon, Henry Simpson, and John Rogers.[34] Among the Aldermen, Garde was a recorder. As Gorgeana did not have a police force, the mayor, twelve Aldermen, twenty-four common council, and the recorder constituted the police of that city. Emery relates that the mayor and Aldermen were justices.[35] Godfrey, an ardent support of the colonization movement, was the first mayor of Gorgeana in 1642. In addition to Godfrey, Garde was one of the mayors of Gorgeana in 1643.[36] Gorges returned to England in the same year when Garde became a mayor of Gorgeana. After the departure of Gorges, Richard Vines assumed management over the government in the province of Maine. Vines was in the service of Sir Gorges for years. He came to New England for the exploration of that region with a plan of establishing a permanent settlement. The editor of the Collections of Maine Historical Society called Vines "the trusted friend of Sir Ferdinando Gorges."[37]

Maine under the Administration of Richard Vines

After the departure of Thomas Gorges to England, government officials in his administration decided to continue the governing operations. As Gorges did not return to Maine, his associates Richard Bonighton, Arthur Mackworth, Edward Small, and Abraham Preble elected Richard Vines as deputy governor for a year. After Vines' election, freemen decided that if Vines left the province, Henry Jocelyn would succeed him as deputy governor. Regarding the government's administration, during the Vines' term, tax assessment for Casco was ten shillings, Saco was eleven, Gorgeana was one pound, and Kittery and Berwick were 2.10 pounds. When Vines sold his patent to Dr. Child in 1645, Jocelyn succeeded him as deputy governor.

Western Maine under Edward Godfrey's Government

The province of Maine was under two administrations, that of the Lygonia and Maine. When Alexander Rigby purchased the Plough patent, the inhabitants of western Maine formed a combination government. In this government, in 1649, they elected Edward Godfrey as the governor by popular vote. Godfrey was in the colony in 1629. In 1634, Samuel Maverick, William Hooke, and Godfrey purchased twelve thousand acres on the north side of the river Agamenticus.[38] Godfrey was a defender of the territorial integrity of Maine. He refused the subjection of settlements in Maine to the control of Massachusetts Bay. During the administration of Gorges in Gorgeana, Godfrey succeeded Roger Garde to the position of mayor. The Maine Historical Society notes that he had a large tract of land on the northern part of Agamenticus river in 1637. In 1639, he procured fifty acres of land on the southern part of the same city. In the municipal government, he served as recorder and Alderman.[39]

The Record of the Collections of the Massachusetts Historical Society recorded the oath reserved for those who served in the municipal government in Gorgeana in 1640. The oath prescribed by Sir Gorges ordered his officials to be faithful to him as well as to his posterities. On June 25th, the officials of Sir Gorges opened an office at Saco. They signed before Richard Vines, Richard Bonighton, Henry Josseline [Jocelyn], and Edward Godfrey, all counsellors to Sir Ferdinando Gorges. On this date, Roger Garde was register and Robert Sankey a provost marshal. Among the deputies were Edward Johnson, John Baker, George Puddington, and Barh.[40] Data indicates that, in 1645, magistrates had the power to settle cases. As the General Court convened at Saco on October 21, 1645, Francis Robinson, Arthur Mackworth, Edward Small, and Abraham Prebble, all magistrates, ordered the selection of Richard Vines as deputy governor of the state as the inhabitants did not hear from Sir Gorges on the affairs of the province.

Alexander Rigby and George Cleeves' Governments

On April 7, 1643, Col. Alexander Rigby, a republican and member of the parliament in England, purchased the province of Lyconia. Its patent belonged to John Dy and his associate. The territory was between Cape Porpus and Cape Elizabeth. While Col. Rigby was the president and the proprietor of the Lyconia province, he appointed George Cleeves as his deputy. After his appointment, Cleeves left England, arriving in Boston in 1643. In the colony, Richard Vines challenged Cleeves, who rejected his authority. Vines' opposition failed to legitimize because he did not have support in England. When the republicans came to power in England, the commissioners granted Col. Rigby the province of Lyconia, making him the rightful proprietor of the province. When Cleeves became the official deputy governor, Vines left the province for Barbados. Henry Jocelyn was his successor as deputy governor of Maine. Jocelyn could not stand the pressure from Cleeves' supporters, he and others submitted to the Rigby and Cleeves government. After Rigby's death in 1650, the opposition against Cleeves was renewed.

Maine Under the Massachusetts Bay Government

Massachusetts Bay was populous and powerful during the period under examination. The officials from this colony coveted the territory occupied by other English traders. This was the case of the provinces of Maine and New Hampshire. Religiously, the inhabitants of Maine were Episcopal. On the other hand, Massachusetts Bay inhabitants were Puritans. The religious visions of these two entities were contradictory. Therefore, the province of Maine was a threat to the existence of the colony of Massachusetts. As a result, Massachusetts Bay officials hoped to incorporate the settlements of Maine into their territory. According to William Willis, in 1652, the Massachusetts Bay authorities materialized their wishes of incorporating the territory of Maine into their own. In this year, the inhabitants of Cape Porpus and Saco voluntarily combined themselves into the administration of Massachusetts Bay. Also, Gorgeana and Kittery signed their voluntary submission into the government of Massachusetts. On July 5, 1653, Wells and Cape Porpus followed the same path as the other towns in joining Massachusetts Bay. In 1658, the inhabitants of the eastern part of Maine submitted to Massachusetts like their brethren had.[41] The inhabitants of Maine unified with Massachusetts Bay liberally. As such, church membership requirements did not apply to the inhabitants of Wells or Cape Porpus. The towns and settlements of Maine belonged to the York County government in Massachusetts Bay. Under the Massachusetts Bay government, the General Court permitted them to elect their own deputies. They had the towns' liberties and power like small governments in the colony. In addition to the subsuming government of Massachusetts Bay, data also indicates that the settlement of Pemaquid was under the government of New York.

Pemaquid under the New York Government

As previously mentioned, various officials governed Maine. In 1664, King Charles II granted the territory of New Netherlands to James the Duke of York. The name of this colony became New York. The Duke of York also had the control of the territory between River Kenebeck and St. Croix. The *Collections of the Maine Historical Society* recorded that the governors appointed by the Duke of York to the colony of York governed few settlements in Maine. Pemaquid was in the county of Cornwall. In the local government of Pemaquid, John Jocelyn was a Justice of Peace under Governor Richard Nicholls of New York. Like Governor Nicholls, Edmund Andros appointed him in the same position. During his administration, Thomas Sharpe was the commander at Pemaquid. John Dollin, Lawrence Dennis, and John Jourdaine also served as Justices of Peace. In 1680, under Sir Andros, Henry Jocelyn was a Justice of Peace in Quorum. In 1681, Lieutenant Governor Anthony Brockholls, appointed Thomas Sharpe and John Allen as Justices of Peace. Richard Pettishall, Alexander Woldrop, and Thomas Gyles were commissioners for the administration of the territories covering the interval of the River Kennebeck and St. Croix. They had the power to enact rules and orders for the better governing of the named settlements. Moreover, they had the power to administer punishments to offenders. Furthermore, during the administration of Thomas Dongan as Governor General, the settlement of Pemaquid was still under the administration of New York. In 1686, due to the distance between Pemaquid and New York, King Charles II ordered the surrender of Pemaquid to Massachusetts Bay.[42]

Under Massachusetts Bay, Pemaquid was under a different form of government. The form of New York's government under Governors Nicholls and Edmund Andros was autocratic. With the administration of Governor Nicholls, the government made laws in accordance with the political vision of the Duke of York. In this colony, the freemen did not have the privilege to elect their own deputies or local officials. The governor had absolute power to appoint and remove government officials from their duties. This form of government was destructive to the inhabitants of the towns, which were under the democratic government of Connecticut. Like Governor Nicholls, Governor Andros governed the colony of New York tyrannically. He observed the orders of the Duke of York with passion. Like the previously named governors, Lieutenant Governor Anthony Brockholls governed the colony like his predecessor. Contrary to Governors Nicholls, Andros, and acting Governor Brockholls, during the administration of Governor Thomas Dongan, New York's inhabitants lived under a democratic form of government. In 1681, Colonel Dongan was the Governor of New York and the regions between St. Croix and Pemaquid, as well as the area situated along River Kenebek. Regarding democratic principles, Governor Dongan allowed the institution of a representative government in the colony. He also introduced the rights granted to English subjects in England. Representatives of the people had the power to make laws for the colony. Moreover, freemen enjoyed the principle of equality. Elections were free and fair throughout the colony. In this colony, the Duke of York declared that "every free holder within this province, and freeman in any corporation, shall have his free choice and vote in the electing of the representatives without any manner of constraint or imposition, and that in all elections, the majority of voices shall carry."[43]

Maine Under the Royal Government

In 1660, Ferdinando Gorges, the grandson of Sir Gorges, claimed the right of the land after the restoration of King Charles II to the throne of England. As a result, Parliament assigned a committee to investigate the matter in question. After the investigation, Parliament ordained Ferdinando Gorges as the territory's rightful owner. In 1677, he sold his right as proprietor to Massachusetts for 1,250 pounds. In 1680, the Massachusetts government organized a government in Maine. During this period, the freemen elected a provincial president each year. In addition to the provincial president, freemen had the privilege to elect eight standing council members and a lower house of deputies from each town. For the formation of the government, Thomas Donforth, a deputy governor in Massachusetts, became the first provincial president in Maine. In 1684 when Massachusetts' charter lapsed, Maine was under the control of the crown of England.[44] The governor and the assistants formed the government. The governor and assistants in Massachusetts appointed the standing council, which served as the supreme judicature.[45]

Maine's freemen did not consent to Massachusetts Bay creating a government. According to John G. Palfrey, hundreds of inhabitants from different towns petitioned the king protesting against the action. They desired a government under the royal authority or a government under the freemen from Maine.[46] Maine's government ended up being different from Massachusetts'. They did not have the same religious views as those of the Puritans in Massachusetts. To illustrate, in 1643, Maine was not part of the United Colonies of New England. Governor Winthrop explained why they excluded them from the union. He stated that,

> Those of Sir Ferdinando Gorges [in] his province, beyond Piscataqua, were not received nor called into the confederation, because they ran a different course from us both in their ministry and civil administration; for they have made Aqumenticus (a poor village) a corporation and had made a tailor the mayor, and had entertained one [Parson] Hull, an excommunication person and very contentious, for their minister.[47]

In Massachusetts, New Hampshire, and Maine, such religious enmity existed against the Puritans. Thomas Warneton, a resident of Strawberry Bank, described the Bay people as rogues and knaves.[48] Regarding the civil government in Maine, Thomas Gorges managed his province as in England by introducing the titles of mayor and alderman.

Chapter 4

Freemen Liberties in the New England Colonies

The historical development of freemen's liberties in New England deserves careful examination. Researchers from political science to history as well as local authors in the region under examination have gathered pertinent data on the emergence of freemen liberties. Richard Frothingham, Jr. in his book, The *History of Charlestown, Massachusetts*, asserts that freemen's liberties in the New England colonies were inviolable. He noted that,

> Our citizens, as a general thing, in an age of restriction and tyranny, enjoyed personal security; inviolability of property; jury trial; freedom to engage in business; town meeting; education for their children, annual elections; a government of laws and not of men; and the right of making the laws, which, if arbitrary, were still tested on those who made them, and could correct them. Such principles were more firmly grasped, and more intelligently defended.[1]

Frothingham, Jr.'s account helps explain how the rule of law was observed, maintained, and defended in the New England colonies. Data from his work indicates that the founders of the New England colonies observed the rule of law, both judiciary and otherwise governmentally, such as with the General Court and House of Representatives, and in business settings. This principle was applied in every sphere of the government, including the establishment of schools, division of land, the establishment of good laws and repealing of unnecessary ones, observance of democratic principles during the elections, and the administration of local government. Like Frothingham, Jr., historians Christopher

Collier, Patrick T. Conley, and A. E. Dick Howard produced their own work on English liberties in the New England colonies.

In their book titled, *The Bill of Rights and the State*s: *The Colonial and Revolutionary Origins of American liberties*, these historians documented the development and embodiment of the English liberties in the New England colonies. Howard discusses the emergence of the liberties of freemen in Massachusetts. His account indicates that the Massachusetts Body of Liberties were similar to some articles in the Magna Carta, the Bill of Rights, and the American and State Constitutions.[2] Like Howard, Collier noted that Connecticut's Fundamental Orders of 1639, Declaration of Rights of 1650, and Royal Charter of 1662 protected the rights of every citizen in that colony.[3] In Connecticut, settlers had the right to suffrage, self-governing, and participation in the management of local affairs. Collier goes on to articulate that the Connecticut Fundamental Orders guaranteed due process rights to the inhabitants of the colony. Regarding due process, he stressed that the Fundamental Orders required the magistrates to administer justice in accordance with the established laws of the colony.[4] The law prohibited magistrates from being partial or going outside of the confines of the law during court proceedings.

Conley examined the emergence of religious freedom in Rhode Island. He praised the architect of the freedom of conscience. According to his work, Roger Williams and John Clarke were the leading men in Rhode Island who introduced the principle of religious liberty. In addition to discussing religious liberty, Conley goes on to note that the previously named leaders advocated the notion of civil liberties.[5] The Rhode Island Charter of 1663 enacted the same. This charter guaranteed a full freedom of religion to the English in Rhode Island.

In the New England colonies, the observation of settlers' liberties was the same as in England. Moreover, they had the liberty to hold property as guaranteed by the laws of the colonies. In addition to previously mentioned liberties, the New England colonists had liberty to bear arms. In colonies such as Rhode Island and Plymouth, settlers enjoyed the liberty of conscience. Historically, the English settlers in New England identified themselves as the subjects of England. From the charters granted to the colonists, the king allowed them English liberties. As an illustration, in the charter granted to the Governor and Company of the Massachusetts Bay in New England, the king allowed the English children born in the colonies the same rights and immunities as those born in England. This indicates that the protection of the liberties of English children were in accordance with the common law of England.'

As mentioned in the charter of Massachusetts, Englishmen in the colonies believed the same. In Rhode Island's settlements of Portsmouth and Newport, the English always identified themselves as subjects of King Charles II. In 1639, the founders of Portsmouth claimed as follows: "we, whose names are under [written do acknowledge] ourself the legal subjects of his Majesty King Charles, and in his name [do hereby bind] ourself into a civil body politic, unto his laws according to matters of justice."[6] This statement indicates that the rights, privileges and immunities that were afforded to the English in England were also extended to them. With that in mind, settlers in Portsmouth opposed violations of their natural rights. As in England, they maintained the same militant spirit regarding the protections of the birth rights of their brethren. Like the founders of Newport and Portsmouth Samuel Gordon and his associates in Warwick believed the same. In fact, the founders of that town did not form a government because they were subjects of the English crown. They believed in the power of the king and his government in England even though they were far from the kingdom. The Pilgrims in New Plymouth identified themselves as the subjects of King James of England in the compact signed on the Mayflower in 1620, identifying King James as their sovereign Lord.[7]

In addition to the previously mentioned colonies, the charters of Rhode Island issued in 1643 and 1663, and that of Connecticut in 1662, granted the rights of self-government, establishment of laws, and the observing of the laws of England. In the charter of 1643 issued to the Rhode Island inhabitants, Sir Robert Earl of Warwick identified the inhabitants of the islands and plantations as the subjects of the King of England. This is another piece of solid evidence revealing the attachment of the settlers of the colony to their mother country. In the same charter, members of the House of Commons and Sir Earl of Warwick, the Governor and Chief, and Lord High Admiral of all those islands and other plantations, granted a free charter of civil incorporation and government to the Rhode Island settlers.[8] Considering the nature of this charter, the colonists in Rhode Island had the right to establish free institutions in the colony, such as a democratic government with freedom of religion, religious tolerance, and freedom of conscience. The Rhode Island Charter of 1647 was created as a free and absolute charter of incorporation known as The Incorporation of Providence Plantations, in the Narragansett-Bay, in New England.[9] Connecticut's was called Governor and Company of the English Colony of Connecticut, in New England, in America.[10] This charter granted the continuations of the free institutions which they had before the issuing of the charters by the King of England in 1662.

Regarding English liberties, English writers had documented various charters granted to them by their kings. To illustrate this, Henry Care, Sir Edward Coke, Sir William Blackstone, and Sir Matthew Hale among others collected authoritative data on the English liberties from the time of the leges non scriptae or known written laws of the kingdom. Henry Care in his book, *English Liberties; Or, the Free-Born Subject's Inheritance*, noted that,

> Every man had a fixed fundamental right born with him, as to freedom of his person and his property in his estate, which he cannot be deprived of, but either by his consent, or some crime, for which the law was imposed such as a penalty or forfeiture.[11]

The English rights enumerated by Care are customary to the English. These liberties can be traced from the traditions of the ancient German tribes who settled in that land. In Germany, according to the work of Frederick Kohlrausch, translated by James D. Hass, the Saxons enjoyed unlimited freedom. It is certain that this culture existed in England during the reign of Saxon kings. The same work of Kohlrausch and Hass, shows that the Saxons established a free form of government in their institutions. Moreover, these authors specified that the ancient Germans were obedient to the laws established in their realms.[12] In the same context of the ancient German liberties, Albert Harkness, in his *Caesar's Commentaries of the Gallic War; with Notes, Dictionary, and a Map of Gaul*, relates that the ancient Germans fully exercised their freedom. He posited that they protected their people from arbitrary aggression.[13] This statement indicates that the Germans believed in the protection of their liberties. They opposed the violation of personal freedom and property rights.

Pertaining the source of the English rights, Sir Matthew Hale noted that,

> The common law asserts, maintains, and with all imaginable care, provides for the safety of the king's royal person, his crown and dignity and all his just rights, revenues, powers, prerogatives, and government; as the great foundation (under God) of the peace, happiness, honor, and justice of his kingdom. And this law is also that which declares and asserts the rights, and liberties, and the properties of the subject; and is justly known, and common rule of justice and right, between man and man, within this kingdom.[14]

Hale's assertion regarding English liberties is that they are the same as those granted in the Magna Carta of King John, and the charters of Kings Henry I and Edward I. Similar views on English liberties were mentioned by Sir Blackstone in his *Commentaries on the Laws of England*. In this book, Blackstone layed out rights of the English. According to him, every English subject enjoyed these liberties, of which he states they had the right to personal security, liberty, and private property. He described these as absolute rights.[15]

Lord Edward Coke stated, in *The Golden Passage in the Great Charter of England, called Magna Carta; Or, the Charter of British Liberties, Granted by King John to His Subjects, in the 17th Year of his Reign, in Running-Mead*, that English liberties had been initially granted by King John. Similarly, John Stow, in his *Survey of London*, detailed liberties in London during the reign of King Henry I, Richard I, and King John, among others. He noted that King Henry entrusted the inhabitants of London with the power to choose or oust their sheriffs as they pleased. King John granted them similar liberties. In his letters patent, he empowered the citizens of London with the liberty to choose their mayor each year.[16]

In the colonies, as subjects of the English crown, inhabitants observed the same mores and folkways as in England. New Englanders observed personal security and liberties, including property liberties with jealousy. In England, Hale wrote, parliament members jealously and vigilantly removed all the obstacles that would obstruct the best laws enacted for the safety of the inhabitants as well as the best provision of laws supporting the administration of the true rule of justice in all cases covering criminal and civil matters.[17] Like their peers in England, the settlers in the New England colonies were protective of their liberties. Francis C. Gray, the author of *Remarks on the Early Laws of Massachusetts Bay*, wrote that "the people [of Massachusetts] early showed, that they were jealous of their liberties."[18] They stood firm in protecting and preserving the same. Note also that, in Massachusetts Bay, deputies were concerned about the despotic power of the magistrates. They believed that the magistrates decided cases according to their own judgements without recourse to the laws. Governor Winthrop wrote that "the people had long desired a body of laws and thought their condition very unsafe, while so much power rested in the discretion of magistrates."[19] As a result, deputies requested the enactment of positive laws parallel to the Magna Carta. Deputies and ministers consented to make the same.

Freemen wanted the enactment of positive laws due to the arbitrary judiciary proceedings of the assistants. They feared violations of their liberties. English liberties were a birth right for each subject. To avoid such despotic procedures in the judicial system in Massachusetts Bay, government officials vested Revs. Nathaniel Ward and John Cotton with the mission of codifying laws. In 1641, Massachusetts Bay authorities codified the Body of Liberties, and these laws became the law of the land. This is the first statutory law ever established in the New England Colonies. The Body of Liberties consisted of 100 laws, as noted by Governor Winthrop. According to him, these laws were composed by Ward, a pastor in Ipswich, Massachusetts. He held the same position as he did in England. In addition to his religious ministry, he was knowledgeable of the common law of England. Governor Winthrop noted that he was a student and practitioner of the common law. After the composition of these laws, freemen and colonial officials revised them and they were altered by the Court.[20] After the elaboration of these 100 laws, colonial officials sent them to every town for their review and consideration. After this process, officials returned the laws to the Court for further revision and amendment. At the completion of the elaboration process, officials approved the Body of Liberties. The laws were in force for a period of three years of observation.[21]

Massachusetts Bay authorities codified the Body of Liberties in the same manner as the Magna Carta. As in Massachusetts, in Connecticut, the Code of 1650 covered the same provisions. Similarly, the code of Rhode Island enacted in 1663 provided the same. In New Hampshire, the Code of Governor Cutt mirrored the provisions of Massachusetts, Connecticut, and Rhode Island regarding English liberties. To comprehend this, it is pertinent to briefly discuss the development of the protections of English liberties.

English liberties are mores and folkways passed down through generations. These liberties emanated from various sources. Lord Coke writes that the Saxons made excellent provisions for their liberties. From his observation, it is sound to conclude that English liberties were of antiquity. The Saxons brought to England liberties that they had in Germany. In England, Sir William Blackstone asserted, English liberties emerged with the Magna Carta and the Petition of Right.[22] Lord Edward Coke argued that, before the securing of English liberties by King John, King Stephen, Henry I, and Richard provided the same. From this, it is reasonable to state that English liberties were part of their customs and culture. English subjects took with them the same liberties to their newly established plantations, settlements, and colonies. This was the case of the New England colonies.

The Massachusetts Bay Body of Liberties

Massachusetts Bay's Body of Liberties contains doctrines found in the Magna Carta and later Constitution of the United States. The Body of Liberties covered all the rights afforded to the English in their native country. As it pertains to personal security, the Body of Liberties stressed clear protections against arbitrary arrest, and for life, honor, and good name. This body of law tells us that colonists in New England valued those liberties as those in England did.

Personal Security

Personal security was highly valued in the colonies. From the earliest days of the settlement, the colonists in New England advocated peaceful methods to deal with their peers. Officials prohibited violence through legal means. For personal security and liberty, honor and good name, the Body of Liberty asserted that,

> No man's life shall be taken away, no man's honor or good name shall be stained, no man's person shall be arrested, restrained, banished, dismembered, nor anyway punished, no man shall be deprived of his wife or children, no man's good, or estates shall be taken away from him, nor anyway indammaged [damaged] under color of law or countenance of authority, unless it be by virtue or equity of some express law of the country warranting the same, established by a general court and sufficiently published, or in case of the defect of a law in any particular case by the word of God. And in capital cases, or in case, concerning dismembering or banishment according to that word to be judged by the General Court. [1641][23]

In addition to the protection against arbitrary detention, arrest, banishment, and other illegal punishment, inhabitants of Massachusetts Bay had protection from bodily injury or the infliction of physical and moral pain by a violent person. For the preservation of peace and security, every man's liberty and security were inviolable. As a result, all fights and quarrels or disturbances were illegal by law. The law which passed for the security of settlers from fights, quarrel, and disturbances reads as follows:

> It is by this court ordered, and by the authority thereof enacted, that no person shall beat, hurt or strike any other person, upon

penalty of paying to the party stricken by fine to the county where the offence is committed, or both, such sum or sums as the county court, magistrate, commissioner or associate, that take cognizance thereof shall determine: and because in his case several circumstances may alter the degree of the offence, as who do smite, who is smitten, with what instrument, the danger of the wood, more or less, time, place and provocation, and other like, it is left to the discretion of the judges aforesaid, upon hearing and consideration to impose such penalty or penalties, as in their discretion shall seem just, equal and proportionable to the merit of the offence.[24]

In 1647, colonial officials in Rhode Island codified English liberties. In this colony, each freemen's life, property, and honor were inviolable. That year, a provision for protection against arbitrary arrest, forcible exile, and due process were codified. In Rhode Island, personal liberty against arbitrary arrest and protection of life reads as follows:

That no person, in this colony, shall be taken or imprisoned; or be disseized of his lands or liberties, or be exiled, or any other otherwise molested or destroyed, but by the lawful judgment of his peers, or by some known law, an according to the letter of it, ratified and confirmed by the major part of the General Assembly lawfully met and orderly managed.[25]

In Connecticut, the Fundamental Orders of 1639 protected the rights of the colonists. This document prescribed the government's framework as well as the administration of justice. That year, the Connecticut General Court granted the freemen liberty to elect their deputies and magistrates. Similarly, the constitution of Connecticut limited the power of elected officers. Freemen in Connecticut had the same liberties as their brethren in England and Massachusetts in accordance with the Code of 1650. Puritans in Connecticut had the same legal mores and folkways as their brethren in Massachusetts Bay. From the *Public Record of Connecticut*, the codified law of 1650 declared as follows:

No man's life shall be taken away, no man's honor or good name shall be stained, no man's person shall be arrested, restrained, banished, dismembered nor any way punished; no man shall be deprived of his wife or children, no man's goods or estate shall be taken away from him, nor any ways indamaged [damaged], under color of law or countenance of authority, unless it be by the virtue or equity of some express law established by a General Court, and sufficiently published, or in case of the defect of law in any particular case, by the word of God.[26]

In Connecticut, laws enacted for personal security covered personal liberty as well as the protection of personal belongings. The punishment of violators of laws regarding personal security, liberty, and properties were determined through legal proceedings established by lawmakers. These laws required the protection of due process rights for each inhabitant of the colony. Regarding personal security, the Connecticut law added protection for each settler's family. Children as well as the wives of the settlers had the same liberties and rights.

In 1215, King John restored English liberties when he signed the Magna Carta. This royal charter guaranteed the ancient rights of the English subjects from a despotic government. The English throughout the world enjoyed these liberties. Countries such as the United States, Canada, Australia, and New Zealand had citizens with rights granted to them in the Magna Carta. Regarding personal security, the Magna Carta declared the following:

No free man shall be taken, or imprisoned, or disseized, or outlawed, or banished, or any ways destroyed; nor will be pass upon him, or commit him to prison, unless by the legal judgment of his peers, or by the legal judgment of his peers, or by the law of the land. We will sell to no man, we will deny to man, or defer right or justice.[27]

This article prioritizes the liberties of every English citizen against despotic judiciary proceedings and arbitrary arrests. Sir Edward Coke, the

Lord Chief justice of England, gave an outstanding interpretation of this article. In his view, the liberties restored in the Magna Carta are the free birth rights of each English subject. According to his understanding of the article noted above, the King prohibited his subjects from losing their country, except by decision of the court.

Colonists in New England were English subjects and observed the same rights as their brethren in England. Like King John, King Edward III granted the same liberties to the English. King Edward III ordered that "no man, of what estate or condition that he be, should be put out of his land or tenements, nor taken nor imprisoned, nor disinherited, nor put to death without being brought to answer by due process of law."[28] This is the first time that the law of England prescribed due process rights for alleged offenders. In this law, judges or magistrates followed all legal steps of judiciary proceedings before making final decisions. Another statute of similar value regarding the English liberties was the Statute 5 Edw. III. C.9. This statute declared that "no man shall be forejudged of life or limb, contrary to the great charter and the law of the land."[29] After tackling the personal security of the English, Sir Blackstone provided a cogent analysis on the subject.

According to Blackstone, the right of personal security covers the legal rights of a person and the continuation of the enjoyment of his life, limbs, body, health, and reputation. The analysis of Sir Blackstone indicates that illegal bodily, psychological, and emotional injuries against English citizens were against the law. The well-being of English subjects was inviolable. Any violations of these rights were punishable by the established laws. Regarding personal well-being, Sir Blackstone stated that it is inviolable because without it, a person would not enjoy the liberties or rights which such person deserves.[30] Before the creation of the Magna Carta, the protections of English liberties were in accordance with the old statutes. During the reign of King Henry I, the statute for the protection of the security of the English subjects reads as follows: "no man shall be taken or imprisoned by suggestion or petition to the king, or his council, unless it be by legal indictment, or the process of the common law."[31] In the same argument regarding English liberties, Roscoe Pound of Harvard University posited that, during the reign of King Henry I, the liberties of the Englishman were enforced, and those liberties were defined by his charter.³² Like King Henry I, King Canute also restored the English liberties during his reign. According to J.A. Giles, King Canute observed all the laws which the ancient kings established, especially those of his predecessor, Ethelred. He ordered the universal observance of those laws and penalties for the violations of the same.³³

Similar Articles to the Body of Liberties in the United States

The Constitution of the United States contains articles like those of the Massachusetts Body of Liberties. Here, for the maintenance of peace and liberty, as well as the protections of the rights of her people, Congress framed an amendment for that purpose. Amendment XIV of the Constitution prohibits the infringement of the rule of law. The foundation of the United States is respect for the rule of law. For the protection of her citizens against arbitrary legal proceedings against their property and personal rights as well as personal security, Amendment XIV of the United States Constitution orders that "no state shall deprive any person of life, liberty, or property, without due process of law; nor deny to any person within its jurisdiction the equal protection of the laws."³⁴ This Amendment covers various protections of rights in which the Constitution guarantees each citizen the enjoyment of the benefit of law and protection against arbitrary arrests, discrimination, prejudicial legal proceedings, and illegal confiscations without recourse through the rule of law. Along with this, Amendment XIV protects citizens from illegal proceedings and arrests without recourse. Based on the protection clause of this Constitution, citizens are equal in a court of law. The same Amendment gives the U.S. Congress enforcement power against violators of it. This amendment is one of the pillars of American liberty. As with personal security, laws of the colonies secured the personal liberty of every inhabitant in the New England colonies.

Personal Liberties

In the New England colonies, officials and colonists valued the notion of personal liberties in the same way as personal security. This was important to everyone in the colony. From the time of settlement, data indicates that settlers moved freely in the area where they saw fit to establish themselves. Their lands, houses, and domestic animals were safe from arbitrary confiscations. Colonial officials established laws for the protections of property. In previous years, every town had to choose a clerk for the recording of each person's land. In Massachusetts Bay, 1641, the protections of properties were in accordance with the Body of Liberties. For the protection of personal goods, the Body of Liberties declared that,

> No man cattle or goods of what kind soever shall be pressed or taken for any public use or service, unless it be by warrant grounded upon some act of the General Court, nor without such reasonable prices and hire as the ordinary rates of the country do afford. And if his cattle or goods shall perish or suffer damage in such service, the owner shall be sufficiently [recompensated].[35]

This law was for the protection of the horses belonging to the colonists from illegal use in the service of the government, such as war or other services. As evidence of ownership, the town clerks kept record of properties. In *The Charters and General Laws of the Colony and Province of Massachusetts Bay*, I discovered clerks certified and recorded houses and lands owned by each inhabitant. Clerks also kept record of marriages, births, and deaths of every person. They were additionally tasked with the keeping of records and wills for each inhabitant in the towns' book.

Aside from their personal belongings, inhabitants in the colony of Massachusetts Bay had the liberty to make their will as they wished. According to the Body of Liberties, "all persons which [were] of the age of 21 years, and of right understanding and memories, whether excommunicated or condemned shall have full power and liberties to make their wills and testaments of their lands and estates."[36] Moreover, a provision was inserted into the Body of Liberties for the freedom of movement. The Body of Liberties stated that "every man of or within this jurisdiction shall have free liberty, notwithstanding any civil power to remove both himself, and his family at their pleasure out of the same, provided be no legal impediment to the contrary."[37] In New

England, settlers moved frequently in search of fertile land to settle on. Settlers founded towns wherever they found an unoccupied land. This was the case in Boston, Charlestown, Medford, Hartford, New Haven, Providence, Newport, and other towns. The protection of freedom in New England was, again, the same as that granted to the English in the Magna Carta of King John. In this charter of liberties was stated, "merchants had liberty to go and come safely to buy and sell, without any manner of evil tolls, by the old and lawful customs." In 1226, the citizens of London had the same liberties. According to John Stow, citizens of London had toll-free passage throughout all of England. The restoration of the rights of the City of London happened during the reign of various kings, such as Edward I, King Henry III, King Stephen, and King Henry II. Like the liberties mentioned above, the inhabitants of Massachusetts Bay and other colonies had judicial liberties as well.

Judicial Proceeding Liberties

In the New England colonies, each settler had protection against arbitrary judicial proceedings. For example, in Massachusetts Bay, deputies were firm defenders of the inhabitants against magistrates' abuses of power. As early as 1635, I discovered ministers setting forth rules for court rulings and the behavior of the magistrates in court and thereafter. Governor Winthrop in his book, *The History of New England*, narrates those rules which the ministers prepared for the magistrates. It is important to note that during this period, the colony did not have a body of positive law. As a result, the assistants, the governor, and deputy governor had judiciary, executive, and legislative powers. They judged cases according to their own discretion. The named officials formed the Massachusetts Bay Court of Assistants. In 1635, ministers in Massachusetts Bay ordered that,

> ... there should be more strictness used in civil government and military disciple, that the magistrates should (as for might be) ripen their consultations beforehand, that their vote in public might beer (as voice of God.), that in meetings out of court, the magistrates should not discuss the business of parties in their

presence, nor deliver their opinions, &c., that trivial things, &c. should be ended in towns, &c., that if differences fall out among them in public meetings, they shall observe these rules:

Not to touch any person differing, but speak to the cause

To express their differences in all modesty and due respect to the court and such as differ, &c., that after sentence, (if all have agreed), none shall intimate his dislike privately, or, if one dissent, he should sit down; without showing any further dislike, publicly or privately, that the magistrates shall be more familiar and open to each other, and more frequent in visitations, and shall, in tenderness and love, admonish one another, (without reserving any secret grudge,) and shall avoid jealousies and suspicions, each seeking the honor of another and all, of the court, not opening the nakedness of one another to private persons in all things seeking safety and credit of the gospel.[38]

These rules were important for the administration of justice during this period. It is pertinent to note that ministers wanted the magistrates to administer justice impartially. The term "credit to the gospel" indicates that ministers desired the magistrates to avoid the applications of unjust procedural methods in court proceedings. They also advised them to communicate to each other freely without jealousy or grudge.

In Plymouth, as a rule, judges could not pass a sentence in a civil case between party or parties if they were related to the defendants or the victims. Government officials made this rule to avoid favoritism. Officials believed where the judge was related to the parties as a father, son, brother, nephew, or uncle, he could not be impartial in his court ruling. Government officials in Plymouth also declared that the judge who was related to his landlord had the same difficulties with impartiality in his court decisions.[39]

In 1641, when the Body of Liberties was codified, the law ordered that,

No man person shall be restrained or imprisoned by any authority whatsoever, before the law has sentenced (him thereto, if he can put sufficient security) bail, or mainprise, for his appearance, and good behavior in the meantime, unless it be in crime capital, and contempt in open court, and in such cases where some express act of court do allow it.[40]

This law was enacted to protect settlers from illegal or arbitrary arrests. In addition, judiciary officers observed the notion of the presumption of innocence until proven guilty. In Massachusetts Bay, the law required the exhaustion of all legal proceedings before the conviction or discharge of the suspect from legal responsibilities. Moreover, the Body of Liberties protected people from self-incrimination and double jeopardy. It appears that sentencing a suspect for the same crime two or more times was a violation of his personal security as well as legal proceedings. To restrict multiple sentences for the same crime, the Body of Liberties ordered that "no man shall be twice sentenced by civil justice for one and the same crime, offence, or trespass."[41] Colonial officials in Massachusetts believed that when the jury have rendered their verdict in a case, the same case could not be resentenced by any judge or jury. Rhode Island passed a similar law against double jeopardy that law stipulated,

> It is ordered, that from henceforth no suite in any court of justice within this jurisdiction, that is heard, judged, and executed served thereon, such suite or action shall not again be heard in any court, either of town, or of General Court of Trials within this colony.[42]

In Massachusetts, the law prohibited the use of illegal proceeding against a suspect. In situations where different means of solving legal cases were present, the Body of Liberties restricted judicial officials from involving needless procedures. To solve such ambiguity, the Body of Liberties declared that,

> No man's person shall be arrested or imprisoned upon execution or judgement for any debt or fine, if the law can find competent means of satisfaction otherwise from his estate, and if not his person may be arrested and imprisoned where he shall be kept at his own charge, not the plaintiff's till satisfaction be

made unless the court that had cognizance of the cause or some superior court shall otherwise provide.[43]

By law in Massachusetts Bay, judges and other judicial officials were ordered to punish a barrator. According to the Body of Liberties, "if any man shall be proved and judged a common barrator vexing others with unjust frequent and endless suites, it shall be in the power of courts both to deny him the benefit of the law, and to punish for his barratry."[44] It is certain that the colonists believed granting to the barrator the benefit of the law was the same as denying justice to the victim. In the Anglo-Saxon as well as Anglo-American' legal systems, frivolous litigations or lawsuits are inadmissible by the system upon the discovery of judges.

Throughout New England, the plaintiffs and defendants had the right to a jury trial. In 1623, the Plymouth Government officials introduced trial by jury. In this colony,

> It was ordained by the court that all criminal facts, and also all matters of trespasses and debts between man and man should be tried by the verdict of twelve honest men to be impanelled [sic] by authority in form of a jury upon their oath.[45]

In later years, the law allowed the selection of jury members from freemen and those who were not. This was the same criteria used by the English courts. In New Plymouth, the law required "that all trial whether capital or between man and man be tried by jury according to the precedents of the law of England as near as may be."[46] In Massachusetts Bay, the Body of Liberties ordered that,

> It shall be in the liberty [of] both plaintiff and defendant, and likewise every delinquent (to be judged by a jury) to challenge any of the jurors. And if his challenge be found just and reasonable by the bench, or the rest of the jury, as the challenger shall choose it should be allowed him and takes de cercumstantibus impanel in their room.[47]

This ability to challenge jurors was one of the rights of Englishmen during court proceedings. Both the defendants and plaintiffs had protections against arbitrary punishment or court proceedings. To avoid misrule among jurors, the Massachusetts Body of Liberties ordered that "all jurors shall be chosen continually by the freemen of the town where they dwell."[48] This law protected both the defendant and the plaintiff from prejudice and discrimination from outsiders. People who dwelt in the same town or plantation with both a defendant and plaintiff were more likely familiar with the case. Therefore, they had better knowledge of the character of both the defendant and the plaintiff as towns were small at that time. In addition to the benefit of a jury, every person had the liberty to have an attorney during court proceedings.

The Body of Liberties declared that,

> Every man that find[s] himself unfit to plead his own cause in any court shall have liberty to employ any man against whom the court do not except, to help him, provide he give him no fee or reward for his pain. This shall not exempt the party himself from answering such questions in person as the court shall think meet to demand of him.[49]

In the modern era, suspects and victims have the right to counsel as well. In Connecticut, government officials thought it was critical to entrust John Winthrop, the son of the governor of Massachusetts, with the power to execute justice. This commission is an ample example indicating that rule of law existed in the colony. In Connecticut, government officials observed the principles of equity and justice in the administration of justice. Like the aforementioned liberties, the administration of punishment was in accordance with the law of the land. In 1635, the General Court of Massachusetts ordered that,

> If any man shall offend in any of the said cases, he shall be punished by fine or imprisonment, according to the quality of the offence, as the court to which he is presented upon lawful trial and conviction shall adjudge.[50]

Protections against unjust and illegal punishment is essential for the observation of the rule of law. In Massachusetts Bay, colonial officials believed in the rule of law as well as its observance. Here, magistrates judged cases according to the law of the land, not their own interpretations of said law. Beyond this, arbitrary criminal convictions were illegal. Like the New England colonists, Caesar Beccaria and Jeremy Bentham were against unjust punishment. Beccaria wrote that no magistrate could inflict punishment on any member of the society according to his own will without recourse to the laws enacted for that purpose. In his conception, officials must administer punishment in conformity with the law made by legislatures. He went on to argue that punishment must fit the crime committed. Beccaria stressed that a magistrate did not have power to increase the punishment for crime beyond what the law allowed for.[51] Beccaria was also against torture which he described as cruel.[52] Bentham was also against cruel and unusual punishment in England.

Like Beccaria, Bentham noted that administration of punishment must follow the principle of utility. According to him, it was illegal for a judge to seek punishment not prescribed by legislators. From the reasoning of both, it is important to note that New England colonial officials valued the notion of the rule of law as well as the spirit and the intent of law in the administration of justice in an era where despotic government prevailed. Like Beccaria and Bentham, Tacitus wrote that the Germans punished criminals according to the committed offense. In other words, according to his research, the ancient German tribes punished offenders proportionate to their offenses. He went on to note that "convicts [were] fined in horses and cattle. The king or the state received a part of the fees paid by the convict, and the injured person or his relatives received the other part court charges.[53]

In New England, cruel and unusual punishments were unlawful. However, it is difficult to ascertain whether officials enforced this law. In Massachusetts Bay, the Body of Liberties restricted physical punishment as barbarous and cruel. In the same code, officials inserted an article for the protection of criminals from torture. Specifically, the Body of Liberties declared,

> ...no man shall be forced by torture to confess any crime against himself nor any other unless it be in some capital case, where he is first fully convicted by clear and sufficient evidence to be guilty, after which if the cause be of that nature, that is very apparent there be other conspirators, or confederates with him, then he may be tortured, yet not with such tortures as be barbarous and inhumane.[54]

This law specified without reserve that torture was not applicable when it was classified as inhumane or barbarous. Pertaining to torture, the Body of Liberties declared that "bodily punishments, we allow amongst us none that are inhumane, barbarous, or cruel."[55] Jeremy Bentham had similar views on crime and punishment. In his book, *An Introduction to the Principle of Morals and Legislation*, he noted that "the punishment ought in no case to be more than what is necessary to bring it into conformity with the rules here given."[56] In this case, Bentham asserts that the punishment for a crime must be proportionate to the crime as codified in the law of the land.

Like the Body of Liberties, the United States Constitution prohibits cruel and unusual punishment. Specifically, it protects U.S. Americans from the imposition of excessive fines and corporal punishment such as torture, long hours of interrogations, and forced confessions. For protections against cruel procedures during judicial proceedings, Amendment VIII of the Constitution declares as follows: "Excessive bail shall not be required, nor excessive fines imposed, no cruel and unusual punishment inflicted."[57] Sir Edward Coke was against the use of excessive fines in England. In the case of Robert Bullen against Richard Godfrey, the Court settled that excessive fines were unreasonable. In this case, the court held that jurors had the power to impose fines, but they had to assess that fine before its application. According to the report of Lord Coke,

> ...the reasonableness of the fine and it appears to them to be excessive, it is against law, and shall not bind; for excessive distress is prohibited by the common law, 41 E.3. 26.a. In Magna

Carta, cap 9k) 14. Excessive amercement is against the law. In 14 Henry 4.9.a, an excessive fine at the will of the lord, shall be said oppression of the people. The reasonableness of the fine shall be determined by the justices[58]

From the account of Lord Coke, it is plausible to conclude that the prohibition of excessive fine or bail in England was of ancient usage. In the United States, Canada, Australia, and New Zealand government officials enforce the same legal standard.

It is important to note that in a society where officials fail to enforce the notion of excessive fines, the rule of law will be impaired. In a more abstract sense, they infringe on democratic norms and principles. As was the case in the colonies and in the United States, torture for the retention of a confession was illegal by common law in England. Contrary to the common law rule, data indicate that during the reign of King Henry VI and Queen Mary, torture and forced confessions were prevalent. From his work, *A Reading of the Use of Torture in the Criminal Laws of England*, David Jardine wrote that Sir John Fortescue, Lord Chief Justice and Lord Chancellor of England, mentioned the existence of such practices during the reign aforementioned. He noted that reprobation and horror, including false accusations were employed by the judiciaries.[59] Even though officials tortured suspects, Jardine posited that "tortures and torment of parties accused were directly against the common laws of England. No law to warrant tortures in this land, nor can they be justified by any prescription, being so lately brought in." He goes on to point out that there are no judicial records indicating that torture or torments were practiced in England during legal proceedings.[60]

A Similar view was taken by Sir Fortescue in his work, *De Laudibus Legum Angliae*, translated from Latin by Selden. In this book, he writes that torture for confession for crimes was illegal in England. Similarly, in Scotland, torture and forcible confession were against the law.[61] To support his claim, Sir Fortescue detailed the court proceedings of an accuser during his period. According to him, an accuser had the liberty to challenge his plaintiff and witnesses, including jurors. He mentioned that when officials charged a suspect with a crime, they called twenty-four good and lawful men of the same neighborhood where the crime allegedly occurred to testify. The selection of witnesses was based on several requirements, such as being unrelated to the accused person and having properties such as land and revenues amounting to 100 shillings. Moreover, the law ordered witnesses to certify before the judge under oath the facts of the incident.[62] In conclusion, he states this process was not cruel or inhumane which would make an innocent person suffer in life or limb. The accused person did not have to fear the prejudices or calumny deriving from his enemies. In addition, he was not put to the rack to gratify the will or pleasure of his adversaries.[63] The process noted above is still in use in the United States. Amendment VI of the United States Constitution permits the accused person to challenge his or her witness during court proceedings. Contrary to the accounts of these previously mentioned authors, Bishop Burnet recorded various incidences where government agents used torture to obtain a confession.[64]

Chapter 5

Principle of Equality in New England

The principle of equality in New England has received attention from various authors and historians. Pertaining to the principle of equality, Alexis De Tocqueville wrote that "equality existed among the emigrants who settled in the shores of New England."[1] Like De Tocqueville, Francis C. Gray recorded the principle of equality before the Body of Liberties in Massachusetts Bay. In Rhode Island, William R. Staples mentioned perfect equality which existed in Providence among the early settlers.[2] Similarly, William H. Whitmore discussed the same articles of the Body of Liberties as Gray. From the work of these authors, I discovered that in Massachusetts Bay, due process of law was the cornerstone of the legal system. Like in Massachusetts, in Rhode Island, New Hampshire, and Connecticut, authorities enforced the notion of equality in the judiciary as well as outside of its spheres.

In New England, colonial officials valued the principle of equality and impartiality from the early years of the colonies onward. Colonists were prudent and avoided the use of arbitrary methods which would have divided the community. To avoid alienating them, colonial officials enacted laws for the regulations of the principles of equality and impartiality. In the New England colonies, committees divided lands in accordance with local or colonial laws. As a result, each settler enjoyed the same privileges. As illustrated, in 1646, the Massachusetts general records declared that all inhabitants in the colony shall have equal right of commonage in their respective town. In addition, each inhabitant belonged to the town where he resided.[3]

Historically, in a society where equality flourishes, citizens believe in a democratic form of government. As a result, citizens are more patriotic than in a state where inequality prevails. This is the case of the

United States of America, Canada, and Germany. In these countries, citizens support and observe democratic principles protectively. Like in the United States, in the New England colonies, most people were patriotic and supportive of the welfare of their local institutions as well as the colony government. They contributed enormously to the development of their local institutions. They were always in town meetings and obeyed laws established for the governing of local as well as colonial institutions. During the various wars in the colonies, data shows that each town provided militiamen for the preservation of peace, security, and safety in their territories. This was true during the French and Indian Wars, as well as during the American Revolution. The New England colonists exhibited patriotic deeds in defending their rights against the arbitrary political and military abuses of King George III. Even Massachusetts and New Haven were under the aristocratic governments, officials and freemen observed democratic principles such as liberty, equality, and equity and their rights as Englishmen.

In the New England colonies, colonists were against troublemakers as well as incorrigible community members. From various colonial era New England books and records, data indicate that government officials banished incorrigible inhabitants from the colony or sent them back to England. Like in Massachusetts, New Plymouth officials banished the same class of people from their territory. Yet, the strict control of behavior did not prevent them from accepting repented criminals in their respective towns.

Regarding the notion of equality, town meetings and general assemblies unified poor and influential planters. In the meetings, these individuals expressed themselves freely. This culture is prevalent in the United States of America. There, in general meetings in Congress and community groups, participants express their views freely. Participants adhere to a code of conduct. Everyone stands on the same footing as others. Due to the principle of equality, many American citizens love their country unconditionally. They are on the whole more patriotic than those of despotic governments in Africa, Asia, and South America, including a few other European countries. In New England, inhabitants worked for the progress of their towns, plantations, and settlements due to the observance of democratic principles which everyone valued even in aristocratic colonies like Massachusetts Bay and New Haven. In New England, ministers and officials governed by example. They approached the rich and poor, along with servants and slaves in public meetings. The General Court and town meetings were open to everyone. Each town ordered their inhabitants to assist poor people, such as Harvard students who were less fortunate. Each colony collected donations for use by those scholars. These donations were for the students so that they would have the same education as the children of rich families. In this case, rich and poor students could have access to equal educational benefits. That meant education at Harvard college was not for rich people only. Children from poor families were on the same footing as children from rich families.

Historically, the principle of equality dates to antiquity. According to Tacitus, the ancient Germans observed this principle. Tacitus wrote that a German king did not have absolute or unlimited power over his people, rather, he was accountable to his subject. From the work of Tacitus, I discovered that Ambriorix, the King of Eburones, valued the notion of equality among his people. Ambriorix asserted that "the nature of his authority was such, that the people had no less power over him, than he over the people."[4] The account of Ambriorix indicates that the Eburones advocated equality. Similar to the Germanic people, in England, King Alfred the Great believed in the notion of equality. Sharon Turner, in his work, *The History of the Anglo-Saxons*, noted that the Anglo-Saxons valued equality of men. He states that King Alfred also enforced the notion of equality among his people.[5] During King Alfred's reign, the law ordered impartiality of the administration of justice. Those who judged cases unjustly received a fine of one hundred and twenty shillings, except if judges could prove that the unjust proceeding was by mistake or made carelessly.[6] King Canute observed the same in England after his conversion to Christianity.

After his trip to Rome, he ordered the universal observance of the just laws throughout his kingdom.[7] For a better understanding of this notion, it is useful to look at the current United States system. In the United States, neither Congressmen and women, Senators, nor the President are above the law. Neither do they have unlimited power over the American citizens. In fact, officials always use the term "fellow

American citizens" to indicate that they are no better than their countrymen. In return, the American citizens owe them respect and support. Religious ministers adhere to the same standard. Contrary to the United States, however, in countries such as the Democratic Republic of Congo, religious ministers and government officials associated with the party in power are untouchable. Their children have unlimited liberties compared to those of poor families. In the developing countries, the courts do not sanction government and religious leaders in the same way as the lower class of citizens. Party leaders in power, influential citizens, the rich, and powerful religious officials receive preferential treatment in the court of law.

Contrary to modern developing country, in New England, laws were the same for influential people, leaders, and the poor. From *The Yale Review Journal*, I discovered that New England officials observed "the law of equity by treating every man fairly, not only on giving him a share in conquered or purchased lands, but also in allotting that share that he might be subject to also the advantages."[8] Accordingly, the colonists brought with them the principle of equality from their native country.[9] This view is in line with the reality of policies of many English kings. In England, King Alfred, Canute, Edgar, and Edward I ordered the observance of the principle of equality. During the reign of King Edgar, he did the same when he converted to Christianity. He did not permit his government officials, regardless of rank, to abuse their power. The King punished officials who engaged in unjust practices.[10] As did King Edgar, King Canute, the king of all England, Denmark, Norway, and part of the Swedes, ordered the observance of equal justice in his kingdoms. To satisfy the same, he commanded his counselors to render equal justice to all the people.

King Edgar prohibited his counselors from rendering favor to powerful people associated with him.[11] He also prohibited his sheriffs and governors throughout the kingdom from committing injustice towards any man, rich or poor, and demanded they render impartial justice to inhabitants of all economic statuses. He also prohibited the amassing of illegal taxes for personal benefit by his officials. He stressed that he did not need the accumulation of money though an unjust exaction.[12] These examples indicate that the settlers in New England were familiar with the notion of equality in their native land before they emigrated to America.

The American Founding Fathers were of the same frame of mind. Equality was stressed by Thomas Jefferson, one of the delegates of the Constitutional Convention from Virginia. In his book, *A Summary View of the Rights of British America*, Jefferson lamented about the disparity existing between American colonists' rights and their British counterparts. He went on to argue that it was pertinent to deal out equality and impartiality to all.[13] His complaints were based on the abuses of King George III and Parliament towards the Americans. For him, 160,000 electors on the island of Great Britain should not rule over 4,000,000 in the colonies. He believed that every individual subject in the colonies was equal to every subject in Great Britain.

The principle of equality in the colonies was also noted during the Constitutional Convention by Charles Pinckney of South Carolina. In his view, the people of the United States were different to those of other countries in terms of social fabrics. He articulated that among them, there were fewer distinctions of wealth, and less rank compared to the inhabitants of other countries. In the United States, he elucidated that,

> Every freeman has a right to some protection and security; and a very moderate share of property entitles them to the possession of all the honors and privileges the public can bestow. Hence, arises a greater equality than is to be found among the people of any other country; more likely to continues. I say, this equality is likely to continues; because in a new country, possessing immense tracts of uncultivated lands, where every temptation is offered to emigration, and where industry must be rewarded with competency, there will be few poor, and few depended. Every member of the society almost will enjoy an equal power of arriving at the supreme offices, and consequently of directing the strength and sentiments of the whole community. None will be excluded by birth, and few by fortune, from voting for proper persons to fill offices of government. The whole community will enjoy, in the fullest sense, that kind of political liberty which consists in the power, the members of the state reserve to

themselves, of arriving at the public offices, or at least of having votes in the nomination of those who fill them.[14]

Pinckney's account of South Carolina supports that of De Tocqueville who mentioned that New England colonists observed the notion of equality among each other. Certainly, Pinckney's perception was based on the cultural backgrounds of the English in America. During the colonial era, New England colonists did not have ranks as nobles, lords, dukes, and knights as in England. Even governors labored lands like servants and slaves. In addition to the previous statement, Pinckney remarked that the people of the United States were more equal in their circumstances than the people of any other country; they have very few rich men among them—meaning those whose riches may have a dangerous influence or were deemed rich in Europe—and perhaps there were not one hundred such people on the continent.

He went on to say that perhaps this number will be greatly increased; that the genius of the people, their mediocrity of situation, and the prospects which were afforded their industry, in a new country which must be a new one for centuries, were unfavorable to the rapid distinction of ranks. Furthermore, he argued that the destruction of the right of primogeniture, and the equal division of the property of intestates, would also influence preserving this mediocrity; for laws invariably affect the manners of a people. On the other hand, that vast extent of unpeopled territory, which opens to the frugal and industrious a sure road to competency and independence, will effectually prevent, for a considerable time, the increase of the poor or discontented, and be the means of preserving that equality of condition which too eminently distinguishes us.[15]

In the United States, the Founding Fathers advocated the principle of equality through the Declaration of Independence. The statement regarding the notion of equality for the American people reads as follows:

> We hold these truths to be self-evident, that all men are created equal, that they are endowed by their creator with certain unalienable rights; that among these are life, liberty and the pursuit of happiness; that to secure these rights are governments

instituted among men, deriving their just powers from the consent of the governed; that whenever any form of government becomes destructive of these ends, it is the right of the people to alter or to abolish it, and to institute new government, laying its foundation on such principles and organizing its powers in such form, as to them shall [see] most likely to effect[,] their safety and happiness.[16]

In New England, at various levels of government, officials as well as religious leaders observed the notion of equality. In any society at any given time when inequality reigns, such society tends to ruin itself. In those places, the economy and security of the people are always in despair. Take England during the reign of King Stephen, for example. The kingdom was in turmoil due to his oppressive rule. The English revolted against him due to his violation of the Charter of Liberties which he previously restored to his people as well as to the church, including nobles. The Earl of Gloucester, the son of King Henry, renounced his allegiance due to King Stephen's breach of oath against him.[17]

England is a better example of citizens battling injustice and despotic government measures. Culturally, the English are protective of their liberties. They do not cede to any despotic officials or authorities. In the colonies, the Americans revolted against King George III due to his abuse of power. Thomas Jefferson, in his book *A Summary View of the Rights of British America*, recorded grievances against the King. He lamented that he and Parliament passed laws which infringed on the rights and liberties of the Americans. During this period, King George III weaponized the colonial judiciary system. As a result, Americans rejected the notion of inequality imposed on them by the King. They believed that they were English citizens and had the same rights as their brethren overseas.[18]

In nations where officials observe the notion of equality, law and order prevail. Regarding New England, freemen, and colonial officials, observed the principle of equality early. In Massachusetts, the Company's letter to Governor John Endicott reveals pertinent information on the notion of equality. The letter advised Endicott to be impartial in his encounter with the planters and servants alike. In matters of law, it tells him to proceed without partiality to the offenders while punishing them. The punishment must also fit the crime. Company officials were obligated to prohibited abuses of power by the governor. In the same letter, the company ordered him to apply the same law equally among servants and planters. To avoid arbitrary proceedings in the court of law and outside it, they sent him a duplicate of the letters patent to consult for better administration of the plantations. In the same letter, they prescribed an oath for the governor advocating the principle of impartiality towards the settlers.[19]

As in Massachusetts, governors and other government officials in Rhode Island and New Plymouth took an oath to observe the principles of equality and the rule of law. In 1638, when William Coddington was elected a judge in the Newport colony, he consented to administer justice and judgement impartially according to the laws of God, and to maintain the fundamental rights and privileges of his body politic, which shall hereafter be ratified according unto God.[20] However, even though each colony championed the notion of impartial justice, laws to this end were not codified. In 1641, colonial officials in Massachusetts codified the principle of equality before the law. In Rhode Island, the officials codified the principle of equality in 1647. Colonial officials in Connecticut codified the principle in 1660.

Equality under Codified Laws in the New England Colonies

In 1641, a statute codified that every freeman was equal before the law. The same legal proceedings, laws, and courts were for the poor and the rich. This statute prohibited abuses of power by government officials. Namely, in Massachusetts, the Body of Liberties created the same laws to the freemen, servants, and strangers. According to the Body of Liberties,

> Every man whether inhabitant or foreigner, free or not free shall have liberty to come to any public court, council, or town meeting, and either by speech or writing to move any lawful, seasonable, and material question, or to present any necessary motion, complaint, petition, bill or information, whereof that meeting

has proper cognizance, so it be done in convenient time, due order, and respective manner.[21]

This law clearly explains the notion of equality in Massachusetts Bay. Inhabitants who were not freemen received the same justice as the freemen. Foreigners had the same legal rights as well. Like in Massachusetts Bay, German laws of hospitality during the time of Caesar were inviolable. Foreigners enjoyed the same liberties as members of the German tribes. In his commentary, Caesar elucidated that the law of hospitality was inviolable. Ancient Germans received refugees with hospitality and offered them the same protection as the Germanic people. Moreover, they welcomed them into their homes and defended them against abuses. Furthermore, they accommodated all their needs.[22] The writings of Caesar indicate that when a foreigner was in these territories, he received the same justice as a native.

In addition to the previous articles, the Body of liberties stressed equal judicial proceedings. Specifically, it ordered that,

> Every person within this jurisdiction, whether inhabitants or foreigner shall enjoy the same justice and law, that is general for the plantation, which we constitute and execute one towards another without partiality or delay.[23]

Delaying justice was an issue in Massachusetts. Before the codification of the Body of Liberties, Thomas Dudley, then an assistant, opposed delaying of justice. Governor Winthrop tells us that tending to hinder and prevent justice created grief for him as well as all the magistrates. As a result, Dudley refused to serve as assistant in the coming term. Governor Winthrop qualified him as "being [of] very wise and just men, and one that be trodden under foot of any man"[24] A conflict happened, for instance, between Dudley and the colonial's elders. The latter did not want the adjudication of cases emanating from their conflict in an open court. They wanted to avoid humiliation because they knew they were in error. A second case was that of Samuel Maverick, who was charged 100 pounds for entertaining Thomas Owen for escaping from prison. Instead, the court reduced his fine to 60 pounds. After this decision, one of the magistrates altered the fine to 80 pounds.²⁵ Such practices were the main causes of hindrance and prevention of justice. Dudley was one of the magistrates in this case. This was a statement from an honorable man, as Governor Winthrop indicated that Assistant Dudley was an advocate of rule of law in the colony. Delaying justice was an offense to others in the colony of the Massachusetts Bay Company. Dudley was deputy governor and governor in that colony.

The Massachusetts Body of Liberties ordered the enforcement of the principles of impartial justice for all causes brought before a judge. Statutes were in place prohibiting the delay of justice. As in the Body of Liberties, the Magna Carta stated that justice cannot be sold or delayed.²⁶ According to the interpretation of Lord Edward Coke, delaying justice is the same as denying it. In his *Golden Passage in the Great Charter*, Lord Coke wrote that the Magna Carta declared that "we shall sell to no man justice or right."²⁷ He went on to state that the same charter ordered that "we shall defer to no man justice or right."²⁸ Pertaining to selling justice, Lord Coke stressed reparations to the victim of a crime. He noted that the court must provide remedies to a victim of a crime committed by any person without exception to their status. For him, the victim must have justice without paying money for it. Judicial proceedings must also be without delay. In his view, justice must be full, free, and right. He lamented that nothing is more odious than justice set to sell. He went on to note that "delay is a kind of denial."²⁹ He added that Parliament expounded the rights of the English subjects stating that,

> ...by no means common right or common law should be disturbed or delayed, no, though it be commanded under the Great Seal or Privy Seal, Order, Wright, Letter, Message or Commandment whatsoever, either from the king or any other; and that the justices shall proceed, as if no such writs, letters, order, message, or other commandment, were come to them: All our judges swear to this: for it is part of their oaths; so that if any should be found wresting the law to serve a court turn, they are perjurer as well as unjust. The common-laws of the realm should by no means be delayed, for the law is the surest sanctuary that man can take, and the strongest forests to protect the

weakest of all; the law is the most safe head-piece; and, no man is deceived whilst the law is his buckler, but the king may stay his own suit, as for the king may respite his fine, and the like.[30]

Like the Magna Carta, the United States' Constitution prohibits the delaying of justice. Amendment VI of the United States Constitution declares as follows:

> In all criminal prosecutions, the accused shall enjoy the right to a speedy and public trial, by an impartial jury of the state and district wherein the crime shall have been committed, which district shall have been previously ascertained by law, and to be informed of the nature and cause of the accusation; to be confronted with the witnesses against him; to have compulsory process for obtaining witnesses in his favor, and to have the assistance of counsel for his defense.[31]

As it was in England, where the king and his public officials were required by law to protect the constitutional rights of the English citizens in a court of law, in the United States, the federal, state, county, district, and local governments are ordered the same. Speedy trial in the United States is a constitutional right. As such, the Constitution of the United States and those of the states prohibit the violation of this procedure. Even though Amendment VI does not mention the delay of cases in courts of law, judiciary officers do not approve of them without a request from the accused and the victim. Moreover, a delay of court proceedings can result in the tampering or contamination of physical evidence. Thus, judges and prosecutors in the United States follow the state and federal government's rules of evidence carefully.

In the same context of the notion of equality, in 1656 in Rhode Island, for better administration of fairness, government officials enacted a law restricting the obstruction of justice. For the notion of equality to be observed, laws established for that purpose cannot be obstructed. To avoid this interference in judicial proceedings by government officials, the Court of Commissioners in Rhode Island made a law which reads as follows:

It is ordered that no law or order appointed and ordained by the general and public authority of this colony, shall anyway obstructed or neglected under pretense of any authority of any of the town charters; but that the general authority shall have it done and placed according to law in all the ways.[32]

It is reasonable to conclude that an illegal act passed by the judiciary had the same effects as the denial of justice, and such acts were prejudicial to the plaintiff or the offender. Furthermore, for the virtue of justice, a testimony given by a plaintiff, offender, or witness had more weight in Rhode Island's judicial system. For better administration of justice, judges had the power to write down any testimony for court given by any parties. The law ordered judges to collect testimony and write the contents of it for the use of the court in legal proceedings. A pre-written testimony of any party was of no value to the court.[33] Equity and justice in Rhode Island were means of peacekeeping in the colony. An unjust formal accusation issued by an elected or appointed state officer was unacceptable. Officers who took a false oath were liable for making an unjust formal accusation. As such, the wronged party received a reward as determined by court officials. The offending judicial officials received punishment by sitting in the stocks six [hours] or paying twenty shillings to their respective court.[34] In Rhode Island, men such as Roger Williams, William Coddington, and John Clarke were advocates for equal justice and freedom of conscience. In 1656, Rhode Island government officials ordered the observance of equal justice for all. The *Records of the Rhode Island and Providence Plantations* stated,

> Inhabitants shall enjoy the benefit of all equal and impartial justice, together with ourselves; as also, they shall be lovingly entertained as freemen of this colony, to have their free votes, in making of laws, choosing of officers in town and colony, with the enjoyment of all privileges belonging to freemen of this jurisdiction according to order established amongst us.[35]

Delay of justice was illegal in Rhode Island. The absence of jurors from their jury duty was also illegal if there were no sound reasons for such absence. From the *Records of Rhode Island and Providence Plantations*, I discovered the Court was concerned about delays at the court of trials. To remedy this condition, the court decided as follows:

> This court having taken into serious consideration the intolerable delays that the court of trials are from time to time put upon, which lies as a great oppression upon the colony, by reason of the non-appearance of jury men; and that because the fines already set are so small that it is to there [their] great advantage to pay the fine and stay at home. Therefore be it enacted, that in case any juror, being chosen by the town or towns, neglect to appear at the general court of trails; being called, he shall be liable to pay a fine of twenty shillings in current pay of this colony; which, if not paid forthwith, shall be taken by distryant by the sheriff as formerly, only in case any lawful excuse shall appear manifest to the present courts, where they should have appeared, then it shall be in the power of the court, according to the way thereof, to lessen the fine to ten shillings, five shillings, or nothing, any, laws to the contrary formerly made, notwithstanding.[36]

Impartial and Equal Justice in New Hampshire

The settlements of Dover and Portsmouth were under the jurisdictions of Massachusetts as early as 1641. During this period, the residents of these settlements observed the laws of the latter. Liberties granted to the settlers in Massachusetts Bay were also enjoyed in the noted towns. In 1643, Exeter received the same liberties when they joined Massachusetts Bay. In 1679, after the separation of New Hampshire and Massachusetts Bay, the former became a royal province. In 1680, President John Cutt, the assistants, and elected representatives of the people codified laws to govern there. The Law of 1680 stipulated "that justice and right be equally and impartially administered unto all; not sold, denied or causelessly deferred into any."[37] This article was the same as that of King Edward in England. Like King Edward, the English received the same right in the Magna Carta. In addition to granting the inhabitants the liberty of equality before the law in New Hampshire, the laws of this colony prohibited government officials from abusing the rights of the people. Moreover, officials took an oath for the observance of equal justice for all. The law of this colony declared that "you shall spare no person for favor or affection, nor any person grieve for hatred or ill will."[38] The wording indicates that favoritism in the administration of justice was illegal. Injustice against the king's subjects in a court of law was unacceptable. The law required judiciary officers to be impartial in civil and criminal cases. Even though by law the notion of impartial justice was observable, during the administration of Granfield, arbitrary justice was prevalent. From this example and others, I can conclude that Granfield employed authoritarian methods in the colony.

Equality and Impartiality Beyond the Judiciary System

Regarding New England, various authors have discussed the notion of the principle of equality. Charles Hudson, in his book *History of the Town of Marlborough, Middlesex County, Massachusetts*, mentioned the observance of social equality in the region. From his work, I found that the freemen in New England enjoyed equal rights and privileges.[39] Like Hudson, data in *The North American Review* revealed that the signers of the Mayflower compact each acted for himself and as an equal to the others. The journal went on to posit that equality of rights and absolute equality were the primordial principles that government officials valued. The same journal also noted that equality was the cornerstone of the establishment of freedom in New England.[40] As in the other New England towns mentioned above, the inhabitants of Lynn celebrated during the *Semi-Centennial of Incorporation Events and Exercises of the 50th Anniversary* the establishment of equality and freedom in that city by their ancestors.

During this celebration, the orator noted that, in Lynn, there were no chosen people. Every citizen enjoyed the principle of equality before the law. The dominant ideas of the settlers were based on freedom and equality.[41] Furthermore, *The Yale Review journal* stressed the same views regarding New England—everyone received equal treatment from other members of the society. The journal noted that the New England settlers brought with them the principle of equality from their native country.[42] Alexis De Tocqueville similarly noted in his book, *Democracy in America*, that the New England settlers did not observe the notion of superiority over one another when they left their native country. It is sound to conclude that De Tocqueville meant that in the New England colonies, the colonists viewed each other as equal even though among them were the best elements of their native country.[43]

Thinkers such as John Locke, De Secondat, and Baron De Montesquieu discussed the notion of equality beyond the judicial system during their era. Each believed equality was important for the maintenance of Democratic principles. Historians have also noted the observance of the principle of equality outside of the judicial system in various countries during the medieval era and thereafter. There is an abundance of data indicating that in Rome and Greece, officials allotted land equally among the tenants.[44] In Greece, William Smith recorded the observance of the notion of equality among its people. In his book, *A History of Greece, from the Earliest Times to the Roman Conquest*, Smith stressed the notion of equality beyond the judicial system. According to him, a perfect equality existed in Greece during the festivals. He elucidated that during the games, there was no distinction of country or race among the participants.[45] He goes on to document that rich and poor were all participants in the games. To illustrate, Cylon, a tyrant of Athens, won a prize during a foot race. Alexander, the son of Amyntos, Prince of Macedon, also participated in one of the races. These examples reveal that the political leaders and inhabitants of Greece valued the notion of equality emanating from the judiciary.[46]

In New England, settlers received the same amount of land during the early years of settlement. Data from various documents indicate that rich and poor received the same acreage from local officials. Namely, in 1629, in Charlestown, Massachusetts, Richard Frothingham, Jr. recorded that each person had two acres for planting. In a 1630 town meeting, local officials agreed to grant each dwelling within the neck two acres of land for a house plot and two acres for every male that was able to plant. Officials followed democratic norms while allotting lands to the freemen.[47] In addition to Frothingham, Jr,' account, William B. Weeden's data reveals the same. He noted that, in New England, government officials divided land equally among the settlers. He recorded that in 1653, Lancaster, Massachusetts local officials equally granted land to the rich and poor. This illustration indicates that in the New England colonies, the notion of equality was a cornerstone for economic development. It is certain that economic disparities were not as prevalent as they are in a modern sense. In 1646, Weeden noted that Boston inhabitants enjoyed the same rights and privileges of the commonage in that town. In addition to the data noted above, local officials in Nahant divided land equally when the settlers from Lynn occupied that portion of land where they found that city.[48] Like in Massachusetts, colonial officials in Plymouth divided land equally among the settlers. From the *Records of Plymouth*, I discovered that in January 1627, it was agreed in a full court that each person would be granted 20 acres of land. The division of land further happened with the consent of community members.[49]

Historically, with the observance of the notion of equality, community members consented freely to the management of affairs of their institutions. It is pertinent to articulate that autocratic features emerge in a society where a segment of the population perceives themselves as being better or more important than the rest of society. Resultantly, in this type of society, powerful elites infringe on democratic norms. Contrarily, in a society prone to democratic norms, inhabitants treat each other as equals. In this case, each citizen contributes to the management of local affairs. This was the case of the colonists in New England. Here, the partition of lands, establishment of schools, and town liberties were in accordance with the principles of equality. Citizens and government officials in the United States advocate the same notion of equality that existed in New England.

Equality in Business

In New England, officials were against the notion of monopoly. Settlers in Plymouth, Massachusetts, Connecticut, Rhode Island, and New Hampshire, and the province of Maine believed in the market economy. As a result, officials established acts or orders for the protection of settlers from arbitrary business procedures and patronage. In Massachusetts Bay, through the Code of 1641, officials included an article prohibiting the same. The Body of Liberties declared as follows: "no monopolies shall be granted or allowed amongst us, but of such new inventions that are profitable to the country, and that for a short time."[50] For them, monopoly in business was an aspect of inequality. Therefore, they did not advocate for the use of it in the colony. Historically, the prohibition of this practice was of ancient usage in England. During the era of Lord Edward Coke, attorney-general; John Popham, Chief Justice; and John Fortescue, Chief Justice, each said that monopoly was against the common law. With that in consideration, English Parliament made the practice illegal.[51]

In Rhode Island, colonial officials passed a law offering the freemen equal opportunity to conduct business as strangers did. In 1652, the General Assembly of Rhode Island ordered that,

> All men of what nation soever they be, that are or shall be hereafter received inhabitant, within any of the towns in this colony shall have equal liberty to buy, sell or trade among us as well as any Englishman, any law or order to the contrary notwithstanding.[52]

This law gives ample evidence as to how the notion of equality was valued in Rhode Island. In this colony, leaders such as Roger Williams, stood for equal justice as well as liberty of the people. He was a defender and advocate of personal liberty as well as the liberty of conscience during his years as minister and government official in the colony.

Equality in the Establishment of Schools and the Treatment of Students

In New England, especially in Massachusetts and Connecticut, local officials established elementary and grammar schools in accordance with the laws of the colonies. The account regarding the Act of 1647, for instance, is in the *Records of the Governor and Company of the Massachusetts Bay in New England*. As in the listed document, the Education of Act of 1647 is also in *The Charters and General Laws of the Colony of Massachusetts Bay*. This was the first law ordering the founding of elementary and grammar schools in New England. The Act of 1647 ordered the establishment of a reading and writing school in each town of 50 families. In addition, in every town of 100 families, the law ordered the founding of a grammar school to prepare students for college or university. In the same act, the towns which did not abide incurred a fine. Failure to establish a grammar school was punishable by fine of ten shillings. In 1671, the law required the establishment of two grammar and writing schools in every town of 500 families. Failure to comply with this law was punishable by a fine of twenty shillings.[53]

In 1650, Connecticut passed a similar law. The language of the Connecticut law advocated the notion of equality. Each town of the same population had the same privilege and liberties to establish a school. The law prescribed a fine for failure of compliance. Like in Connecticut, in 1656, in the colony of New Haven, the education law championed the notion of equality. In New Haven, officers of each plantation enforced educational law firmly to their brethren for the training of their children.[54] Government officials used the term brethren as an indication of fellow religious members or brothers. In this case, there is no question the principle of equality flourished among them.

Equality and Impartiality in Dorchester Schools

Historically, the founders of the New England colonies believed in the principles of equality and impartiality. These principles were in their legal, social, and judiciary systems. As early as 1645, in Dorchester, government officials stressed dearly these notions. The *Dorchester Town Records* noted that local officials ordered schoolmasters to treat students equally and impartially. The Order of the Selectmen of this town regarding the treatments of students by the schoolmaster reads as follows:

> He shall equally and impartially receive and instruct such as shall be sent and committed to him for that end whether their parents be poor or rich not refusing any who have Right and Interest in the school.[55]

This is the first order ever enacted in the colony for the protection of students against discriminatory practices. The prohibition of discriminatory practices in schools was subsequently observed in the education system at the federal, state, and local levels in the United States. In Dorchester, Massachusetts, the violation of the rights of students weas under the jurisdiction of school wardens. In 1645, the Dorchester's town government ordered the election of three wardens for the management of the schools. The chosen officials had various mandates for the regulation of the schools. One of the mandates was the protection of the students from the school masters' abuses, such as missing school, arriving late to school, not dispensing classes in accordance with the schools' town orders, and teaching materials that was not beneficial to the students.[56]

Chapter 6

Liberty of Conscience in the New England Colonies

Historians and social scientists have shown interests in the notion and practice of liberty of conscience, especially in a religious sense. This topic merits attention in the United States and in other parts of the world. To note, pure liberty of religion emerged in Rhode Island during the period under investigation. As to date, scholars and historians do not contest Rhode Island's founders being the pioneers of this practice. Even European scholars agree that religious freedom existed in colonial Rhode Island.

Rhode Island historians, such as Thomas W. Bicknell, Edward Peterson, William B. Weeden, Samuel Greene Arnold, Richard M. Bayles, and William R. Staples, have documented factual data on the evolution of freedom of religion and the architects of the principle in Rhode Island. In addition to the authors listed above, Professor Patrick T. Conley has made major contributions in explaining the historical emergence of freedom of religion in that colony and during its later statehood. His work on this subject remains relevant. In the work of the aforementioned authors, pertinent data is recorded on the character as well as religious beliefs of the founders of Rhode Island. As illustrated by William Staples, in his *Annals of the Town of Providence from Its First Settlement to the Organization of the City Government, in June, 1832*, authoritative evidence on the religious and political culture from Roger Williams exists. From Staples' work, I discovered that, in addition to his advocacy for religious freedom, Williams, the founder of Providence, was also a champion of human rights. Staples credits him as being the first religious leader in our modern era to oppose the interference of government in the matter of religion. He articulated that Williams was receptive to the political opinions of other people even if they did not have the same opinions as him.[1]

Williams was an advocate of civil and religious rights. He endured humiliations at the hands of Massachusetts Bay authorities. The work of Governor John Winthrop has similar information on religious opinions of Williams. Governor Winthrop in his book, *The History of New England from 1630 to 1649, Vol. 1*, asserted that Williams was against the interference of the civil government into religious affairs. In 1635, a fearless Williams taught in public that "magistrate ought not to tender on oath to an unregenerate man, for that we thereby have communion with a wicked man in the worship of God, and cause him to take the name of God in vain."[2] His speech was heard by all the ministers who were present. Williams' opinions were offensive to religious leaders in Salem and Boston, including colonial officials. Consequently, they began to document his religious violations so that they had evidence to censor him. In addition to his offensive public speeches before the ministers, Governor Winthrop stated that one of the charges against Williams concerned a letter that he wrote detailing the abuses of magistrates towards the inhabitants of the colony.

In this letter, Williams declared that the magistrates were unjust and employed extreme oppression against the people. Moreover, officials and church ministers accused him of convincing his church to renounce communion with all the churches in Massachusetts Bay.[3] From this case, it is clear that Williams was against the use of the communion procedures of the Church of England. Due to these charges, the Court decided to banish him from the colony. He had six weeks only to reside in the colony before his departure. Governor Winthrop tells us that religious and government officials consented to sending him back to England. However, they failed to do so because he left the town of Salem before the arrival of government messengers. He departed from the Massachusetts Bay colony accompanied by more than twenty others.

In Rhode Island, Williams became the architect of the principle of freedom of conscience. Historian Samuel Greene Arnold identified him "as a scholar, an ardent friend of popular liberty as well for the mind as for the body."[4] He stated that Williams was the great and earliest assertor of religious freedom. Arnold's account is based on the struggle and persecutions which Williams endured. Williams was not afraid to challenge magistrates and religious ministers' policies and regulations towards his fellow colonists. From the work of Charles Francis Adams, I found that Williams and Sir Henry Vane represented the ideas of extreme civil liberty and religious tolerance during the early days of the colony when these principles were unwelcomed by political and religious leaders in Massachusetts Bay.[5] In regard to his perceptions of the government of that colony, Oscar S. Straus notes that Williams' political and religious principles were offensive to government authorities in Massachusetts. Furthermore, Straus said that for years, Williams devoted his energy and time to religious liberty. As a result, he qualifies as a pioneer of it in the colony.[6] Richard P. Hallowell, in his book *The Quaker Invasion of Massachusetts*, identifies Williams as the apostle of liberty.[7] In an undated letter written by Williams to the inhabitants of Providence, he noted the struggle which he faced during his fight for religious freedom in his life. In a portion of his letter recorded in the *Records of the Colony of Rhode Island and Providence Plantations*, he stated, "I have been charged with folly for the freedom and liberty which I have always stood for; I say liberty and equality, both in land and government."[8] This quote reveals the experience of Williams with regard to the treatments he received in Massachusetts Bay during his stay in that colony.

Aside from Williams, Governor Winthrop mentioned the names of religious and government officials who advocated freedom of religion in Massachusetts Bay. As early as 1635, religious leaders with different opinions were influential in cities, such as Boston. Additionally, he noted the names of Massachusetts government officials who left that colony and founded the towns of Newport and Portsmouth. From his recollections, he wrote that William Coddington, John Coggeshall, William Aspinwall, and John Clarke resided in the colony of Massachusetts before they emigrated to Rhode Island. Coggeshall was a deputy in Massachusetts Bay and the Court disfranchised him due to his religious opinion. Coddington was an assistant and the colony treasurer in Massachusetts Bay. In Winthrop's *History of New England from 1630 to 1649, Vol. 1*, he mentioned Coddington as a gentleman of great influence in the town of Boston and reported that he was the first Englishman who built a brick house in the city.[9] In addition to this accolade, he was among the leading men in Massachusetts who believed in the liberty of conscience. In 1636, he lost his magistracy through an election. Contrary to Coddington and Coggeshall, Clarke was a physician and a preacher. These men were the founders of Newport and Portsmouth. Regarding religious activities, Aspinwall had the same view as John Wheelwright. According to Governor Winthrop, he joined Wheelwright in advocating for freedom of religion. As a result, the Massachusetts General Court banished him, but after a reconciliation with members of his church in Boston, colonial officials rescinded his banishment.[10] Like Coddington, Nicholas Easton was also an advocate of freedom of religion. He was among the founders of Newport, Rhode Island.

Regarding religious freedom in Newport, Coddington and Clarke deserve credit for its implementation. John Callender in his work, *An Historical Discourse, on the Civil and Religious Affairs of the Colony of Rhode-Island*, documented evidence of Dr. Clarke's contribution to religious freedom. He asserted that Dr. Clarke was a pioneer who pushed for the foundation of the first government in the world where equal and civil rights to all was supreme. He went on to note his advocacy on religious liberty was the same as equal and civil rights. According to Callender, Dr. Clarke had the same religious philosophy as Roger Williams.[11] From the account of John Hayward, Dr. Clarke was a physician in London before his emigration to Massachusetts. In addition to his medical practice, he was a distinguished Baptist minister. In the colony, he was the first founder of the Baptist church in Newport. According to Hayward, Dr. Clarke's Baptist church in Newport was the second to be established in America.[12] As with the previously mentioned authors, Edward Peterson wrote that Dr. Clarke and Coddington have the honor of being the architects and pioneers in the advocacy of liberty and independence in Rhode Island.[13] His view indicates that the principles of equality, civil liberty, and freedom of conscience in Newport and Portsmouth were implemented by these men. Therefore, it is plausible to state from the above that Coddington, Dr. Clarke and Williams were the pioneers of religious freedom in Rhode Island.

Regarding religious militancy, it is appropriate to shed light on events which occurred in Boston pertaining to advocacy for freedom of religion. In Boston, freemen were against the interference of the government in the matter of religion. In various congregations, revolts occurred against ministers due to their religious doctrine. William I. Buddington in his book, *The History of the First Church, Charlestown, in Nine Lecture, with Notes*, documented how Boston men resisted against the influence of the Puritans towards their religious beliefs. He cited the case of Thomas Gould and Thomas Osborn who had Baptist religious ideologies. During his time in the First Church, Gould refused to have his child be baptized. To avoid being reprimanded by church officials, Gould withdrew from its communion. As early as 1665, Gould and Osborn along with others formed their own church. After self-exclusion, church officials invited them to explain their indignation. However, Gould and Osborn refused to appear before church officials. Consequently, Gould and his associates appeared before the Court Assistants where they were charged and prosecuted. The magistrate of the court of assistant imprisoned them for being disobedient to laws of the colony.[14]

In the New England colonies, freemen had freedom of conscience to elect government officials, decide a verdict in court, and other such town liberties. In Massachusetts, even though officials infringed on liberty of worship, freemen enjoyed other liberties of conscience. Members of the jury decided verdicts based on their own conscience for cases entrusted to them. As was the case with Massachusetts, in Plymouth, Rhode Island, Connecticut, New Hampshire, and Maine, freemen had freedom of conscience. Each freeman acted freely by his conscience. In Massachusetts Bay, deputies took an oath to decide cases according to their conscience. The oath reads as follows:

> I do swear by the most great and dreadful name of the ever living God, that in all cases wherein I am to deliver any vote or sentence, against any criminal offence, or between parties in any civil case; I will deal uprightly and justly, according to my judgement and conscience; and I will according to my skill and ability, assist in all other public affairs of this court, faithfully and truly, according to the duty of my place when I shall be present to attend the service.[15]

In New England, colonial officials managed religious laws according to their own beliefs and political agendas. Here, liberty of conscience was not parallel. To specify, in Massachusetts Bay, colonial officials did not permit religious freedom to churches which held religious views contrary to theirs. Contrarily, in Connecticut, officials observed a separation of the church and state. In Rhode Island, the protection of worship was in accordance with the law of the colony. In this colony, people of different religious denominations were free to worship without constraint from authorities. In settlements such as those of New Hampshire and Maine, religion did not have any impact on the administration of local government. Furthermore, in New Plymouth, evidence indicates that religious tolerance was prevalent. In this chapter, I will discuss the freedom of worship, liberty of conscience for jurors, liberty of conscience to vote for laws without the interference of the government, and election of local and colonial officials.

Freedom of Worship in Providence

In New England, freedom of worship was legal for the first time in Providence, Rhode Island. In this town, Roger Williams and his associates passed an order granting liberty of conscience to all. From the beginning of the settlement, town officials in Providence did not punish a single person based on his religious opinions and beliefs. Regarding the first religious order, William R. Staples wrote that "no man should be molested for his conscience."[16] With this order, servants, children, and women were able to participate in all religious meetings without any constraints. When Roger Williams and his associate founded Providence, religious freedom was inviolable. According to the *Records of the Colony of Rhode Island and Providence Plantation in New England*, Verin, one of the first settlers in the town of Providence, did not observe the religious order of the town by restraining his wife from going to a religious meeting. As a result, town officials censured him. Due to his violation of the religious order, the court "agreed that Joshua Verin upon the breach of a covenant for restraining of the liberty of conscience, shall be withheld from the liberty of voting till he shall declare the contrary."[17] After being disenfranchised, Verin moved to Salem, Massachusetts. This is the first evidence indicating the enforcement of liberty of conscience in New England. In 1640, local officials continued to observe liberty of conscience in Providence.[18] Like Providence, in Newport, government officials perpetuated the law for the protection of liberty of conscience.

In 1647, when the four towns in Rhode Island united into a body politic under the patent of 1643, colonial officials passed a law for the protection of the liberty of conscience. That year, each man enjoyed peaceable rights and liberties. William B. Weeden in his, book *Early Rhode Island. A Social History of the People*, noted that the fundamental right of religious liberty which was advocated by Roger Williams was recognized in the law of 1647 in Rhode Island and then in the charter of Charles II of 1663.[19] Like Weeden, in the Proceedings of the First General Assembly of the "Incorporation of Providence Plantation," and the *Code of Laws Adopted by that Assembly in 1647 with Notes Historical and Explanatory*, the law protecting the principle of liberty in 1647 was recorded. In this document, colonial officials declared as follows:

> These are the laws that concern all men, and those are the penalties for the transgression thereof, which, by common consent, are ratified and established throughout the whole colony, and otherwise then thus what is herein forbidden, all men may walk as their consciences persuade them, everyone are in the name of his God; and let the saints of the most High walk in his colony without molestation, in name of Jehovah their God, from ever and ever.[20]

This law explicitly indicates that Rhode Island inhabitants were free from molestation and other abuses based on religious opinions. In Rhode Island, officials prohibited religious persecution. For example, officials did not abuse Quakers based on their religious opinions as Massachusetts Bay had done. They enjoyed the same rights as other colonists.

Protection of Quakers from the United Colonies and Massachusetts Bay Colony

Due to their religious beliefs, government officials in the United Colonies restricted Quakers from entering their territories. The United Colonies was composed of Massachusetts Bay, Plymouth, Connecticut, and New Haven. This confederation had the same security policy toward each other. It is plausible that Puritans were in the majority in the New England colonies. Quakers were seen as fanatics, heretics, and dangerous. The New England United Colonies emerged in 1643 from the union of the colonies previously mentioned.

Historically, Quakers made their appearance in Massachusetts Bay in 1656. According to Hallowell, Ann Austin and Mary Fisher were the first identified Quakers in the colony. He went on to note that, upon their arrival, Deputy Governor Richard Bellingham dispatched officers to search their belongings and arrest them. After searching them, officials burned their books. Austin and Fisher were imprisoned for five weeks. After serving their time, they were deported to Barbados. In the same year, colonial officials in Massachusetts enacted laws prohibiting the entrance of Quakers in the colony as well as against those who entertained with them.[21] Fearing such persecution, Quakers preferred to live in Rhode Island. Quakers believed in the notion of human rights as did Rhode Island colonists.

Regarding the protection of Quakers in Rhode Island, in 1657, evidence indicates that the commissioners of the United Colonies wrote a letter to officials there, requesting Quakers' banishment from that colony. In their letter, the commissioners qualified Quakers as dangerous for the colonies. In their view, Quakers, and other heretics, did not have the right to reside in any colony. They also requested the refusal of any Quakers wanting to move to Rhode Island in the future. Rhode Island officials did not succumb to their demand. In their response, they stressed that Quakers were not criminals or subjected to any legal proceedings in the United Colonies. Like the commissioners of the United Colonies, when Massachusetts Bay officials sent a letter to the Rhode Island government for the same purpose, their request was rejected.

The response of the Rhode Island officials was that freedom of different consciences was dear to them and protected from enforcements.[22] According to them, Parliament in England authorized freemen in Rhode Island to enjoy their freedom of conscience. Freedom was the greatest prize that any man could have in the world. Regarding Quakers, Rhode Island officials believed that the best solution for their case must come from England. They went further in stating that Parliament had the power and the final say to accept or banish Quakers from Rhode Island.[23] As a result, in Rhode Island, Quakers and other religious denominations worshiped their religions freely without infringement or molestation. It is pertinent to note that Puritans in Rhode Island hade the same protections as Quakers. Likewise, believers of the Church of England had also the same privileges as both.

Religious Freedom in Newport and Portsmouth

In Newport and Portsmouth, freedom of religion emerged from the work of John Clarke and his associates. Bicknell recorded that these settlements and plantations have the honor and distinction of primacy in the establishment of a pure democracy, coupled with freedom in all ordered civil magistracy. He also pointed out that the progenitor of the civil and religious liberty in America or even in the world, should be Rhode Island, the smallest political unit in the western hemisphere. In addition to advocating religious freedom, Dr. Clarke was also the founder of the Baptist church in Newport. As with Dr. Clarke, Samuel Gorton, the founder of Warwick, was an early advocate for religious freedom. Bicknell noted that Gorton declared,

> I yearned for a country where I could be free to worship God according to what the Bible taught me, as God enable[s] me to understand it. I left my native country [England] to enjoy liberty of conscience in respect to faith toward God and for no other end.[24]

Due to his religious views, Massachusetts officials imprisoned and subsequently banished Gorton from their colony. From there, he went to

Rhode Island, and thereafter to Plymouth. In 1646, in association with Randal Holden and John Greene, Gorton made a complaint against the colony of Massachusetts to the Lord High Admiral and Commissioners for the Plantations in England. In the petition, Gorton and his associates railed against the rigorous proceedings employed against them by Massachusetts Bay officials. They also denounced the laws enacted for the banishment of the Anabaptist.

The Lord High Admiral and Commissioners saw Gorton's side of the dispute. As a result, they returned to the colony without abuse by any government officials.[25] Historically, the founders of Rhode Island were religious exiles from the Massachusetts Bay. Among these groups I can cite Roger Williams, William Harris, Anne Hutchinson, William Arnold, John Coggeshall, Nicholas Eaton, Chad Brown, and John Clarke. The listed names had different religious views while they resided in Massachusetts. Governor Winthrop in his book, *The History of New England*, treated them as Anabaptists. On Mrs. Hutchinson, Governor Winthrop wrote that,

> Mrs. Hutchinson and those of [Aquidneck Island] broached new heresies every year. Divers of them turned professed anabaptists, and would not wear any arms, and denied all magistracy among Christians, and maintained that there were no churches since those founded by apostles and evangelists, nor could any be, nor any pastors ordained, nor seals administered unit.[26]

This statement from Governor Winthrop illustrates how the religious views of Mrs. Hutchinson and her associates were contradictory to those of the Massachusetts Bay Puritans. For them, such opinions were destructive. Governor Winthrop believed that the Anabaptists were ignorant. This was the case with Nicholas Easton, a pastor in the settlement of Newport. Regarding this case, the governor noted that,

> Nicholas Easton, a tanner, a man very bold, though ignorant, where Coddington their governor lived, maintained that man has power or will in himself, but as he is acted by God, and that seeing God filled all thing, nothing could be or move but by

him, and so he must needs be the author of sin, &c., and that a Christian is united to essence of God.[27]

Freedom of religion in Rhode Island was also noted by Governor Winthrop. He wrote that many inhabitants in Newport became Anabaptists. He went on to note that they freely maintained that there were no churches since those founded by the Apostles and evangelists.[28] The enjoyment of religious freedom in Newport is an indication that government officials tolerated its practices.

Religious Freedom Granted to the Rhode Island Freemen in the 1663 Charter

In 1663, when King Charles II granted a charter of incorporation to the Rhode Island freemen, he preserved their religious liberties. Accordingly, the charter granted them a full liberty in "religious concernment." Regarding religious freedom, the charter stipulated the following:

> No person within the said colony, at any time hereafter, shall be any wise molested, punished, disquieted, or called in question, for any differences in opinion in matters of religion, and do not actually disturb the civil peace of our said colony; every person from time to time freely and fully enjoy his and their judgements and consciences in the matters of religious concernment throughout the tract of land hereafter mentioned, they behaving themselves peaceably and quietly, and not using this liberty to licentiousness and profaneness, nor to the civil injury or outward disturbance of others; any law, statute, or clause, therein contained, or to be contained usage or custom of this realm, to the contrary thereof in any wise, notwithstanding. And that they may in the better capacity to defend themselves, in their just rights and liberties, against all the enemies of the Christian faith, and others, in all respects, we have further thought fit, and at the humble petition of the persons aforesaid are graciously pleased to declare, that they shall have and enjoy the benefit of our late act of indemnity and free pardon, as the rest

of our subjects in other our dominions and territories have, and to create and make them a body politic or corporate, with the power and privileges hereinafter mentioned.[29]

In addition to granting religious freedom, the charter entrusted the colonists in Rhode Island with the power to defend it. The charter stated that they may defend themselves against the enemies of the Christian faith or others who would interfere with their rights and liberties pertaining to religious freedom. There is no question that this clause concerned the Puritans in Massachusetts Bay. As previously mentioned, government officials there attempted to dictate to the officials in the colony of Rhode Island how they should treat the Quakers. Rhode Island government officials, including religious leaders, remained firm on their protection of religious liberties as ordained by law.

Rhode Island freemen believed in the religious works of their ancestors. In the constitution of this state, the framers credited their ancestors as inspiration and guaranteed the subsequent use of religious liberties to their posterities. The Constitution of Rhode Island adopted in 1842, stipulates as follows:

> We, the people of the state of Rhode Island and Providence Plantations, grateful to Almighty God for the civil and religious liberty which He hath so long permitted us to enjoy, and looking to Him for a blessing upon our endeavors to secure and to transmit the same, unimpaired to succeeding generations, do ordain and establish this Constitution of Government.[30]

In the same constitution, under the Declaration of Certain Constitutional Rights and Principles, the framers of the Rhode Island constitution declared that,

> In order effectually to secure the religious and political freedom established by our venerated ancestors, and to preserve the same for our posterity, we do declare that essential and unquestionable rights and principles herein after mentioned, shall be established,

maintained, and preserved, and shall be a paramount obligation in all legislative, judicial and executive proceedings.[31]

Like in Rhode Island, the framers of the constitution in Massachusetts also granted religious liberties. Article II stipulated,

> It is the right as well as the duty of all men in society, publicly, and at stated seasons, to worship the SUPREME BEING the great Creator and preserver of the Universe, and no subject shall be hurt, molested, or restrained, in his person, liberty, or estate, for worshiping God in the manner and reason most agreeable to the dictate of his own conscience; or for his religious profession or sentiment; provided he doth not disturb the public peace or obstruct others in their religious worship.[32]

The language utilized for religious freedom in the constitution of Massachusetts was the same as that of New Hampshire.[33]

In the state of Connecticut, legislatures adopted a law prohibiting infringement of religious freedoms. Sect. 3–5 of the constitution of this state orders that,

> The exercise and enjoyment of religious profession and worship, without discrimination, shall forever be free to all persons in this state; provided, that the right hereby declared and established, shall not be so construed as to excuse acts of licentiousness, or to justify practices inconsistent with the peace and safety of the state. Sect. 4. No preference shall be given by law to any Christian Sect or mode of wordship. Sect.5. Every citizen may freely speak, write, and publish his sentiments on all subjects, being responsible for the abuse of that liberty.[34]

Similar laws for the protection of liberty of conscience are in the United States Constitution. Amendment I declares that,

> Congress shall make no law respecting an establishment of religion, or prohibiting the free exercise thereof; or abridging the

freedom of Speech, or of the press; or the right of the people peaceably to assemble, and to petition the Government for a redress of grievances."[35]

Religious Freedom in New Hampshire and Maine

In New Hampshire, local officials did not control religious activities. The *Laws of New Hampshire* documented that the settlers had "little concern about the establishment of a state or a church, the conservation of religious freedom, and the propagation of the gospel."[36] As in Rhode Island, in New Hampshire, settlers were also against any interference from Massachusetts Bay regarding liberty of conscience. In 1638, when Rev. John Wheelwright, a Puritan clergyman, escaped to Piscataqua, the freemen in New Hampshire received him with civility. In New Hampshire, Puritans and members of other religious denominations worshiped their religions freely. To expand on this, Antinomian believers banished from Massachusetts Bay took refuge in New Hampshire. When Massachusetts Bay officials opposed the entertainment of the Antinomians by New Hampshire, Rev. Burnett and others of the plantation refused to obey.[37] Wheelwright was among those banished from Massachusetts.

In 1641, when Portsmouth and Dover combined with Massachusetts Bay, the inhabitants of these towns had their religious freedom. There is no indication that the inhabitants of these settlements converted to Puritanism. In a similar fashion, in 1643 when the settlement of Exeter joined Massachusetts Bay, freemen in that city kept their religious liberty. From the period when these settlements joined the Massachusetts Bay colony to 1679 when they separated, religious freedom existed in New Hampshire. In 1680, the inhabitants of New Hampshire had the freedom of conscience as granted by a positive law. That year, New Hampshire government officials passed a law for the regulation of religious activities. The regulation of religion reads as follows:

> We do by all possible care for the discountenancing of vice and encouraging of virtue and good living; and the such examples the infidels may be [evited] and desire to partake of the

Christian religion, and for the greater ease and satisfaction of the said loving subjects in matters of religion, the liberty of conscience shall be allowed into all protestants; that such especially as shall be conformable to the rites of the Church of England shall be particularly countenanced and encouraged.[38]

In Maine, settlers had the same views on religion as settlers in New Hampshire. Maine was composed of royalists and those of Episcopal faith. Sources indicate that Sir Ferdinando Gorges was a royalist and an adamant friend of the king. From the work of Rev. Joshua Millet, evidence further shows that few people observed religious principles in Maine. According to him, portions of the population were lawless and wicked. In this province, Puritans, Baptists, and others expressed their religious opinions freely. Like in New Hampshire, banished religious ministers and leaders took refuge in the Province of Maine.

Chapter 7

Town Liberties and Self-Governing in the New England Colonies

The investigation of town governments and liberties is a subject of continuing investigation to historians and political scientists. Researchers and historians have written extensively on the historical development of town government in New England. Pertaining to the subject of town liberties, Josiah Quincy authored an informed work relating pertinent information on the municipal government instituted by colonists in Boston. Charles Francis, Abner C. Goodel, Jr., Mellen Chamberlain, and Edward Channing similarly authored, *The Genesis of the Massachusetts Town, and the Development of Town Meeting Government*, which sheds light on town and county governments in Massachusetts Bay. In addition to the authors previously mentioned, John A. Fairlie's *Local Government in Counties, Towns and Villages* provides the same. Here, in addition to the management of towns' affairs, Fairlie examined the duties of town officers during this period.

As in Massachusetts Bay, William E. Foster examined town government in Rhode Island. In his study, he made a sharp distinction between town governments in Massachusetts, Connecticut, New Hampshire, and those of the Rhode Island colony. Like Fairlie, Edward Channing authored an authoritative book on town and county government in the colonies in North America. As is the case with the American writers, Alexis de Tocqueville, in his book *Democracy in America*, discussed the organization of town governments in New England. Various scholars credit his work. In the United States, Josiah Quincy authored, *A Municipal History of the Town and City of Boston during Two Centuries: From September 17, 1630, to September 17, 1830*. This book contains important information on the municipal government of Boston. Moreover, Richard

Frothingham, Jr. in his book, *The History of Charlestown, Massachusetts*, documented the means of governing towns in New England. Furthermore, in his book, *The History of New England*, Governor Winthrop recorded the emergence of town governments in Massachusetts Bay and Connecticut. Similar documentation on town governments in New England can be found in Charles H. Bell's *History of the Town of Exeter, New Hampshire*. Bell covered the early town governments in the Piscataqua settlements. In Connecticut, William Chauncey Fowler, in his *Local Law in the Massachusetts and Connecticut*, wrote the same. In New Hampshire, the account of towns' liberties is in the *Laws of New Hampshire*. *Provincial Documents and Records Relating to the Province of New Hampshire*, also contains evidence of the emergence of the settlements, including the liberties of the freemen. As in New Hampshire, in Rhode Island, Edward Peterson in his book, *History of Rhode Island*, documented the emergence of town government and liberties in that colony.

The accounts of the previously named authors regarding New England town governments are enlightening. In Connecticut and Massachusetts, Fowler wrote that each town in both colonies was a republic for its own purpose.[1] Like Fowler, Bell noted that Exeter was an independent republic in the Piscataqua region.[2] Frothingham, Jr. framed the New England colonies as little independent nations, noting that New England town governments were not like those in England. The town governments in New England were closer to that of the Anglo-Saxons', which were independent nations of the free citizens where every office was elective.[3] A similar view was held by De Tocqueville. During his visit to America, he viewed towns as independent entities. He saw each town as self-governing.

The Emergence of Self-Government in New England

The history of self-government in New England starts with the Mayflower Compact, the patent of the Massachusetts Bay colony, and voluntary associations made by the settlers, including a commission from Massachusetts Bay issued to the Connecticut settlers, and the Fundamental Orders of Connecticut. When looking at New England as a whole, settlers did not inherit lands, towns, or plantations from their ancestors. They occupied or purchased land without the assistance of a lord. As a result, titles indicating notability did not exist like in England or other European countries and kingdoms. In the New England colonies, settlers tooled land, cultivated, and established their own plantations or towns. This was the case of the first settlers of the Plymouth colony. The historical record indicates that private people established plantations and towns in this colony for communal use. From there, every plantation or town established a self-governing institution. In this colony, sources indicate that the settlements of Plymouth, Scituate, Duxbury, and Marshfield among others, were not government established towns or plantations. Freemen established these settlements by common consent. As the towns were founded by voluntary association, there was no imposition of town laws, orders, and by-laws by any external power. Additionally, they elected their own officers without the interference of the general government. This is ample evidence indicating the existence of the self-governing system in the colony of Plymouth.

The founding of settlements by English in New England was a policy that was subsequently observed by the Americans. For better understanding of the emergence of self-government in New England, it is imperative that I examine the Mayflower Compact, the letter patents of the Massachusetts Bay colony, and the combination of voluntary associations made by the settlers before the establishment of the plantations, villages, or towns. The above are important in the history of the political system in the New England colonies as well as in the United States.

The Mayflower Compact

The Mayflower Compact is an important document in the history of the colonies but also in the emergence of the United States. The language utilized in this document points to the emergence of the self-government system in New England. From William Bradford's *History of Plymouth Plantation*, I discovered that the Pilgrims wrote a constitution for the better governing of their institutions. Each Pilgrim signed the compact willingly without impositions from any power or lord. Regarding the combination written in the Mayflower Compact, Governor

Bradford wrote that "the combination was the first foundation of their government in the colony." Additionally, Bradford noted the Pilgrims were obligated to self-govern because they did not have an authorization from the king or the Virginia Company to begin a settlement in the New England territory.[4] Governor Bradford articulated authoritatively that the region where they established the plantation was not under the control of the Virginia Company. He stated that that region belonged to the Plymouth Company. As such, the Virginia Company which they associated with did not have any power over that sphere.[5] Like Bradford, William Douglass noted that the Pilgrims in Plymouth did not have a grant or royal charter or patent for the New England region. He went on to posit that they did even not have a territory assigned to them. Due to these conditions, they established a voluntary settlement.[6] As a result, they formed a consensual government for the welfare of their community. On that basis, they formed a civil body politic. This organization had as mission and mandate, the better ordering, and the preservation of unity. To accomplish this, they consented to frame just and equal laws, ordinances, acts, and a constitution. In the same way, they agreed to appoint or elect government officials.[7]

The Massachusetts Bay Company Letters Patent

Contrary to the Plymouth colony, Massachusetts Bay had letters patent from the crown of England. This document was the constitution of the company that put forth the form of government for the colony. In addition to the letters patent, the instructions from the Massachusetts Bay Company in accordance with the letters patent was another instrument which facilitated the emergence of self-government in Massachusetts Bay. The evidence of Massachusetts Bay Company's governing power can be found in *Records of the Company of the Massachusetts Bay in New England from 1628 to 1641*. The records (italic) stated that the governor and his deputy had the power to appoint officers. The power bestowed on them granted authority from his majesty, to make, ordain, and established reasonable orders, laws, statutes, and ordinances not conflictual with the laws of England. The laws made by the governor, his deputies, and councilors were for the management of the affairs of the plantation and the residents inhabited within the limits of the Massachusetts Bay Company's plantations.[8] Even though this letters patent granted the Massachusetts Bay Company the power to erect towns, such authorization seemed difficult to control. Stockholders freely selected the locations of where to grow and establish a plantation.

Immigrants from Dorchester under the leadership of Rev. John Maverick, John Warham, Roger Ludlow, Gaylord, and Rockwell, selected Mattapan as a location for their settlement.[9] By the order of the General Court, colonial officials re-named this town Dorchester. From Governor Winthrop's *The History of New England*, I discovered that Ludlow was one of the founders of Dorchester.[10] Notably, Rossiter and Rev. Maverick were co-founders of Dorchester. This plantation was independent from the others in the colony. Like Dorchester, Alexander Young tells us that Sir Richard Saltonstall and other English emigrants founded Watertown. He also pointed out that William Pynchon and others established a plantation at Roxbury which was located between Dorchester and Boston. Regarding the colonists of Roxbury, Francis S. Drake tells us that they were people of substance and came from London and the surrounding area. Among them were those who came from the western part of England. He went on to reveal that many of them were farmers and none were of humble means.[11] Drake also pointed out that Pynchon was the principal founder of Roxbury.[12] Furthermore, Governor Dudley and Bradstreet in association with others, founded Newtown, which was subsequently named Cambridge.[13] Similar to the previously noted towns, Medford was also a privately owned plantation before it became a town. According to Charles Brooks, Governor Mathew Cradock owned a large farm in Medford. Governor Winthrop chose this portion of land for its establishment. For the management of his farm, Governor Cradock dispatched his servant to Governor Winthrop who assisted with a mandate. Unlike these settlements, Salem and Charlestown were started before the arrival of Governor Winthrop.

Salem and Charlestown were the oldest towns in Massachusetts Bay. Before their forming, freemen agreed on their location. Regarding Salem, this settlement was inhabited by colonists from Dorchester after the failure of their fishing industry in Cape Ann. According to Joseph B.

Felt, Roger Conant, John Woodbury, John Balch, Peter Palfrey, and others moved from Cape Anne to Salem.[14] Felt also noted that "Salem was indebted for its first settlement to the failure of a planting, fishing, and trading enterprise at Cape Ann."[15] The Dorchester colonists who inhabited Salem were always called old planters. In 1628 when Governor Endicott and his associates arrived in Salem, they met the old planters in that settlement. According to Roger Conant, the old and new planters consented to the formation of a body politic lead by Governor Endicott. Conant went on to estimate that the total population was about 300 people.[16]

Some documents from Conant collected by Felt said that among the 300, 200 of them remained in Salem and the rest relocated to Massachusetts Bay and built the town of Charlestown.[17] Pertaining to Charlestown, Richard Frothingham, Jr. tells us that Ralph, Richard, and William Sprague, with three or four others, did with Endicott's permission build the town of Charlestown in 1629.[18] Thomas Walford was the first English settler in that location before the arrival of Endicott. In addition to Charlestown, in 1629, Rev. Edmund Ingalls and his brother Francis Ingalls settled at Lynn. Along with these two brothers, William Dixey, the servant of Isaac Johnson, was among those who settled in Saugus. Alonzo Lewis noted that Dixey came to Salem with Isaac Johnson. From Dixey's account, Lewis noted that Salem's planters requested permission from Governor Endicott to establish a new plantation in a different location. The Governor approved their request. As such, they went to Saugus and established a plantation in the name of Isaac Johnson. Among the founders of Saugus, John Wood was the principal person for its existence.[19] In 1630, Deputy Governor Thomas Dudley confirmed that Puritans settled at Saugus in 1630. He also noted that others went to Charlestown and Boston in the same year. According to him, the rest of the English began new settlements at Roxbury, Dorchester, Watertown, and Medford. From the narrations of the authors previously noted and that of Deputy Governor Dudley, it is comprehensible that the emergence of self-government began with the formation of independent plantations. As Lewis put it, "each town was itself a little colony, a miniature republic, and the history of one is almost the history of all."[20]

With the existence of uncultivated lands in New England, English immigrants established plantations and towns. As the number of settlements grew, self-government took shape. Like Plymouth and Massachusetts Bay, Dover, Portsmouth, and Exeter in New Hampshire were independent republics. They were entities separate from each other even when they were under the jurisdiction of the Massachusetts Bay. Similarly, in Connecticut and Rhode Island, the freemen observed the same system. In New Haven, each town was also independent from the next. They emerged into union government for security reasons. New Haven, Guilford, Milford, Stamford, and Branford were independent republics established by a group of individual people. Like the above, Greenwich was also an independent republic even though it was not under the government of the New Haven colony due to its revolutionary spirit. Like all these towns, in Maine, self-government was dominant.

Edward R. Lamber wrote that in New Haven,

> It was their plan that each town should govern themselves independently, as far as local interest were concerned, and as far as the public interests or commonwealth was interested, to organize an authoritative governmental and judiciary council, to which all should submit and be in subordination.[21]

Self-governing was also expanded to new settlements established by the English in territories outside the jurisdiction of Plymouth, Massachusetts Bay, and New Haven colonies. Afterwards, Vermont conformed to self-government as well.

The Expansion of Self-Government by New England Freemen in New York and New Jersey

Historically, there is an array of sources documenting New England's form of self-government in other regions. According to historians, New England Puritans established settlements in New York and New Jersey, including South Carolina and Georgia. In 1670, Daniel Denton, a settler, wrote that New England Puritans established towns in Long Island and New Jersey. He also stated that after the founding of towns in that region, more people from New England came to settle in new settlements in Rhode Island and New Jersey every day.[22] In regard to Denton, Rev. Edwin F. Hatfield wrote that he was with Rev. Richard Denton when he emigrated to Watertown, Massachusetts in 1634. His father, Rev. Denton, moved to Wethersfield after a short stay in Watertown. After Wethersfield, he moved to Stamford in 1641, and in 1644, he emigrated to Hempstead. In 1658, Rev. Denton returned to England, and died in 1662 at Essex.[23] Denton, in his book *Brief Description of New York*, gives an authoritative account of the migration of New England colonists to Long Island and New Jersey. According to Rev. Hatfield, Daniel Denton and his bother Nathaniel were the first planters of Jamaica, Long Island.[24] According to the *Records of the Towns of Jamaica Long Island, New York*, Daniel and Nathaniel Denton, Robert Coe, and his son Benjamin Coe were in the town meeting held on February 18, 1656. There, Nathaniel Denton was named clerk for Jamaica.[25] Robert Coe was one of the founders of Stamford, Connecticut after emigrating from Wethersfield. He was with Andrew Ward when Wethersfield freemen dispatched him for the purchase of land to found Stamford.[26]

Various documents record that New England Puritans were ardent pioneers in terms of plantations and town building. As already mentioned, due to an abundance of uncultivated land, New England colonists were able to establish new plantations willingly. As illustrated when the Massachusetts Bay settlers heard about the fertility of land in Connecticut, colonists in Watertown, Dorchester, and Newtown moved to Connecticut and founded new plantations. While in Connecticut, they continued the same territorial expansions. By the Order of the Connecticut General Court, officials renamed Watertown as Wethersfield, and Windsor as Dorchester. On the other hand, Newtown was re-named Hartford.[27] Similar to Connecticut and New Haven, colonists from Lynn, Massachusetts founded the town of South Hampton in Long Island. Those of New Haven founded the town of Southold. George Rogers Howell noted that colonists in Lynn migrated to Southampton, Long Island in 1640. In his view, this was the first town settled by the English in New York. He points out that freemen emphasized self-government in this town. According to him, in its early history, Southampton was a little republic. He goes further in stating that this town instituted a pure democracy without a parallel except for the short-lived republics of ancient Greece. In this town, equal justice as well as the protections of individual rights were inviolable.[28]

Regarding Connecticut, I note that settlers in Wethersfield established new plantations in other locations outside of their original sphere. Wethersfield freemen established the plantation of Stamford. Freemen often identified this plantation as "Wethersfield Man's Plantation."[29] Rev. E.B. Huntington, in his *History of Stamford, Connecticut*, related that dissatisfied and restless men in Wethersfield founded Stamford.[30] From this example, I would like to note that Newtown settlers found new settlements after their departure from Massachusetts Bay. In addition to expanding in Connecticut, sources reveal that the same people established plantations in New Jersey and New York. Similarly, documents indicate that the Dorchester freemen from Massachusetts planted new settlements in South Carolina and Georgia where they introduced a system of self-government inspired by those in New England.

Self-Governing under Puritans in New York and New Jersey

On previous pages, I noted that the settlers from Wethersfield established Stamford. Benjamin Trumbull wrote that, on October 30, 1640, Andrew Ward and Robert Coe of Wethersfield purchased a portion of land in Long Island for themselves and twenty other planters.[31] Benjamin F. Thompson associates the inhabitants of Wethersfield and Stamford with the establishment of Hempstead in Long Island. He tells us that Robert Coe and Rev. Richard Denton were among those who settled in Hempstead. Rev. Denton lived in Watertown, Massachusetts when he emigrated from England in 1630. When the Watertown freemen moved to Connecticut, he was among the first settlers in Wethersfield. Additionally, he moved to Stamford with Coe and others. In 1644, he was also among those who settled in Hempstead, Long Island.[32] Like the previously mentioned authors, Silas Wood gives further light on Hempstead, Long Island.

In his book, *A Sketch of the First, Settlement of the Several Towns of the Island, With their Political Condition to the end of the American Revolution,*

Wood recorded that the founders of Hempstead resided shortly in Wethersfield as well as in Stamford before their arrival in that newly founded town. Pertaining to the system of government, he noted that the English settlements in Long Island were independent of each other politically. They were not under the control of a colonial government.[33] Wood's work indicates that Puritan settlements in Long Island had the same forms of government found in New England. Hugh Hasting, the State Historian, mentioned the emergence of Hempstead and its founders in Long Island. He noted that Rev. M. Alfred recorded that the first settlers of Hempstead passed from Watertown to Wethersfield before they settled there.[34] In addition to the settlement noted above, the same Wethersfield freemen founded Jamaica. Thompson wrote that Robert Jackson and others founded the plantation of Jamaica in 1656 with the permission of colonial Governor Peter Stuyvesant.[35] Robert Coe was among the founders.[36]

Like other settlements, New Englanders also founded the village of Middelbury. James Ricker, Jr. mentioned in his book, *The foundation of Middelbury by the New England Puritans,* the same information. In *The Annals of Newton, in Queens County, New York*, Riker Jr. stated that in 1652, New England freemen founded the village of Middelbury. According to him, after settlement, new settlers from Greenwich, Stamford, Fairfield, and other villages along the Connecticut shore followed thereafter. In addition to the Connecticut people, Thomas Hazard from Boston was also among the settlers in Middelbury. Furthermore, the experienced town founder Robert Coe was the first magistrate of Middlebury. Along with them, Richard Gildersleive, William Wood, Thomas Hazard, Edward Jessup, and William Herrick were also magistrates.[37] His biographer identified Robert Coe as "a Puritan founder of New England." He came to New England when he was thirty-eight years old with his three children—John Coe, age eight, Robert Coe, age seven, and Benjamin Coe, age five. When the elder Coe came to Massachusetts Bay, he settled first at Watertown. At the time of his arrival, settlers who came with Governor Winthrop settled there. In 1635, he was associated with the Watertown people who founded the plantation of Wethersfield. Before his departure to Wethersfield, church officials in Dorchester dismissed him from the church with his townsmen,

Andrew Warde, John Sherman, John Stickland, Robert Reynall and Jonas Weede.[38]

Like New York, the New England Puritans established a plantation in the colony of New Jersey. According to Joseph Atkinson, the founders of the plantation of Newark were the inhabitants from Milford. The Milford people introduced a self-government system similar to other New England towns. Regarding the founding of Newark, Atkinson noted that Robert Treat was the earliest inhabitant of Newark.[39] In addition to the Milford freemen, Branford's inhabitants resided in Newark as well. According to Atkinson, Treat from Milford and Samuel Swaine from Branford signed an agreement for a unified government between the two groups. Moreover, Guilford freemen were also among those who settled in Newark with their Puritan brethren from Milford and Branford. In this town, freemen established the same local government principles as in New England.

Atkinson wrote that local affairs were managed through a consensus of all the community members.[40] Regarding the Branford freemen, Atkinson recorded that twenty-three heads of family members of this town desired to form a town union with the Milford freemen in Newark.[41] In his book, *The History of Newark, New Jersey*, Atkinson noted that Newark was first settled by freemen from the colony of Connecticut, especially Milford.[42] From the accounts of the authors previously mentioned, sources reveal that the New England political culture's containing elements like town meetings, building towns by a group of individual people, governing through the majority, and independency of each town or plantation were preserved and observed with great care. Like New York and New Jersey, New Englanders settled in Southern states. And like the Watertown freemen, colonists from Dorchester were also pioneers by way of Southern settlement.

Dorchester, Massachusetts Freemen in South Carolina and Georgia

The accounts on the settlements founded by the Puritans from Dorchester, Massachusetts in South Carolina and Georgia indicate the extension of the New England self-government far from their native region.

In the same context, these accounts reveal the expansion of democratic principles from New England to Southern states. Documents from various towns founded by New Englanders indicate that each town established was independent from other neighboring towns. Town meetings were subsequently used like the ones that took place in New England. Furthermore, freemen observed democracy and held the of rule of law. *Records of the First Church at Dorchester in New England* indicate that, on October 20, 1695, Rev. Joseph Lord, Increase Sumner, and William Pratt were dismissed for planning to establish a church in South Carolina.[43] According to the book written by William H. Sumner, a son of Governor Increase Sumner, in 1696, Rev. Lord, Increase, and others from Dorchester, Massachusetts went to South Carolina to form a settlement which they named Dorchester. This settlement was in Berkley County.[44] Like the Dorchester named above, Samuel Sumner, the father of Increase, was also among those who went to South Carolina. His son Increase was a selectman of Dorchester in 1693.[45]

In South Carolina, after few years in Dorchester, they migrated to the colony of Georgia where they established the town of Midway. According to George Howe, Benjamin Baker, Samuel Bacon and their families went to Georgia to form the settlement of Midway on December 6, 1752. After Baker and Bacon, Parmenus Way, William Baker, John Elliott, John Winn, Edward Sumner, and John Quarterman emigrated from Dorchester, South Carolina to Midway, Georgia.[46] In addition to the settlement of Midway, a group of New Englanders went to reside in Sunbury. Charles C. Jones, in his book *The Dead Towns of Georgia*, wrote that the early population of Sunbury were from the Midway Congregation. He went on to note that the inhabitants of the Midway settlement were Puritans who emigrated from Dorchester, Roxbury, and Milton under the leadership of Rev. Joseph Lord.[47]

Regarding government and political structure, Jones says that the Midway colonists had the same parentage, religion, and political education as their brethren in Boston. During the American Revolution, the Midway and Sunbury colonists sided with their brethren in New England. Even inhabitants of St. John's Parish chose this side. According to Jones Jr., Midway people stated their allegiance early to the Revolution. He went on to note that Sunbury and St. John's Parish were effective resistance fiefs. Dr. Lyman Hall, a native of Connecticut and a member of the Midway Congregation, was the leading physician in the settlement and the surrounding area. On March 21, 1775, the colonists in the settlement elected him as a delegate from St. John's Parish to the General Congress. He was also a delegate to the Provincial Congress from Georgia. Additionally, he was a signer of the Declaration of Independence.[48]

Early Town Orders, Power, and Liberties

In New England, colonial officials as well as locals had limited power. At each level of government during this colonial period, officials enforced law and order according to the acts or orders of the colonial government or those of the towns' government. At local levels, officials' powers emanated from the laws made in town meetings by the consent of the freemen. In addition to local laws, officials at the local level enforced colonial laws in their respective towns. Specifically, in Massachusetts, Connecticut, and Rhode Island, including New Hampshire, freemen in each colony observed the codified laws. Before the codifications of laws as well as the enactment of colonial laws, principal men of each town in association with the freemen made town orders for the management of town affairs. As the principal chief freemen of the towns, religious ministers were among the regulators of town affairs. To illustrate, in Dorchester, Massachusetts, the clergymen, with the assistance of the principal men, managed the affairs of the town. According to the *Dorchester Antiquarian and Historical Society*, Roger Ludlow and Rossiter were magistrates associated with the clergymen in management of the plantation there. Due to the limited number of freemen, a civil government was not operational until the spring of 1631. When the numbers of the freemen increased, orders were enacted for the regulation of the plantation. In 1633, nine freemen had the power to regulate the affairs of the town.[49]

Orders for the Regulation of Towns

In the early years of settlement, various towns lost their town records. However, the town of Dorchester kept early records of the plantation. In this town, in 1633, officials passed an order with the consent of the freemen at a town meeting for the better ordering of the plantation. The order made in Dorchester was the first ever recorded in the Massachusetts Bay colony. Before this order, sources reveal that throughout the towns in the colony, freemen obeyed the orders made by the General Court. Despite the orders of the General Court, it is certain that the chief principal men of the town continued to make orders with the consent of the freemen in their respective town. *The Dorchester Antiquarian Society and Historical Society* noted that the town of Dorchester did not have a special government before the order of 1633. The order made by the Dorchester freemen for the regulation of town affairs reads as follows:

> On October 8, 1633, "it has ordered that for the general good and well ordering of the affairs of the plantation, there shall be every Monday before the court, by 8 o'clock A.M., and presently by the beating of the drum, a general meeting of the inhabitants of the plantation at the meeting house, there to settle and set down such orders as may tend to the general good as aforesaid, and every man to be bound thereby, without gainsaying or resistance. It is also agreed that there shall be twelve men selected out of the company, that may, or the greatest part of them, meet as aforesaid to determine as aforesaid; yet so far as it is desired that the most of the plantation will keep the meeting constantly, and all that are there, though not of the twelve, shall have a free voice as any of the twelve, and that the greater vote both of the twelve and the other shall be of force and efficacy as aforesaid. And it is likewise ordered, that all things concluded as aforesaid shall stand in force and be obeyed until the next monthly meeting, and afterwards if it be contradicted and otherwise ordered at said monthly meeting by the greatest vote of those that are present as aforesaid.[50]

From this order, I can stipulate that in the Massachusetts Bay colony, democratic principles began under the leadership of local officials. Freemen approved the notion of the majority rule. They also accepted the decision made by a major part of local officials. Moreover, local affairs were determined by the consent of the freemen. In addition to the democratic principles noted above, the order prescribed the number of local officials who managed the town's affairs.

Freemen had freedom of expression regarding matters of their concern. The selected twelve men were local elected officials and had the power from the freemen to exercise authority. These officers served in the local government for a year only. After the end of their terms, the town organized a new election for the selection of new officers. The election and town meetings took place at a meeting house. In Dorchester, the first town meeting was in 1631 in the meeting house built on Allen's Plain near the Corner of Pleasant and Cottage Street. At this site, the first settlers of Roxbury with those of Dorchester worshipped together.[51]

In 1634, Boston freemen had the power to manage their own affairs as well. In that year, Governor Winthrop, William Coddington, Capt. John Underhill, Thomas Oliver, Thomas Leverett, Giles Firmin, John Coggeshall, William Peirce or Pierce, Robert Harding, and William Brenton had the duty of ordering the affairs of Boston. Among these officials, Firmin was overseer of the landing place [dock]. He supervised the landing place and deterred inhabitants from committing offences at that location. He had the power of levying fines from violators. The selection of these ten officials happened at a town meeting of the freemen. When Firmin died and Harding moved to Virginia, Richard Bellingham and John Cogan, a merchant, replaced Firmin and Harding to make ten officials for that governing body. While Boston had ten officials for the regulation of town affairs, in Cambridge, seven officials were selectmen. According to *The Records of the Town of Cambridge (Formerly Newtown) Massachusetts, 1630-1703*, on February 3, 1634, John Haynes, Simon Bradstreet, William Westwood, John White, William Wadswood, John Taylcott, and James Olmsted managed the whole business of the town for a year's term until new officers were elected the following November. On November 23, 1635, nine people regulated the affairs of the same town.[52]

The Emergence of Municipal Government in New England

In Plymouth and Massachusetts Bay, the General Courts did not establish a law empowering towns with certain liberties. From various documents, evidence indicates that in 1636, in Massachusetts Bay and Plymouth, local town officers had the power to manage their own affairs. In Massachusetts Bay, the Acts Respecting towns reads as follows:

> Sec. 1. Whereas particular town have many things which concern only themselves and the ordering their own affairs, and disposing of business in their own town: it is therefore ordered, that the freemen of every town, with such others as are allowed, or the major part of them, shall have power to dispose of their own lands and wood, with all the privileges and appurtenances of the said towns, to grant lots, and also to choose their own particular officers as constables, surveyors for the highways, and the like annually, or otherwise as need requires; and to make such laws and constitutions as may concern the welfare of their town; provided they be not of a criminal, but of a prudential nature, and that their penalties exceed not twenty shillings for one offence, and that they be not repugnant to the public laws and orders of the country. And if any man shall behave himself offensively at any town meeting, the rest then present shall have power to sentence him for such offence, so as the penalty exceed not twenty shillings.
>
> Sec. 2. And every township has power to choose yearly or for less time, a convenient number of fit men to order the planting and prudential affairs of their towns, according to instruction given them in writing, provided also that the number of Selectmen be not above nine. And if any inhabitant should neglect or refuse to observe them, they shall have power to levy the appointed penalty by distress. It is ordered, that all towns shall take care to order, and dispose of single persons, and inmates within their town, to service, or otherwise; and if any be grieved at the order of a town, the parties to have liberty to appeal to the governor and council, or the court.[53]

This Act was effective when the colonists of Connecticut were under the administration of Massachusetts Bay. As in Connecticut, towns founded after the passage of this Act were under the same conditions. In 1636, each town in Connecticut had a constable.

According to *The Public Records of the Colony of Connecticut*, Henry Walcott was constable for Windsor. In Hartford, the freemen elected Samuel Wakeman as constable. Daniel Finch was constable for Wethersfield. Like the election of constables, each town in Connecticut maintained its own watch.[54] These examples are solid proof to support the existence of self-government in Connecticut. On October 10, 1639, in Connecticut, the General Court ordered that the towns of Hartford, Windsor, and Wethersfield, and any other of the towns within this colony's authority would have power of disposing their commodities as bounded out to them by the Court. Each town also made orders and by-laws not being repugnant to the established colonial laws. Moreover, each town government had the power to punish and fine violators of the laws.[55] In the same order of the Court, each had the power to select three, five, or seven of their chief inhabitants to serve as local government officials for the management of the town's affairs. The selection of a moderator was among the elected officials.[56]

Similarly, in Rhode Island, groups of emigrants from Massachusetts established towns. In 1636, Providence, Rhode Island was like a little republic. Portsmouth, Newport, and Warwick were the same. These towns were far away from each other. In 1640, by an order, the self-government came to fruition in Rhode Island. This system emerged from the Union of Portsmouth and Newport. The order enacted by the officials of both towns reads as follows:

> It is ordered, that each town shall have the transaction of the affairs that shall fall withing their own town, and that the magistrates of each town shall have liberty to call a court every first Tuesday in the month at Newport; and every first Thursday in the month at Portsmouth.[57]

In 1647, when Providence, Portsmouth, Newport, and Warwick were united into one government, Roger Williams proposed the observance of self-government. According to Williams, each town needed to have the power and liberty to choose, ordain, authorize, and confirm officers of the town for the management of their respective town's affairs. He went on to reject the intermixture of the general and local officers in their duties. According to him, colonial and local officials had the right to know their boundaries and limits. He also pointed out that each town should have a charter of incorporation, apart for the transaction of their town affairs.[58] In 1648, each town in Rhode Island had the power to govern its local affairs.[59]

As was the case in Massachusetts, Connecticut, Rhode Island, and Plymouth contained towns with liberty to self-govern. It appears that before 1636, Plymouth did not have a formal government. In this colony, the governor, one assistant and the whole body of freemen managed its affairs. In 1636, Plymouth and Scituate had the power to self-govern. In *The Compact with the Charter and Laws of the Colony of New Plymouth*, records indicate that the purchasers of land and the freemen of Plymouth had the liberty to dispose their lands, the power to make orders for their town, and could accept new immigrants. They did not have the right to make orders or by-laws which were contrary to the public ordinances of the government. In 1637, Duxbury became a township with the same town liberties as Plymouth and Scituate.[60] In 1639, the General Court passed an order for the same purpose. The act for the towns to make orders reads as follows:

> All the townships within this government allowed or to be allowed shall have liberty to meet together and to make such town orders as shall be needful and requisite for the heading of Cattel and doing other things as shall be needful for the maintenance of good neighborhood, and to set penalties upon delinquent; provided that their orders be not repugnant nor infringe any public acts, and that the fines and penalties shall be disposed of afterwards to their particular town, also that the fine exceed not the sum of ten shillings for any one fine.[61]

This order clearly defined the power and liberties of each town in the Plymouth colony. It is plausible to conclude that each town was a body politic. With these statutes, town officers regulated their town's affairs concerning electing officers, judging minor cases, and controlling the behavior of the freemen. Moreover, the order specified limitations of power placed on town officials.

Towns' Statutory Powers in the New England Colonies

Before the codification of laws in New England, officials enforced towns' liberties by the orders and acts of the General Courts of each colony. The codification of laws in Massachusetts Bay happened in 1641. At the time when the Body of Liberties became the law of the land, Dover and Portsmouth, New Hampshire were under the jurisdiction of Massachusetts Bay. As such, they were governed with such immunities, power, and liberties as other towns in Massachusetts Bay. In 1643, when the town of Exeter came under the administration of Massachusetts Bay, it enjoyed the same liberties. When Maine joined Massachusetts Bay in 1652, they enjoyed identical liberties. As a reminder, in 1641, Portsmouth and Dover were in union with Massachusetts Bay. In Massachusetts, the Statute of 1641 ordered as follows:

> The freemen of every town or township, shall have full power to choose yearly or for less time out of themselves a convenient number of fit men to order the plantation or prudential occasions of the Town, according to instruction given them in writing. Provided nothing be done by them contrary to the public laws and orders of the country, determined that the number of such select persons be not above nine.[62]

According to this statute, the power of towns' officials was in accordance with the laws of the colony. In addition to the power of officials, the selection of town's officers was in accordance with the 1641 statute. Only people fit for this nature of employment served as regulators and government officials. Furthermore, limitation of power for local officials was in accordance with this statute. The law authorized the regulation of town affairs by nine people or less. In 1642, Portsmouth and Dover had the same authority as other towns of Massachusetts in accordance with the statute of 1641. On September 27, 1642, the General Court of Massachusetts stipulated that,

It is ordered that all the present inhabitants of Piscataqua who formerly were free there shall have liberty of freemen in their several towns to manage all their town affairs, and shall each send a deputy to the General Court, though they not at present [be] church members.[63]

In New Hampshire, the Statute of 1680 similarly ordered,

> ...that the freemen of each town to choose their officers and make orders for their town, set penalty for not observing town acts, and to choose particular officers such as constables, grand-jurors, and jury for trial, surveyors for the highways and officers annually. They were also given the power to make laws and constitutions as may concern the welfare of their towns provided that those laws and orders were not of criminal nature, but of a prudential nature: And that the penalty exceed not twenty shillings for one offence: And that they be not repugnant to the public laws and orders of this province: And if an inhabitant shall neglect or refuse to observe them, they shall have power to levy the appointed penalty by distress. And if any man shall behave himself offensively at any town meeting, the rest then present shall have power, to sentence him for such offence: so as the penalty exceed not twenty shillings.[64]

The New Hampshire Statute of 1680 prescribed the duties of the prudential officers or selectmen. According to this Statute, inhabitants elected selectmen each year from each town. The number of these officers could not exceed seven for each town. For their duties, the selectmen of each town had the power of managing their town's affairs. This act is like that of Massachusetts Bay. It is possible that President John Cutt consulted the laws of Massachusetts Bay when he codified these laws.

Chapter 8

Representative Democracy in the New England Colonies

It is evident from the referenced source that representative government in New England has been a point of interest for many prominent figures. In various historical documents of this region and time, historians, researchers, and scholars have documented the emergence of the representative system. For example, Thomas Hutchinson, a former governor of the Massachusetts Bay, documented the emergence of the representative system in that colony. Like Hutchinson, Governor John Winthrop revealed authoritative information on the development of the representative system in his colony. As a participant in that process, his account remains prominent in the history of the New England colonies. Regarding Connecticut, information pertaining to the representative system is found in *The Public Records of the Colony of Connecticut*. Furthermore, similar accounts regarding the development of the representative system in Rhode Island can be found in the *Records of the Colony of Rhode Island and Providence Plantation*.

In the *Charters and General Laws of the Colony and Province of Massachusetts Bay*, the act respecting deputies for the Massachusetts General Court is found. The twenty-three members of the House of Deputies from each town in Massachusetts Bay were listed in the *Records of the Governor and Company of the Massachusetts Bay, in New England, 1644-1657, Vol .3*. This document is important for researchers who seek to produce scholarship on this topic. In Maine, William D. Williamson, in his work, *The History of State of Maine*, revealed what representative government meant while under the jurisdiction of Massachusetts Bay. In Plymouth, data pertaining to the representative system is in *The Compact with the Charter and Laws of the Colony of New Plymouth*.

Representative System in Massachusetts Bay Colony

The emergence of the representative system in New England developed initially in Massachusetts Bay. Before the institutionalization of this system, the freemen advocated for implementations of democratic norms. In keeping with this vision, the majority of the freemen were against unlimited power of the Massachusetts Bay officials. In the case of Watertown in 1632, the freemen revolted against the government due to it levying taxes against them without representation. As Government officials did not have the power to collect taxes, the elders and the freemen in Watertown questioned the validity of that process. According to the Newtown freemen, Massachusetts Bay's government was like that of the mayor and the Alderman of London. As such, they did not have parliamentary power to collect taxes without the consent of the people. The governor and the assistants challenged their arguments which they affirmed as being in error. According to Governor Winthrop, the Massachusetts Bay Company had the same power as the Parliament in England.

After the revolution of the Watertown freemen, Governor Winthrop tells us that the freemen were eager to know the contents of the patent of the Company. When they discovered that they had the right to make their laws, they asked the Governor to advise them on how to involve themselves in that process. They also wanted the repeal of unnecessary laws which they believed were unproductive for the colony, such as the killing of swine in corn. After carefully listening to them, Governor Winthrop revealed to the freemen that when the patent was issued, freemen were few like any other corporation. But as the number of the freemen increased in various towns, it was impossible to assemble everyone in the General Court to make or ordain laws and orders. These points considered, the Governor had them to choose their representatives for this purpose. As a result, the process of selecting people to assist the governor in minor affairs became democratized.

In 1632, the General Court passed an act ordering each town to send two men to assist the governor and assistants for the raising of public stocks. Governor Winthrop noted that everyone should be committed to the consensus made by the committee of public stocks.[3] That same year, Roger Conant and Peter Palfrey were elected as representatives from Salem to fulfill these roles.[4] In Watertown, John Oldham and John Masters were listed as members of the committee to assist the governor and the deputy for the same purpose.[5] In Boston, I discovered that William Colborn and William Chesbrough were deputies to the Massachusetts Bay General Court for raising the public stocks in 1632.[6] In Roxbury, Robert Coles and John Johnson were elected as committee members for raising the colony taxes in 1632. In Saugus, Richard Wright served on the committee for raising public stocks. Like other towns, William Phelps and John Gallard represented Dorchester in the same General Court. Moreover, Abraham Palmer and Edward Gibbons served the same role at the General Court in 1632, representing Charlestown. In Newtown [Cambridge], Edmund Lockwood and William Spencer were among those who assisted the governor and the deputy in collecting taxes for the colony in 1632.[7] The election of two committee members from the eight towns was described by Thomas Prince as paving way for a House of Representatives in the General Courts.[8] Like Prince, Samuel Drake believed that the committee established in 1632 for the collection of taxes with the inclusion of freemen was a sort of House of Representatives.[9] While listing the names of the deputies which formed the General Court, James Savage noted that those who served believed this process was the beginning of a representative democracy in the Massachusetts Bay colony.

Deputy Israel Stoughton detailed the emergence of the representative democracy in Massachusetts Bay with precision. He served in that council in 1632 as a representative from Dorchester. From his letter to his brother, John Stoughton, he took detailed notes on that process. In the letter, he mentioned to his brother abuses of power by the magistrates toward the freemen. He also revealed that the magistrates were fighting internally. According to him, a group of magistrates did not approve of the power they had over the people. He did note that some magistrates liked such power and others were against it. The magistrates believed that their power was based on the language of the patent. As the freemen and church ministers did not have knowledge on the contents of the patent, it was difficult for them to challenge the magistrates. He stressed that at the time when he emigrated to Massachusetts, the government was totally under the control of these magistrates. Freemen elected them to enact laws, dispose of lands, raise taxes, and punish offenders. At that time, the people did not know the patent nor the prerogatives of their liberties according to it.[10] He went on to stipulate that with the implication of the raising of taxes in the colony, the freemen were interested in reading the patent. With this in consideration, Governor Winthrop gave them the patent. There is no question that after reading the patent, the freemen discovered the rights granted to them by King Charles I. To support the change of the magistrates' government policy to include the freemen in the affairs of the colony, Deputy Stoughton wrote that, by way of charity, the magistrates consented to admit the people to join with them in the governance of the colony. As a result, each town elected three deputies to serve as representatives of the people.[11]

On May 14, 1634, government officials ordered that the colony had to convene four General Courts every year. Officials also decided that the entire body of the freemen be present at the Court of Election to choose their officials, including as magistrates. In the other three courts, the Act of the Court allowed freemen to send their deputies to the General Court with a mandate to make laws, dispose lands, and manage other affairs of the colony.[12] A notice was sent by the Massachusetts General Court ordering each town to select three freemen to serve as their representatives to that Court. According to Governor Winthrop, the Order of 1634 entrusted the representatives of the freemen with the taking of the General Court's orders, revising all laws, and correcting those which were out of place.[13] They were also empowered to make laws and make orders for the welfare of the towns and the colony.[14] This was the first time that the democratically elected members of the House of Deputies took their seats in the General Court. In this year, there were eight towns in the colony.

Twenty-four members were elected as the representatives of the freemen to the General Court of Massachusetts. In Charlestown, Abraham Palmer, Robert Moulton, and Thomas Beecher served as representatives of that body in 1634. Palmer was a merchant and prominent in Charlestown. Richard Frothingham, Jr. wrote that, on May 30, 1628, he signed the instructions which was sent to Governor John

Endecott for the management of the newly founded plantation in Salem.[15] In Boston, John Coggeshall, Edmund Quincy, and Capt. John Underhill represented this town to the General Court in 1634.[16] In the same year and General Court, William Phelps, Israel Stoughton and George Hull were elected as representatives of the freemen from that town.[17] The freemen of Watertown were represented by John Oldham, Robert Feake and Richard Browne [Brown] at the General Court of May 14, 1634.[18]

In 1636, the Act of the General Court prescribed the duties and numbers of the representatives of the people in the Massachusetts Bay. From thereon, the representative system developed in Massachusetts Bay. In the same year, this system was also in Connecticut while under the jurisdiction of Massachusetts Bay. The officials did not codify the Act of 1632 which ordered the selection of two members from each town to assist the governor and his deputy in the collection of taxes. The Act of 1636 respecting the Massachusetts Bay deputies reads as follows:

> Sect. 1. It is ordered by this court and the authority hereof, that henceforth it shall be lawful for the freemen of every town, to choose (by papers) deputies for the general court, who have liberty to meet together, to confer and prepare such public business, as by them shall be thought fit to be considered of at the next general court, who also shall have the full power of all the freemen deputed to them for the making and establishing of laws, granting lands, and to deal in all other affairs of the commonwealth, wherein the freemen have to do, the matter of election of magistrates and other officers only, excepted; wherein every freemen is to give in his vote; provided that no town shall send more than two deputies, and no town that has not the number of twenty freemen shall send more than one deputy; and such plantations as have not ten freemen shall send none, but such freemen may vote with the next town, in the choice of their deputies, till this court take further order. And all towns that have not more than thirty freemen, shall be at liberty of sending or not sending deputies to the general court [1636, 38, 53].

Sect 2. And the freemen or any shire or town, have liberty to choose such deputies for the general court either in their own shire town, or elsewhere or they judge fit, so be it by freemen, and inhabiting this jurisdiction. And when the deputies for several towns are met together at any general court, it shall be lawful for them or the major part of them, to hear and determine any difference that may arise about the election of any of their members, and to order what may concern the well ordering of their body. And because we cannot foresee what variety and weight of occasions may fall into future consideration, and what counsels we may stand in need of; it is ordered that the deputies of the general court, shall not at any time be stated and continue but from court to court, or at most but for a year, that the country may have an annual liberty, to do in that case what is most behoofull [hopeful] for the welfare thereof [1641, 34, 35].

Sect. And it is further ordered, that no man, although a freeman, shall be accepted as a deputy in the general court, that is unsound in judgement, concerning the main points of Christian religion, as they have been held forth and acknowledged by the generality of the protestant orthodox writers; or that is scandalous in his conversation, or that is unfaithful to this government.

Sect. 4. And it is further, ordered, that it shall not be lawful for any freeman to make choice of any such person as aforesaid, that is known to himself to be under such offence or offences specified, upon pain or penalty of five pounds, and the case of such persons to be tried by the whole general court [1654].

Sect.5. And henceforth the constables of each town, shall return the name of the person or persons chosen by the freemen to be deputies for the general court, and the time for which they are chosen, whether for the first session or for the whole year. And every constable that shall fail in his duty herein shall forfeit the sum of twenty shillings; to be paid to the common treasury;

and all persons so chosen as aforesaid, accepting thereof, which shall be absent from the house, during the time of their sitting, without just grounds so judged by the house, shall pay twenty shillings a day for every such defect, and the several returns of each constable, shall be kept on file by the clerk of the deputies until the court be ended [1654].

Sect. 6. It is ordered by this court and the authority thereof, that no person who is an usual and common attorney in any inferior court, shall be admitted to sit as a deputy in this court [October 1663].[19]

The Act of 1636 gives us trustworthy information regarding the election laws in Massachusetts Bay. From these acts, it is important to note that people who were antagonistic to the Puritan religion did not vote or engage in the election process. Moreover, officials punished those who dared to vote for freemen who did not support or believe in the Massachusetts Bay's mixed form of government. Furthermore, colonial laws sanctioned constables who refused to enforce election laws. This was the first time colonial officials established laws for regulating elections. Like the election of minor officers, elected deputies received a punishment for an unjustified absence. Even though the acts prohibited the election of more than two deputies from each town, in 1636, three freemen were deputies from Boston. According to *The Second Report of the Record Commissioners, of the City of Boston*, William Hutchinson, John Coggeshall and William Brenton were deputies or committees to the General Court.[20]

In New Hampshire, this system emerged in 1641 when the settlement of Hampton was under the jurisdiction of Massachusetts. In Dover and Portsmouth, the representative system developed in 1642 after being united with Massachusetts Bay. According to *The Provincial Papers of the colony of New Hampshire*, on September 8, 1642, James Parker was deputy to the Massachusetts General Court from Portsmouth. Parker was re-elected on May 10, 1643, representing the same town. On May 29, 1644, William Hilton was a deputy for Dover in the Massachusetts General Court. In the same year, Stephen Winthrop represented the freemen of

Strawberry Bank in the same assembly. In this province, two government officials served as speakers for the session at the Massachusetts General Court; Capt. Richard Walderne from Dover and Richard Waldron. These deputies served in that position for various sessions. Capt. Walderne was Speaker in 1666, 1668–1669. On the other hand, Capt. Waldron held the same position from 1673–1678 with an interruption in 1678. In 1682, Capt. Waldron was the President of the Council after the death of President John Cutt on March 27, 1681, until the arrival of Edward Cranfield on October 4, 1682.[21]

In Maine, data from the work of William D. Williamson indicates that the first deputies represented freemen of Kittery and York in 1653. According to him, in May 1653, John Wincoln of Kittery and Edward Rishworth served as representatives to the Massachusetts Court for towns mentioned above. While Kittery and York were privileged with sending representatives to the Massachusetts court, the towns of Wells, Saco, and Cape Porpoise were not. The General Court allowed them to elect town commissioners and selectmen. In Wells, Henry Bood, Thomas Wheelwright, and Ezekiel Knight were commissioners elected in that city. As commissioners, they had powers like those of magistrates in Massachusetts Bay. In Saco, Thomas William, Robert Boothe and John West were commissioners in addition to the position of selectmen.[22]

The division of the Massachusetts General Court into two chambers happened in 1644. From this date, the colony had the House of Assistants and the House of Deputies. From there onwards, Assistants worked in the General Court with deputies. Each parliamentary house decided the affairs of the colony separately. Regarding those affairs, a decision agreed to by the assistants or magistrates was sent to the deputies and vice versa. From the decisions of both houses, the final decision on the matter reached a resolution.[23] According to Thomas Hutchinson, before the division of both houses, the assistants sat together with the deputies. He noted that, as the numbers of the towns increased, the colony had to augment the number of deputies. Consequently, there were more deputies than magistrates. In this case, the assistants were in the minority in the General Court. This resulted in them losing legislative power. They preferred to convene on public affairs among themselves without the deputies.[24] He also pointed out that, in May 1634, there was a General Court where there were agitations. It was during this General Court that he served as a deputy from Dorchester.[25]

Historically, the representative system in North American emerged in the colony of Virginia. The date in which this system is said to have developed in Virginia varies. There are authors who believe that Governor George Yeardley convened the first assembly in Virginia in 1619. Others believe the Virginia system of representation happened in 1620. William Stith in his *History of the First Discovery and Settlement of Virginia*, wrote that at the end of June 1619, Governor Yeardley called the first General Assembly in Virginia. Furthermore, he said that before the emergence of counties, each town did not elect its representatives. Jamestown, Henrico, Bermuda Hundred, and the rest, each sent their members to the Assembly. From that year onwards, the first House of Burgesses emerged in Virginia.[26] Charles Campbell, the author of the *History of the Colony and Ancient Dominion of Virginia*, informs us that,

> In June, Governor Yeardley summoned the first legislative assembly that ever met in America. It assembled at James city or Jamestown, on Friday, the 30th of July, 1619, upwards a year before the Mayflower left England with the Pilgrims.[27]

In this assembly, John Pory, secretary of the colony was the speaker, and John Twine, the clerk. Thomas Pierse was the sergeant. The lower house was composed of 22 burgesses.[28]

Regardless of a dispute over dates, the most import fact is that Virginia is the architect and pioneer of instituting the representative form of government in North America. The freemen had the right to suffrage without exceptions. They voted by proxy by sending the name of their choice on paper. Later, every freeman had the right to vote in person. Before the formation of counties, there was no law prescribing the number of burgesses representing freemen in each town. In 1634, Virginia had eight counties. Each county elected four burgesses as representatives of the freemen. In 1645, each county elected four burgesses to represent them to the General Assembly except for Jamestown, which could send only one deputy because it was the metropolis of the colony. In 1660, the law allowed each county two burgesses.

The Impact of Deputies on the General Court of Massachusetts Bay

In Massachusetts, deputies played a significant role in the implementation of democratic norms and the observance of the rule of law. From the work of Governor Winthrop, it is plausible to conclude that Massachusetts Bay's deputies were advocates of liberties. This is evident from 1634, when most deputies supported the migration of Watertown freemen to Connecticut. According to Governor Winthrop, fifteen deputies advocated for them, and the governor and two assistants also gave support. On the other hand, the rest of the assistants opposed the migration of the inhabitants of Watertown to Connecticut.[29] This is the first convincing piece of evidence indicating democratic views among the Massachusetts deputies. The Massachusetts Body of Liberties allowed freedom of movement. In addition to the freedom of movement, deputies were against the arbitrary power of the assistants. The complaints of the deputies recorded by Governor Winthrop reads as follows:

> Deputies having conceived great danger to our state, in regard that our magistrate, for want of positive laws, in many cases, might proceed according to their discretions, it was agreed, that some men should be appointed to form a body of grounds of law, in resemblance to a Magna Carta.[30]

The freemen in the colony also complained about the excess power of the assistants. In the early years of the colony, civil and criminal cases were under the jurisdiction of the Courts of Assistants. This body had executive, legislative, and judiciary powers before the codification of the Body of Liberties. As such, they used their discretionary power in judging cases brought before them. As a result, assistants or magistrates abused their power at will. Regarding the lamentations of the freemen on the abuse of the magistrates' powers, Governor Winthrop wrote the following:

> The people had long desired a body of laws, and thought their condition very unsafe, while so much power rested in the discretion of magistrates. Diverse attempts had been made at former courts, and the matter referred to some of the magistrates

and some of the elders; but still it came to no effect; for, being committed to the care of many, whatsoever was done by some, was still dislike or neglected by others. At last it was referred to Mr. [John] Cotton and Mr. Nathaniel Warde [ward], etc.., and each of them framed a model which was presented to this general court, and by them committed to the governor and deputy, and some others to consider of, and so prepare it for the court in the 3rd month next.[31]

This statement from Governor Winthrop reveals pertinent information regarding the history of the judicial system in the colony. In this colony, the assistants were aristocrats who did not believe in democratic principles. Magistrates had different legal opinions among them regarding laws. As a result, two ministers had the power to codify the laws of the colony following the Magna Carta model. Rev Nathaniel Ward served as elaborator and codifier of the colonial laws because he was a legal scholar of the common law of England. From the complaints of the freemen and that of the deputies, it is sound to note that their views and opinions on the laws of the colony were the same. On the contrary, assistants or magistrates believed in their own interpretation of laws. Assistants advocated mosaic laws in their legal proceedings. Concerning the freemen and deputies, Rev. Ward advocated a code with the protection of English liberties in it.

Regarding religious liberty, various records indicate that deputies were from time to time sanctioned for supporting the religious views of ministers or other religious leaders who were antagonistic to the Puritans' religious opinions. The General Court of Massachusetts dismissed Deputies John Coggeshall and William Aspinwall as deputies from the General Court for supporting the views of Rev. John Wheelwright. Deputy Aspinwall was among those who wrote a petition which claimed that Rev. Wheelwright was innocent from these charges. Deputy Coggeshall approved the religious opinions of Rev. Wheelwright. As a consequence, the Assembly dismissed him from the court after disenfranchising him. Governor Winthrop wrote that the Court sent a warrant for their replacement by the Boston freemen, but they wanted to send them to the Court as their Representatives.[32]

Introduction of the Representative System in the Plymouth Colony

The emergence of the representative system in Plymouth did not develop like in Massachusetts Bay. In this colony, the entire body of the freemen had legislative power. The legislative system changed when freemen expanded the number of plantations. Freemen from various towns went to the General Court for the regulation of the colony's affairs, like making laws and repealing others. This new order of things was not satisfactory to the freemen. They had to travel to Plymouth so that they could participate in government affairs. As a result, freemen complained to officials about the inconvenience of deserting their plantations when they traveled to Plymouth for the General Court. In *The Compact, Charter and Laws of the Colony of New Plymouth*, it was stated that "complaints were made that the freemen were put to many inconveniences and great expense by their continued attendance at the courts."[33] Due to these circumstances, in 1638, by the order of the court, each town was ordered to send two freemen as their representatives to the General Court. The town of Plymouth was privileged with four representatives. The same order also detailed the duties and mandates of the representatives. According to the order, representatives had the power to make laws and ordinances for the good and welfare of the colony. The laws made by the deputies were subject to repeal by the freemen if they discovered discrepancies therein. Moreover, the freemen had the power to enact new laws at the General Court. Family masters who were paid taxes but not freemen had the right to vote for their respective representatives in towns.[34]

In Plymouth, the first democratic assembly of the free elected representatives developed in 1638. From Francis Baylies' *Historical Memoir of the Colony of New Plymouth*, I found that William Paddy and Manasseh Kempton, Jr., John Cooke, Jr, and John Dunham were representatives from Plymouth to the General Court. As the law required this town to elect four representatives, the freemen complied with the law. Jonathan Brewster and Edmund Chandler both represented Duxbury at the General Court. Finally, Scituate sent Anthony Annable and Edward Foster as their representatives to the General Court of that town. After a town was built, each had two representatives, like Duxbury and Scituate. In later years, John Gilbert and Henry Andrew were representatives from Taunton to the General Court. Like other towns, Sandwich sent Richard Bourne and John Vincent to the General Court. Thomas Payne and Philip Tabor were representatives from Yarmouth to the General Court. Barnstable's representatives to the General Court were Joseph Hull and Thomas Dimmock.[35] In 1641, towns such as Duxbury, Scituate, Sandwich, Taunton, Barnstable, Yarmouth, and Marshfield each sent two representatives to the General Court. In 1649, the town of Plymouth had the power to send two representatives to the General Court like other towns in the colony.[36]

Among town representatives for the General Court in Plymouth, I found the names of the Mayflower's passengers and signers of the compact. These were John Alden, George Soule, and John Howland. Alden was for years a deputy representing the town of Plymouth. In addition to the position of deputy, he also served as assistant for the colony. In 1641–1643 and 1649, he served as deputy for Plymouth at the General Court.[37] From the work of Justin Winsor, data indicates that Alden went to Holland with the Pilgrims. He lived with them in Amsterdam as well as in Leyden. He also came to America with them. He was the youngest Pilgrim. In the colony, he served as member of the Board of Assistants in 1633.[38] Like Winsor, Augustus E. Alden also documented details of his life. A.E. Alden tells us that Governor Bradford identified Deputy Alden as a hired cooper. He was often also a surveyor of the highways for the colony. From 1640 to 1650, he represented Duxbury in the General Court at Plymouth.[39] Like John Alden, George Soule, another one of the signers of the Mayflower Compact, was deputy from Duxbury to the General Court at Plymouth in 1642, 1645–1646, and 1650–1651.[40]

John Howland, one of the signers of the Compact in the cabin of the Mayflower, served for years as a deputy representing the town of Plymouth. Henry R. Howland in his article "A Biographical Sketch of John Howland," documented pertinent information about the services of this Howland in the Plymouth colony. He was the thirteenth Pilgrim to sign the Mayflower Compact. According to H.R. Howland, John Howland served as assistant under Governors John Caver and William Bradford. During the administration of Thomas Prince, he was also an assistant in the colony. H.R. Howland noted also that John Howland served in different committees while in the House of Deputies. He was in the committee of leasing and protection of the Kennebec trade, for instance. He also awarded land grants and settled boundary disputes.[41] In Marshfield, Baylies tells us that Thomas Bourne and Kenelm Winslow were the first elected deputies from that town to the General Court of Plymouth.[42]

Representative System in Connecticut and New Haven

In the colonies of Connecticut and New Haven, representative government was resembled that in Massachusetts Bay. From the record in 1639, the elective representative system of government developed in Connecticut. In 1643, after the formation of the New Haven colony government, the General Court established the representative system. In Connecticut, the representative system worked in accordance with the Constitution of 1639. It was a constitutional representative democracy. In the constitution, eleven orders were inserted for the management of the colony. In those orders, two, five, seven, and eight prescribed the elections of deputies as well as their duties in the General Court. The Constitution of 1639 divided the courts into two general assemblies. One of the assemblies or courts was for the election of officers such as magistrates and other public officials.[43] During the Court of Election, by law, each town had the right to send its deputies. After the end of the election, deputies managed public affairs as if they were in other courts. In the court of the second Thursday in April, deputies made laws and discussed other public affairs which concerned the welfare of the colony.[44] In order seven, the procedure for the election of deputies was clarified. According to it, admitted freemen who have taken an oath of fidelity in each town were legal voters. The election laws of this colony excluded colonists who were not freemen from the election process. That is, such a person could not be elected or select a candidate for the election in the commonwealth of Connecticut.[45] The election of deputies was done by paper. A candidate who had the majority of votes was the winner of the election.[46]

Regarding the number of deputies from each town, the law prescribed that Windsor, Hartford and Wethersfield had power to send four deputies to the General Court. In the same order, a provision for forthcoming towns was made. Order eight of the Fundamental Orders of Connecticut declared towns established after the framing of the constitution had the rights and privilege to send as many deputies as the Court shall think fit. The Court took into consideration the proportion of freemen while deciding the number of deputies for each town. Deputies made orders in the name of the commonwealth. The entire population in the colony obeyed the same orders.[47] The information pertaining to the legal numbers for each town's deputies can be found in The Connecticut Code of 1650.

In addition to the previously noted mandates, deputies had the power to meet before the General Court to consult amongst themselves on issues concerning public welfare, such as the elections of officials. Regarding the elections, deputies had the duty to review whether they had reason to nullify an election and recommence it. They could nullify the entire process of the elections or part of it. They were also given the power to sanction those who committed election frauds.[48] Regarding the first representatives of the three towns, various sources indicate that John Talcott, John Steele, Edward Stebbins, William Spencer, John Pratt, George Hull, George Hubbard, and William Gaylord were deputies elected to the General Court of Connecticut in 1639 after the adoption of the Fundamental Orders.

In Hartford, John Talcott held the position of deputy to the General Court in 1639. Before his migration to Connecticut, he served as deputy from Cambridge to the General Court of Massachusetts from 1634–1636. In addition to his deputy positions, in Connecticut, he served as assistant from 1652–1660. Moreover, he was treasurer of the colony from 1654–1660. And finally, he served as a commissioner of the United Colonies from 1652–1658.[49] Like Talcott, Stebbins served also as deputy from Hartford to the General Court of Connecticut in 1639. He continued to serve as such for years. Similarly, John Steel was also a deputy from Hartford to the General Court of Connecticut in 1639.[50] Similar to noted deputies and government officials in Connecticut, William Spencer served as deputy in the colony of Massachusetts Bay from Cambridge for several years. He was a lieutenant of the Newtown militia. He also served as representative in the first Connecticut General Court in 1639 from Hartford.[51]

In the case of Windsor, Hull and Gaylor were deputies who served the Connecticut General Court in 1639 after the adoption of the constitution. Hull and Gaylor were both from Massachusetts Bay. In Massachusetts Bay, they served in the same capacity. Hull was deputy from Dorchester to the Massachusetts General Court in 1634 and 1636. Like Hull, Gaylor was a deputy from Dorchester to the Massachusetts General Court in 1635–1636, and 1638. In Connecticut, Gaylor served as deputy. Regarding Hull, he served also as deputy from Fairfield to the Connecticut General Court from 1649–1651.[52] In addition to the previously mentioned officials, William Phelps served as deputy in Massachusetts Bay before his arrival in Connecticut. He was one of the commissioners to govern Connecticut while under the Massachusetts Bay government. Like Gaylor and Hull, Thomas Ford served as deputy from Windsor to the General Court of Connecticut.[53]

Like Hartford and Windsor, the town of Wethersfield also had the privilege to send four deputies to the General Court of 1639. That year, Richard Law, George Hubbard, Richard Treat, and John Plum represented this town to the General Court. In 1637, he was a deputy from Wethersfield to the General Court of Connecticut.[54] In 1637, Richard Treat of Wethersfield served as deputy to the first General Court in Connecticut. He held that position from 1637–1644 with an interval. From 1657–1665, he continued to serve as deputy.[55] Deputies from Windsor, Hartford, and Wethersfield were on committees during the adoption of the Fundamental Orders. Forest Morgan wrote that eleven committees from Windsor, Hartford, and Wethersfield were present during the adoption of the constitution of 1639. According to him, George Hull, Capt. Mason, Thomas Ford, and Thomas Marshell were from Windsor. From Hartford, he noted that John Webster, John Talcott, John Steele, and Edward Hopkins were committees during the adoption of the Fundamental Orders. He goes on to note that Andrew Ward, Thurston Reynor, and George Hubbard were on committees during the same event.[56]

Roger Welles in his article "Constitutional History of Connecticut" wrote that in addition to the eleven committee members, eight magistrates participated in the framing of the Fundamental Orders and its adoption.[57] Among the magistrates, Roger Ludlow and John Hayne were of that committee. In New Haven, sources indicate that the representative system of government emerged in 1643. On October 23, the New Haven freemen convened the first General Court after the formation of the government. In this year, the towns of New Haven, Milford, Guilford, and Stamford united into one government. In this first General Court, government officials passed an act for the election of deputies. From the *Records of the Colony of New Haven from 1638 to 1649*, an order can be found permitting every plantation to choose two deputies to represent their constituents in the General Court.[58] In New Haven, each government official was a member of an approved church in New England. The same requirement was also for the selection of the deputies. In Milford, John Astwood and John Sherman were representatives of the people to the General Court. William Leete and Samuel Disbrough were representatives from Guilford. As in the previously noted towns, Richard Gildersleeve and John Whitmore were representatives from Stamford to the General Court at New Haven.[59] There, George Lamberton and Nathaniel Turner served as representatives from the town to the General Court.[60] Like the House of Representatives, the governor, deputy governor, magistrates, and assistants from each town comprised another elective branch of the General Court. Elected members of both houses were freemen who were church members under the jurisdiction of New Haven. Both branches had the power to make and repeal laws or orders in the New Haven colony.[61] Even though the colony had two branches of legislatures, both sat always together in the same room. The election of deputies occurred twice annually, and the magistrates once.[62] The representative system developed in Rhode Island and New Hampshire as it did in the colonies of Massachusetts, Plymouth, Connecticut, and New Haven.

Development of Representative Government in Rhode Island

In Rhode Island, the representative system developed in 1647 during the union of four towns—Portsmouth, Providence, Warwick, and Newport under the Charter of 1643. In the Charter of 1643, the Rhode Island freemen received permission from the General Court to form a government according to their design. In this charter, there was no provision regarding the formation of a representative government. But when the committees from the four towns combined themselves into a body politic, this provision was in the laws and orders enacted in 1647. The *Records of the Colony of Rhode Island and Providence Plantation, in New England, 1636 to 1663*, stated that on May 16, 1648, at the General Court held in Providence, each town had the right to elect six discreet men to represent them in the General Assembly or General Court. The order also required that if any town neglected to elect a representative, the General Court had the power of electing commissioners to substitute one for them.[63] The *Records of the Colony of Rhode Island and Providence Plantations* lists the names of deputies elected from each town.[64]

In 1650, the deputies had the full power of the General Assembly. They received two shillings per day for their services to that court. Each respective town paid the allowances for the deputies during their service to the General Court.[65] With such power, they made and repealed laws and orders for the common good of the colony. They had also the power to establish rules and penalties for the ordering of themselves during their sessions.[66] On May 23, 1650, at the General Court of Election held at Newport, authorities passed another order for the substitution of the deputies in case the number of such members was insufficient. The order reads as follows: "It is ordered, that in case the committee shall fall short of six out of each town, that then they appear from town shall have liberty to choose and make up their number."[67] On October 26, 1650, the representatives of the people in Rhode Island further passed an act that reads as follows:

> It is ordered, that from henceforth the representative committee being assembled and having enacted law or laws, the said laws shall be returned within six days after the breaking up or adjournment of that assembly; and then within three days after, the chief officer of the town shall call the town to the hearing of the laws so made; and if any freeman shall mislike any law then made, they shall then send their votes with their names fixed thereto unto the General Recorder within ten days after the reading of those laws and no longer. And if it appear that major vote within that time prefixed shall come in and declare

it to be a nullity, then shall the Record signify it to the president, and the president shall forthwith signify to the towns that such or such laws is a null, and the silence to the rest shall be taken for approbation and confirmation of the laws made; and it is ordered further, that the eleventh law made at Portsmouth, May 20, 21, 1647 is repealed.[68]

In 1650, after the enactment of laws by deputies, they returned the same for revisions and amendments in accordance with the act of October 26, 1650. Furthermore, freemen had a voice on the adoption of newly established laws. They had the right to accept or reject laws made by their representatives. According to the procedural law of the colony, time limits were set forth for the rectification of laws. After the legal limitation for the rejections of laws by the freemen, any claim made thereafter was illegal. Furthermore, the General Court gave government officials a reasonable amount of time to inform the freemen of the nullification or acceptance of a law. In the same year, by an act, the General Court specified the number of town representatives for each town. The General Court also became the Representative Court. In the order pertaining to the Representative Court, the law declared,

> ... that the representative committee for the colony shall always consist of six discreet, able men, and chosen out of each town for the transacting of the affairs of the commonwealth; and being met, they shall have power to make and establish rules, and penalties for the ordering of themselves during their sessions.[69]

Similar to Rhode Island, the representative system was also instituted in New Hampshire after separation from the Massachusetts Bay.

Representative System in New Hampshire under the Royal Province

The emergence of the representative system in New Hampshire as a royal province happened under the administration of President John Cutt. In 1680, Government officials passed an order for the incorporation of the representative system. From Judge John M. Shirley's "The Early Jurisprudence of New Hampshire," on March 1, 1680, freemen assembled themselves for the selection of town representatives to the General Court. On March 16, 1680, the freemen of New Hampshire held an election at Portsmouth for the selection of their representatives. According to Shirley, at this time, there were seventy-one freemen in Portsmouth, sixty-one freemen in Dover, fifty-seven freemen in Hampton, and twenty freemen in Exeter.[70] Charles W. Brewster noted that, on March 16, 1680, Portsmouth, Dover, and Hampton sent three representatives to the General Court, and Exeter sent two of the same government officials. According to him, there were 209 registered voters in the province in this year.[71] The election of representatives from each town was in accordance with the Law of 1680. This law ordered the towns of Portsmouth, Dover, and Hampton to send three representatives of the people to the General Court. In the same law, Exeter had to send two representatives to the General Court.[72]

Regarding the names of the first representatives for New Hampshire, Rev. Jeremy Belknap, and John Farmer listed Robert Elliot, Philip Lewis, and John Pickering as representatives from Portsmouth to the General Court. From Dover, Peter Coffin, Anthony Nutter, and Richard Waldron, Jr. were representatives of the freemen from that town to the General Court. Thirdly, Anthony Stanyan, Thomas Marston, and Edward Gove were representatives of the freemen from Hampton to the General Court in 1680. Finally, Bartholomew Tipper and Ralph Hall were representatives of the freemen to the General Court in the same year.[73] In addition to Rev. Belknap and Farmer, Charles H. Bell, in the *History of the Town of Exeter, New Hampshire* named the representatives of the freemen in Exeter during the period under investigation. According to him, Bartholomew Tippen and Ralph Hall served in 1680; William Moore and Robert Wadleigh served in 1681. Wadleigh continued to serve for years as a representative of the people. In 1692, he was a deputy from Exeter to the General Court. In 1684, Robert Smart and Thomas Wiggin were representatives of the Exeter freemen to the General Court. Samuel Leavitt served in that capacity in 1685, 1692, 1696, and 1700.[74]

Chapter 9

Summary and Conclusion

Democracy, Theocracy, Aristocracy and The Rule of Law in the New England colonies, 1620– 1686 tackles the forms of government instituted by the English in Plymouth, Massachusetts, Connecticut, and Rhode Island, with consideration given to the provinces of New Hampshire and Maine. This book also detailed the principles of democratic government in Rhode Island, Connecticut, the provinces of New Hampshire, and Maine. Moreover, mixed forms of government instituted by the Puritans in Massachusetts Bay and New Haven were considered. This work also discussed the forms of government established by the New England freemen in New Jersey, New York, and the Puritan settlements in South Carolina and Georgia.

The principles of the rule of law established by the English in the New England colonies were also examined. Additionally, readers will note an analysis of liberties granted to the freemen in the previously named colonies. In addition to freemen liberties, this book also discussed town liberties in each colony. For better understanding of town liberties, detail has been given concerning town orders and colonial laws established for this purpose. This study also explored the emergence of self-government in New England. In the same context, this study documented the historical development of religious liberties in Rhode Island and their subsequent emergence in the New England states under the United States government. Furthermore, this book discussed the emergence of the representative system of government in the New England colonies. In the same case of town liberties and the self-governing system, laws covering the same received due investigation. Colonial acts and orders for the observations of towns' liberties and self-government systems received the same attention.

This book also detailed legal instruments used by the colonists in their quest for more efficient forms of government. Relative sources included the Mayflower Compact, the Connecticut Fundamental Orders, the New Haven Fundamentals, the Massachusetts Body of Liberties, The Rhode Island Code of 1647, The Connecticut Code of 1650, the Rhode Island Charters of 1643 and 1663, the Connecticut Charter of 1662, and the Magna Carta. I also incorporated the United States Constitution, several constitutions of the New England states, and the early use of those liberties to state their correlation to the modern era. Finally, this study mentioned the contributions of the architects of the New England forms of government. The impacts made by governors such as John Winthrop, Thomas Dudley, John Endicott, John Haynes, Henry Vane, Theophilus Eaton, and Richard Bellingham were given appropriate attention. In addition to these government officials, this work also noted the contributions of religious authorities such as John Cotton, Thomas Hooker, Roger Williams, John Clarke, John Davenport, and Nathanial Ward insofar as their contributions to the forms of government in the New England colonies are concerned. Along with the previously noted officials, this study detailed the efforts made by the freemen in the England colonies for the maintenance of democratic principles and government.

Endnotes

Notes to Chapter 1

1. George Bancroft, *Address at Hartford, Before the Delegates, to the Democratic Convention of the Young Men of Connecticut, on the Evening of February 18, 1840*, ([Hartford, CT, 1840]). See also George Bancroft, *Bancroft's Oration. An Oration Delivered before the Democracy of Springfield and Neighboring Towns, July 4, 1836* (Springfield, [Mass.]: George and Charles Marriam, 1836).

2. Ibid.,11-12. See the *Oration of Springfield* on July 4, 1836.

3. Oliver Gray Hall, *The Mayflower Democracy. The Last Public Address of Oliver Gray Hall, Given before the Maine Society of Mayflower Descendants, November, 1913. Together with A Memorial of His Life by Haltie Vose Hall* (Bangor, ME: C. H. Glass & Co., 1916).

4. See *Records of the Company of the Massachusetts Bay in New England from 1628 to 1641* (Cambridge: Bolles and Houghton, 1850), xviii.

5. See *The Compact with the Charter and Laws of the Colony of New Plymouth* (Boston: Dutton and Wentworth, Printers to the State, 1836), 28.

6. George Bancroft, *History of the United States, from the Discovery of the American Continent, vol.*1 (Boston: Charles C. Little and James Brown, 1848), 319.

7. Ibid., 310.

8. William Elliot Griffis, *The Pilgrims in their Three Homes England, Holland, America* (Boston and New York: Houghton, Mifflin and Company, 1898), 185.

9. Ibid., 254.

10. See William Bradford, *History of Plymouth Plantation* (Boston: Privately Printed, 1856), 370.

11. Paul E. Lauer, *Church and State in New England* (Baltimore: The Johns Hopkins Press, 1892), 24.

12. Ibid.

13. See *The Compact with Charter and Laws of the Colony of New Plymouth* (Boston: Dutton and Wentworth, Printing to the State, 1836), 36.

14. John Fortescue and Francis Gregor, *Delaudibus Legum Angliae. A Treatise in Commendation of the Laws of England* (Cincinnati: Robert Clarke & Co., 1874), 142-143.

15. See *The Constitution of the State of Massachusetts, adopted 1780, With the Amendments Annexed* (Boston: Printed for Benjamin Russell, Printer to the State, 1822), 12. See also the *Constitution of the State of Maine, formed in Convention at Portland, October Twenty-Ninth, and adopted by the People in Town Meetings, on the Sixth Day of December A.D. 1819, and of the Forty-Fourth. Together with Amendments subsequently made thereto, and arranged, as amended, in Pursuance of a Resolve of the Legislature approved February Twenty-Fourth A.D. 1875, with Amendments adopted since the Last named date* (Augusta: Burleigh & Flynt, Printers to the State, 1893), 12.

16. *The Compact with Charter and Laws of the Colony of New Plymouth* (Boston: Dutton and Wentworth, Printer to the State, 1836), 36.

17. Ibid.

18. Lauer, 26.

19. See *The Compact with Charter and Laws of the Colony of New Plymouth* (Boston: Dutton and Wentworth, Printing of the State, 1836), 62. See also Samuel Deane, *History of Scituate, Massachusetts, From Its First Settlement to 1831* (Boston: James Loring, 1831), 98.

20. See William Braford, *History of Plymouth Plantation* (Boston: Privately Printed, 1856), 90.

21. William Brigham, *The Compact with the Charter and Laws of the Colony of New England Plymouth: Together with the Charter of the Council at Plymouth and an appendix, Articles of Confederation of the United Colonies, of New England, and other valuable documents* (Boston: Dutton and Wentworth, Printers to the State, 1836), 19.

22. Ibid., 30.

23. See John G. Palfrey "The Eligibility of Women for Public Office under the Constitution of Massachusetts Bay" Massachusetts Law Quarterly. January 1922, Vol. vii, 147-153.

24. Deane, *History of Scituate, Massachusetts from Its First Settlement to 1831* (Boston: James Loring, 1831), 4-8.

25. See *The Compact with Charter and Laws of the Colony of New Plymouth* (Boston: Dutton and Wentworth, Printing to the State, 1836), 28.

26. John S. Barry, *The History of Massachusetts. The Colonial Period* (Boston: Phillips, Sampson and Company, 1855), 182.

27. Twichell, Joseph H., *John Winthrop. First Governor of the Massachusetts Colony* (New York: Dodd, Mead, and Company Publishers, 1891), 232.

28. John Winthrop and James Savage, ed., *The History of New England from 1630 to 1649, Vol.1* (Boston: Phelps and Farnham, 1825), 178.

29. Ibid.

30. Ibid., 82-83.
31. Ibid., 132.
32. Ibid., 73.
33. Ibid., 151.
34. Ibid.
35. Ibid., 160.
36. Francis C. Gray, *Remarks on the Early Laws of Massachusetts Bay; with the Code Adopted in the Year 1641, And called the Body of Liberties, Now First* (Boston: Charles C. Little and James Brown, 1843), 16.
37. See Thomas Hutchinson, *The History of the Colony of Massachusetts Bay, from the First Settlement Thereof in 1628, until its Incorporation with the Colony of Plymouth, Province of Main, &c. By the Charter of King William and Queen Mary, in 1691* (London: Printed for M. Richardson, 1760), 25.
38. *The Charter and General Laws of the Colony and Province of Massachusetts Bay* (Boston: T. B. Wait and Co., 1814), 17.
39. Hutchinson, 34.
40. Samuel Roads, Jr., *The History and Traditions of Marblehead* (Boston: Osgood and Company, 1880), 13-15.
41. *Records of the Company of the Massachusetts Bay in New England from 1628 to 1641* (Cambridge: Bolles and Houghton, 1858), xiii.
42. William Stubbs, *Constitutional History of England in Its Origin and Development, Vol.3* (Oxford: The Clarendon Press, 1890), 247. Stubbs quoted the work of John Fortescue.
43. Bradford, *Bradford's History "of Plimoth Plantation" From the Original Manuscript with a Report of the Proceeding Incident to the return of the Manuscript to Massachusetts* (Boston: Wright & Porter Printing Co., State Printers, 1899), 316-317.
44. See The Company's First General Letter of Instructions to Endecott and His Council. *Records of the Company of the Massachusetts Bay in New England from 1641 to 1641* (Cambridge: Bolles and Houghton, 1850), 38-40.
45. See *The Company's Second General Letter of Instruction to Endicott and His Council, London, 28 May, 1629. Records of the Company of the Massachusetts Bay in New England from 1628 to 1641* (Cambridge: Bolles and Houghton, 1850), 94-105.
46. Winthrop and Savage, ed., 70.
47. Ibid., 73.
48. Ibid., 177.
49. Ibid.
50. Ibid., 284.

51. Thomas Hutchinson, *The History of the Colony of Massachusetts Bay, from the First Settlement Thereof in 1628* (Boston, New England: Thomas & John Fleet, 1764), 61.

52. Winthrop, 158.

53. Ibid.

54. See *The Constitution of the State of Massachusetts, Adopted 1780. With the Amendments* (Boston: Russell and Gardner, 1820) 7.

55. Ibid., 8.

56. See Jacob B. Moore "Sketches of the Governors and Chief Magistrates of New England from 1620 to 1820" The American Quarterly Register. Vol. 14 (Boston: Press of T. R. Marvin, 1842), 5-17.

57. Ibid.

58. Winthrop, 31-33.

59. Ibid., 159.

60. Richard Frothingham, Jr., *The History of Charlestown, Massachusetts* (Boston: Charles C. Little and James Brown, 1845), 100.

61. Ibid.

62. Joshua Coffin, *A Sketch of the History of Newbury, Newburyport, and West Newbury, from 1635 to 1845* (Boston: Samuel G. Drake, 1845), 19.

63. Ibid.

64. Charles H. Bell, *History of the Town of Exeter* (Exeter: The Quarter-Millennial Year, 1888), 44.

65. Ibid.

66. J. B. Clarke *The Government and Laws of New Hampshire before the Establishment of the Province 1623-1679. A Monograph Consisting the Introduction to the First Volume of the Province Laws* (Manchester, NH: The John B. Clark Company, 1904), 27.

67. Bell, 44.

68. Samuel Roads, Jr, *The History and Traditions of Marblehead* (Boston: Osgood and Company, 1880), 15.

69. Ibid., 14-16.

70. Ibid., 26.

71. Winthrop, 128-129.

72. See *Records of Massachusetts, 1642-1649, Vol.2* (Boston: William White, 1853), 95.

73. John Winthrop, Winthrop's Journal "History of New England" 1630-1649, Vol.1 (New York: Charles Scribner's Sons, 1908), 125.

74. John Windsor, *The Memorial History of Boston, including Suffolk County, Massachusetts 1630-1880, Vol.1* (Boston: James R. Osgood & Co., 1880), 61.

75. Hutchinson, 34.

76. H. F. Uhden, *The New England Theocracy. A History of the Congregationalists in New England to the Revivals of 1740* (Boston: Gould and Lincoln, 1858), 71.

77. Hutchinson, 25.

78. Winthrop, 1825, 152.

79. Joseph Story, *Commentaries on the Constitution of the United States; with A Preliminary Review of the Constitutional History of the Colonies and States, before the Adoption of the Constitution, Vol.1* (Boston: Hilliard, Gray, and Company, 1833), 44.

80. Charles McLean Andrews, *The River Towns of Connecticut. A Study of Wethersfield, Hartford, and* Windsor (Baltimore: John Hopkins University, 1889), 27.

81. See *Records of Massachusetts, 1642-1649, Vol.2* (Boston: William White, 1853), 95.

82. Winthrop and James Savage, ed., *The History of New England from 1630 to 1640, Vol.1* (Boston: Little, Brown and Company, 1853), 157.

Notes to Chapter 2

1. Alexander Johnston, *American Commonwealth. Connecticut. A Study of a Commonwealth-Democracy* (Boston and New York: Houghton, Mifflin and Company, 1887), viii, 63.

2. Willis Mason West, *History of the American People* (Boston: Allyn and Bacon, 1918), 103.

3. See *Records of the Colony of Rhode Island and Province Plantations, in New England, 1636 to 1663, Vol.1* (Providence: RI: A. Crawford Greene and Brother, States Printers, 1856), 12.

4. William G. Goddard, *An Address to the People of Rhode Island, delivered in Newport, on Wednesday, May 3, 1843, in presence of the General Assembly, on the Occasion of the Chance in the Civil Government of Rhode Island. The Adoption of the Constitution, which superseded the Charter of 1663* (Providence: Knowles and Vose, Printers, 1843, 12.

5. *Records of the Colony of Rhode Island and Province Plantations, in New England, 1636 to 1663, Vol.1* (Providence, RI : A. Crawford Greene and Brothers, State Printers, 1856), 156.

6. Ibid., 42-42.

7. Ibid., 143-147.

8. Ibid., 14.

9. Ibid., 149-150.

10. Ibid.

11. Thomas Williams Bicknell, *The History of Rhode Island and Providence Plantations, Vol.2* (New York: The American Historical Society, Inc., 1920), 53.

12. Rayner Wickersham Kelsey, *Friends and the Indians* (Philadelphia: The Associated Executive Committee of Friends on Rhode Island Indian Affairs, 1917), 55-61.

13. *Records of the Colony of Rhode Island and Providence Plantations, in New England, 1636 to 1663, Vol.1* (Providence, RI: A. Crawford Greene and Brothers, State Printers, 1856), 149-150.

14. Ibid.

15. See *The Famous Old Charter of Rhode Island, Granted by King Charles II., in 1663. Also, the Rhode Island Bill of Rights, and the Declaration of Religious Freedom* (Providence, RI: I. H. Cody, 1842), 3.

16. See *Charter of the Colony of Connecticut. 1662* (Hartford: The Case, Lockwood & Brainard Company, 1900), 3-5.

17. Ibid.

18. See Increase N. Tarbox "Organization of Civil Government" in *The Memorial History of Hartford County Connecticut, 1633-1884, Vol.1* (Boston: Edward L. Osgood Publisher, 1886), 38.

19. Isaac William Stuart and W.M. B. Hartley, *Hartford in the Olden Time. First Thirty Years* (Hartford: F. A. Brown, 1853), 51.

20. Hammond J. Trumbull, *The Memorial History of Hartford County Connecticut, 1633-1884, Vol.1* (Boston: Edward L. Osgood Publisher, 1886), 40.

21. See *The Public Records of the Colony of Connecticut, prior to the Union with New Have Colony, May, 1665.* (Hartford: Brown & Parsons, 1850), 21.

22. Trumbull, 40.

23. Loomis and Calhoun, 9.

24. See *The Public Records of the Colony of Connecticut, prior to the Union with New Haven Colony, May, 1665.* (Hartford: Brown & Parsons, 1850), 256.

25. John Fiske, *The Beginnings of New England or The Puritan Theocracy in Its Relations to Civil and Religious Liberty* (Boston and New York: Houghton, Mifflin and Company, 1891), 127-128.

26. Leonard Bacon, *A Discourse on the Early Constitutional History of Connecticut, Delivered before the Connecticut Historical Society, Hartford, May, 17, 1843* (Hartford: Case, Tiffany & Burnham, Printers, 1843), 5-6.

27. Trumbull, *Historical Notes on the Constitutions of Connecticut, 1639-1818 particularly on the Origin and Progress of the Movement which Resulted in the Convention of 1818 and the Adoption of the Present Constitution* (Hartford: Brown & Gross, 1873), 22.

28. Alexander Johnston, *Connecticut. Study of A Commonwealth Democracy* (Boston and New York: Houghton, Mifflin and Company, 1887), viii.

29. Johnston, 70-71.

30. Alan F. Hattersley, *A Short History of Democracy* (Cambridge: University Press, 1930), 116.

31. Henry R. Stiles, *The History of Ancient Windsor, Connecticut* (New York: Charles B. Norton, 1859), 45.

32. See *The Public Records of the Colony of Connecticut, 1636-1665. Prior to the Union with New Haven Colony, May, 1665* (Hartford: Brown & Parsons, 1850), 21.

33. George Sidney Camp, *Democracy* (New York: Harper and Brothers, 1841), 9.

34. See *The Public Records of the Colony of Connecticut, 1636-1665 Prior to the Union with New Haven Colony, May 1665* (Hartford: Brown & Parsons, 1850), 24.

35. See "Abstracts of two Sermons by Rev. Thomas Hooker from the Short-Hand Notes of Mr. Henry Wolcott" Collections of the Connecticut Historical Society, Vol.1 (The Society, 1860), 20.

36. Ibid.

37. Thomas Keightley, *The History of Greece* (London: Longman, Orme, Brown, Green and Longmans, 1839), 38.

38. John Winthrop and James Savage, ed. *The History of New England from 1630 to 1649, Vol.1* (Boston: Phelps and Farnham, 1825), 75-84.

39. Walter Seth Logan, *Thomas Hooker, The First American Democrat. An Address delivered before the New York Society of the Order of the Founders and Patriots of America, February 19. 1904.*

40. George Leon Walker, *Thomas Hooker, Preacher, Founder, Democrat* (New York: Dodd, Mead, and Company Publishers, 1891).

41. Johnston, 72.

42. Baron De Montesquieu and Thomas Nugent, ed. *The Spirit of Laws* (London: Printed for J. Nourse, and P. Waillant, 1766), 11-17.

43. Henry Stiles, *The History of Ancient Windsor, Connecticut* (New York: Charles B. Norton, 1859), 45.

44. Winthrop, 159.

45. Ibid.

46. *Records of the Colony and Plantation of New Haven, from 1638 to 1649* (Hartford: Case, Tiffany and Company, 1857), 9.

47. Ibid., 13.

48. Ibid.,

49. Ibid., 13-17.

50. Ibid., 17.

51. Ibid., 17-19.
52. Ibid., 20.
53. Ibid., 21.
54. Ibid., 21-25.
55. Edward R. Lambert, *History of the Colony of New Haven, before and after the Union with Connecticut. Containing a Particular Description of the Towns which Composed that Government* (New Haven: Hitchcock & Stafford, 1838), 44.
56. *Records of the Colony and Plantation of New Haven, from 1638 to 1649*, 69.
57. Ibid., 110.
58. Lambert, 23.
59. Ibid., 23.
60. Ibid.

Notes to Chapter 3

1. J. B. Clarke, *The Government and Laws of New Hampshire before the Establishment of the Province, 1623-1679* (Manchester, N.H.: The John B. Clarke Company, 1904), 14.
2. Charles H. Bell, *History of the Town of Exeter, New Hampshire* (Exeter, N.H.: The Quarter-Millennial Year, 1888), 14.
3. Ibid, 3.
4. James Phinney Baxter, *George Cleeve of Casco Bay, 1630-1667, with Collateral Documents* (Printed for the Gorges Society, Portland, Maine, 1885), 28.
5. John Winthrop and James Savage, ed., *The History of New England from 1630 to 1649, Vol.1* (Boston: Phelps and Farnham, 1825), 63. In 1630, Governor Winthrop in his book writes that "Capt. Neal and three other gentlemen came hither to us. He came in the bark this summer to Pascataqua [Piscataqua] sent as governor there for Sir. Ferdinando Gorges and others." (38). On page 62, he says that "Thomas Wigging was agent or governor of the upper plantation. [Capt.] Neal was the [agent or governor] for the lower [plantation]."
6. Winthrop and Savage, ed., 155, 116, 146. Governor Winthrop writes that Capt. Wiggin arrived at Salem with thirty people with him. Among them was Leveridge, a goodly minister for the church at Piscataqua. He went on that Lord Say and Lord Brooke purchased land for them from the Bristol men. It appears that Capt. Wiggin believed in the power of Governor Winthrop and his government. In 1633, when one of his settlers was stabbed by another resident, he requested the adjudication of the case in the jurisdiction of the Massachusetts Bay in case if the victim died. In a similar case, Lord Say and Brooke requested the assistance of Governor Winthrop and

Richard Bellingham to assist Capt. Wiggin in Kenebeck where one of the residents was killed. In 1634, Capt. Wiggin at Piscataqua sent a letter to Governor Winthrop requesting the settling a case pertaining two accused suspects from Piscataqua to Massachusetts Bay. These illustrated cases indicate that the government of Capt. Wiggin did not have a settled government with a strong judiciary system.

7. *Provincial Papers. Documents and Records Relating to the Province of New Hampshire, from the Earliest Period of Its Settlement: 1623-1686* (Concord: George E. Jenks, State Printer, 1867, Vol.1), 119. In this documents, Capt. Wiggin, Rev. George Burdett, Capt. John Underhill, and Thomas Roberts were identified as magistrates at Dover.

8. John Scales, *History of Dover New Hampshire (Tercentenary Edition) Containing Historical, Genealogical and Industrial Date of Its Early Settlers. Their Struggles and Triumphs* (Manchester, NH: John B. Clark Co., 1923), 3, 22-23, 90, 92, 105, 107, 151.

9. Scales, 23.

10. Everett S. Stackpole, *Old Kittery and Her Families* (Lewiston, ME: Press Lewiston Journal Company, 1903), 20.

11. An Old Mountaineer, *Laconia; Legends of the White Mountains and Merry Meeting Bay* (Boston: Ashel A. Kelly, 1855), 30.

12. Scales, 3.

13. Jeremy Belknap, *The History of New Hampshire, Vol.1* (Dover: SC Stevens and Ela & Wadleigh, 1831), 14.

14. Data for Capt. Walter Neal see *Calender of State Papers, Colonial Series, 1574-1660. Preserved in the State Paper Department of Her Majesty's Public Record Office* (London: Longman, Green, Longman, & Roberts, 1860), 285.

15. Winthrop, 289.

16. Joseph Dow, *History of the Town of Hampton, New Hampshire from Its Settlement in 1638, to the Autumn of 1892.* (Salem, MA: The Salem Press Publishing and Printing Co., 1893), 12.

17. Ibid., 12-13.

18. Winthrop, 290.

19. Bell, 148.

20. See *Records of the Governor and Company of the Massachusetts Bay in New England, 1642-1649, Vol.2* (Boston: William White, 1853), 43.

21. Ibid., 32.

22. Ibid., 29.

23. See *Laws of New Hampshire*. (Manchester, N.H.: The John B. Clerk Company, 1904), 774-776.

24. *Records of the Governor and Company of the Massachusetts Bay in New England, 1642-1649, Vol.2* (Boston: William White, 1853), 29.

25. *Records of the Governor and Company of the Massachusetts Bay in New England, 1642-1649, Vol.2* (Boston: William White, 1853), 38.

26. Joseph Dow, *History of Hampton, New Hampshire from Its Settlement in 1638, to the Autumn of 1892* (Salem, MA: The Salem Press Publishers and Printing Co., 1893), 87.

27. See *The New Hampshire Provincial Papers. Documents and Records Relating to the Province of New-Hampshire, from the Earliest Period of Its Settlement, 1623-1686* (Concord: George E. Jenks, State Printers, 1867), 396-408.

28. William Willis, *The History of Portland, from its First Settlement with Notices of the Neighboring Towns, and the Changes of Government in Maine* (Portland: Day, Fraser & Co., 1831), 44.

29. George Folsom, *History of Saco and Biddeford, with Notices of other Early Settlements and the Proprietary Government including the Provinces of New Somersetshire in Maine* (Saco: Alex. G. Putnam, 1830), 49.

30. John Josselyn, *An Account of Two Voyages to New England* (London: Giles Widdows, 1674), 200-207.

31. William D. Williamson, *The History of the State of Maine, Vol.1* (Hallowell: Glazier, Masters, & Smith, 1839), 266-267.

32. Willis, 43.

33. Ibid.

34. Emery, 41.

35. Ibid., 42.

36. Folsom, 44-45.

37. See *Collections of the Maine Historical Society, vol.1 Third Series* (Portland: Published by the Society, 1904), 77.

38. Clayton, 16-17.

39. See *Maine Historical Society, York Deeds Book I* (Portland: John T. Hull, 1887), 5.

40. See "Extracts from the Records of the Province of Maine. Form of an Oath appointed to be taken by Sir Ferdinando Gorges." [*From ancient Records of the Province of Main] Collections of the Massachusetts Historical Society, for the Year 1792, Vol.1* (Re-Printed by Munroe & Francis, 1806), 110.

41. Willis, "The Political Affairs of the Province from the Great Paten in 1620, to the Submission to the Jurisdiction of Massachusetts in 1658" in Collection of the Maine Historical Society, Vol.1. Reprinted for the Society with Correction and Additions (Portland : Bailey & Noyes, 1865), 90-102.

42. James Grant Wilson, *The Memorial History of the City of New-York. From Its First Settlement to the York 1892, Vol.1* (New York: New York History Company, 1892), 307-316.

43. Ibid., 399, 405-407.

44. William MacDonald, *The Government of Maine. Its History and Administration.* (New York: The MacMillan Company, 1902), 8-10.

45. John Gorham Palfrey, *History of New England, Vol.3* (Boston: Brown, and Company, 1892), 400.

46. Palfrey, 40.

47. Winthrop, 99.

48. John Scribner Jenness, *The Isles of Sholes an Historical Sketch* (Boston: Houghton, Mifflin and Company, 1888), 168.

Notes to Chapter 4

1. Richard Frothingham, Jr., (*The History of Charlestown, Massachusetts* (Boston: Charles C. Little and James Brown, 1845), 103.

2. A.E. Dick Howard, "Right in Passage: English Liberties in Early America. Massachusetts" in *The Bill of Rights and the States. The Colonial and Revolutionary Origins of American Liberties* (Madison, WI: Madison House Publishers, 1992), 3-6.

3. Ibid. See also Christopher Collier "Connecticut: Liberty, Justice, and No Bill of Rights Protecting Natural Rights in a Common-law Commonwealth" 100-101.

4. Ibid.,

5. Ibid. See also Patrick T. Conley, "Rhode Island Laboratory for the "Lively Experiment", 123

6. See *Records of the Colony of Rhode Island and Providence Plantations, in New England, 1636 to 1663, Vol.1* (Providence, RI: A. Crawford Greene and Brothers, State Printers, 1856), 71.

7. See *The Compact with the Charter and Laws of The Colony of New Plymouth: Together with the Charter of the Council at Plymouth and an Appendix, Articles of Confederation of the United States Colonies of New England, and other Valuable Documents* (Boston: Dutton and Wentworth, Printers to the State, 1836), 19.

8. See *Records of the Colony of Rhode Island and Providence Plantations, in New England, Vol.1* (Providence, RI: A. Crawford Greene and Brother, State Printers, 1856), 143-145.

9. Ibid., 146.

10. See *Charter of the Colony of Connecticut of 1662* (Hartford: The Case, Lockwood, & Brainard Company, 1900), 5.

11. Henry Care, *English Liberties, Or, the Free-Born Subject's Inheritance* (London: Printed by G. Larkin, for Benjamin Harris, 1680), 2.

12. Frederick Kohlrausch and James D. Haas, *A History of Germany: from the Earliest Period to the Present Time* (New York: D. Appleton and Company, 1852), 23-26.

13. Albert Harkness, *Caesar's Commentaries of the Gallic War; with Notes, Dictionary; and a Map of Gaul* (New York: D. Appleton & Company, 1870), 20.

14. Matthew Hale, *The History of the Common Law of England* (London: Printed for Henry Butterworth, Law-Bookseller, 1820), 47.

15. William Blackstone, *Commentaries on the Laws of England* (Dublin: Printed for the Company of Booksellers, 1775, the Sixth Edition), 128-129.

16. John Stow, *Survey of London, Written in the Year 1598* (London: Whitaker and Co., 1842), 186.

17. Hale, 48.

18. Francis C. Gray, *Remarks on the Early Laws of Massachusetts Bay; with the Code Adopted in the Year 1641, And Called the Body of Liberties, Now First Printed* (Boston: C. Little and James Brown, 1843), 13.

19. John Winthrop, *The History of New England from 1630 to 1649, Vol.1* (Boston: Little, Brown and Company, 1853), 388.

20. John Winthrop and James Savage, ed., *The History of New England from 1630 to 1649, Vol.2* (Boston: Thomas B. Wait and Son, 1826), 55.

21. Ibid.

22. Blackstone, 127-128.

23. See *The Charters and General Laws of the Colony and Providence of Massachusetts Bay* (Boston: T. E. Wait and Company, 1814), 44.

24. Ibid., 54.

25. *Records of the Colony of Rhode Island and Providence Plantations, in New England, 1636 to 1663, Vol.1* (Providence, RI: A. Crawford Greene and Brothers, State Printers, 1856), 157.

26. See *The Code of 1650, Being a Compilation of the Earliest Laws and Orders of the General Court of Connecticut* (Hartford, CT: Andrus & Judd, 1833), 19.

27. See Edward Coke, *The Golden Passage in the Great Charter of England, called Magna Carta. Or, The Charter of British Liberties, Granted by King John to His Subjects, in the 17th Year of his reign, in Running-Mead Between Stains and Windsor, June 15, in the Year 1215, and 560 Years Ago. With Lord Coke's*

Remarks and Explanation (Printed for the Use of the London Association in 1776), 2, 7.

28. See William Blackstone, *Commentaries of the Laws of England. In Four Books* (Oxford: Printed at the Clarendon Press, 1770), 4.

29. Ibid., 133.

30. Ibid., 134.

31. Ibid., 135.

32. Roscoe Pound, *Magna Carta and Constitutional Guarantees of Liberty. Address of Dr. Roscoe Pound, of Harvard University Law School, at Ceremonies in the Coolidge Auditorium of the Library of Congress on Sunday Afternoon, December 15, 1946*, 5.

33. J. A. Giles, *William of Malmesbury's Chronicle of the Kings of England from the Earliest Period to the Reign of King Stephen. With Notes and Illustrations* (London: George Bell and Sons, 1895), 202.

34. See *The Constitution of the United States of America with the Amendments. [Compared with the Original in the Department of State April 13, 1891, And Found to be Correct]* (Washington: Government Printing Office, 1891), 25.

35. Gray, 30.

36. Ibid.

37. Ibid., 31.

38. John Winthrop and James Savage, ed., *The History of New England from 1630 to 1649* (Boston: Little, Brown and Company, 1853), 213-214.

39. *The Compact with the Charter and Laws of the Colony of New Plymouth* (Boston: Dutton and Wentworth, Printers to the State, 1836), 198.

40. Gray, 31.

41. See *The Charters and General Laws of the Colony and Province of Massachusetts Bay* (Boston: T. E. Wait and Company, 1814), 180.

42. See *Records of the Colony of Rhode Island and Providence Plantations, in New England, 1636 to 1663, Vol.1* (Providence, RI: A. Crawford Greene and Brothers, State Printers, 1856), 222.

43. Gray, 34.

44. See *The Charters and General Laws of the Colony and Province of Massachusetts Bay* (Boston: T.E. Wait and Company, 1814), 51.

45. See *The Compact with the Charter and Laws of the Colony of New Plymouth* (Boston: Dutton and Wentworth, Printers, to the State, 1836), 28.

46. Ibid., 42.

47. Gray, 33.

48. Ibid., 36.

49. Ibid., 33.

50. *The Charters and General Laws of the Colony and Province of Massachusetts Bay* (Boston: T. E. Wait and Company, 1814), 172.

51. Caesar Bonesana, Marquis Beccaria, *A Essay of Crime and Punishments, Translated from the Italian of Caesar Bonesana, Marquis Beccaria to Which is Added, A Commentary by M. D. Voltaire. Translated from the French by Edward D. Ingraham* (Philadelphia: Philip H. Nicklin, 1818), 20.

52. Ibid., 59.

53. See *The Works of Tacitus. The Oxford Translation, Revised With Notes. The History, Germany, Agricola, and Dialogue on Orators* (London: George Bell & Son, 1889, Vol.2), 302.

54. See *The Charters and General Laws of the Colony and Province of Massachusetts Bay* (Boston: T. E. Wait and Company, 1814), 180.

55. Ibid.

56. Jeremy Bentham, *An Introduction to the Principles of Morals and Legislation, Vol.2* (London: W. Pickering and E. Wilson, Royal Exchange, 1823), 5, 21.

57. See *Constitution of the United States of America. With the Amendments. [Compared with the Original in the Department of State April 13, 1891, and Found to be Correct]* Washington: Government Printing Office, 1891), 23.

58. See *The Eleventh Part of the Report of Sir Edward Coke, KT. Chief Justice of England, of Please to be Held before the King himself assigned, and of the Privy Council of State: of Divers Resolutions and Judgements given on Solemn deliberation and Conference of the Most Reverent Judges and Sages of the Law, of Cases in Law, which were never resolved or adjudicated before: And the Reason and Causes of the said Resolutions and Judgements* (In the Savor: Printed by E. and Nutt, and R. Gosling, 1727), 42.

59. David Jardine, *A Reading of the Use of Torture in the Criminal Laws of England Previously to the Commonwealth: Delivered at New Inn Hall in Michaelmas Term, 1836, By Appointment of the Honourable Society of the Middle Temple* (London: Baldwin and Cradock, 1837), 7-8.

60. Ibid.

61. John Fortescue, *De Laudibus Legum Angliae. Written Originally in Latin by Sir John Fortescue Lord Chief Justice, and After Lord Chancellor to King Henry VI. Translated by Mr. Selden* (Savoy: Henry Lintot, 1741), 43.

62. Ibid., 58-60.

63. Ibid.

64. Bishop Burnet and His Son, *Burnet's History of the Reformation, of the Church of England, Chiefly as Abridged from the Larger History* (London: John

W. Parker, 1847), 439, 441-444. Bishop Burnet writes that "on June 9, 1555, letters were send to the Lord North and others, to torture such obstinate persons as would not confess at their discretion; and another to the lieutenant of the tower to the same effect." He also mentioned in his book that "orders were given to draw by torture confessions from those suspect of plotting against the king in Dorsetshire and Essex."

Notes to Chapter 5

1. Alexis De Tocqueville, *Democracy in America, Vol.1* (Cambridge: Sever and Francis, 1863), 58.

2. William R. Staples, *Annals of the Town of Providence, from its First Settlement, to the Organization of the City Government, in June, 1832* (Providence: Knowles and Vose, 1843), 38.

3. *Second Report of the Record Commissioners, of the City of Boston. 1877* (Boston: Rockwell and Churchill, City Printers, 1877), 88.

4. See *The Works of Tacitus. The Oxford Translation, Revised. With notes, vol.2. The History, Germany, Agricola, and Dialogue on Orators* (London: George Bell & Sons, 1889), 295.

5. Sharon Turner, *The History of the Anglo-Saxons, from the Earliest Period to the Norman Conquest, Vol.3* (London: Longman, Brown, Green, and Longmans, 1852), 198.

6. Ibid., 204.

7. Ibid., 1898.

8. See "The Connecticut Intestacy Law" *The Yale Review. A Quarterly Journal of History and Political Science, vol.3, May, 1894, to February, 1895* (New Haven, CT: Tuttle, Morehouse & Taylor, 1895), 263.

9. Ibid, 262.

10. J. A. Giles, *William of Malmesbury's Chronicle of the Kings of England from the Earliest Period to the Reign of King Stephen. With Notes and Illustrations* (London: George Bell and Sons, 1896), 158.

11. Ibid, 198-201.

12. Ibid.

13. See Thomas Jefferson, *A Summary View of the Rights of British America set Forth in Some Resolutions Intended for the Inspector of the Present Delegates of the People of Virginia, Now in Convention* (Williamsburg, Printed by Clementina Rind. London: Re-printed for G. Kearsley, 1774), 42.

14. See E. H. Scott, *Journal of the Constitutional Convention Kept by James Madison* (Chicago: Scott, Foresman and Company, 1893), 229.

15. Ibid., 232.

16. Carl Becker, *The Declaration of Independence. A Study in the History of Political Ideas* (New York: Harcourt, Brace, and Company, 1922), 8.

17. J. A. Giles, *William of Malmesbury's Chronicle of the Kings of England from the Earliest Period to the Reign of King Stephen. With Notes and Illustrations* (London: George Bell and Sons, 1896, 497.

18. Thomas Jefferson, *A Summary View of the Rights of British America Set Forth in Some Resolutions Intended for the Inspector of the Present Delegates of the People of Virginia, Now in Convention* (Williamsburg, Printed by Clementina Rind. London: re-printed for G. Kearsly, 1774), 1-20, 41-42.

19. See "The Company's First General Letter of Instructions to Endicott and His Council Written in Gravesend, the 17th of April, 1629" in *Records of the Company of the Massachusetts in New England from 1628 to 1641* (Cambridge: Bolles and Houghton, vol.1, 1850), 79-89.

20. *Records of the Colony of Rhode Island and Providence Plantations, in New England, 1626 to 1663* (Providence, R.I.: A. Crawford Greene and Brother, State Printers, 1856), 52-54.

21. Francis C. Gray, *Remarks on the Early Laws of Massachusetts Bay; With the Code Adopted in the Year 1641, and Called the Body of Liberties, Now First Printed* (Boston: Charles C. Little and James Brown, 1843), 30.

22. William Duncan, *The Commentary of Caesar. Translated into English to which is Prefixed a Discourse Concerning the Roman Art of War, Vol.1* (London: Printed for J. and R. Tonson and S. Draper, and R and J. Dodsley, 1755), 192.

23. Gray, 29.

24. John Winthrop, *The History of New England from 1630 to 1649, vol.2* (Boston: Thomas B. Wait and Son, 1826), 55.

25. Ibid.

26. William Blackstone, Commentaries of the Laws of England in Four Books (Oxford, Printed at the Clarendon Press, 1770), 9.

27. See *The Golden Passage in the Great Charter of England called Magna Carta. Or, the Charter of British Liberties, Granted by King John to His Subjects, in the 17th Year of his Reign, in Running-Mead, Between Stains and Windsor, June 15, in the Year 1215, and 560 Years Ago. With Lord Coke's Remarks and Explanations* (Printed for the use of London Association in 1776), 8.

28. Ibid.

29. Ibid., 13.

30. Ibid., 13-15.

31. See *Constitution of the United States of America with the Amendments. [Compared with the Original in the Department of State April 13, 1891, and Found to be Correct]* (Washington: Government Printing Office, 1891), 22.

32. See *Records of the Colony of Rhode Island and Providence Plantations, in New England, 163 to 1663, Vol.1* (Providence, RI: A. Crawford Greene and Brothers, State Printers, 1856), 333.

33. Ibid., 227.

34. Ibid., 128.

35. Ibid., 340.

36. See *Records of the Colony of Rhode Island and Providence Plantations, in New England, 1636 to 1663, Vol.1* (Providence, RI: A. Crawford Greene and Brothers, State Printers, 1856), 502.

37. See *Laws of New Hampshire including Public and Private Acts and Resolves and the Royal Commission and Instructions; With Historical and Descriptive Notes, and Appendix* (Manchester, NH: The John B. Clarke Company, 1904), 11.

38. *Provincial Papers. Documents and Records Relating to the Province of New Hampshire from the Earliest Period of Its Settlement, 1623-1686, Vol.1* (Concord: George E. Jenks, 1867), 377.

39. Charles Hudson, *History of the Town of Marlborough, Middlesex County, Massachusetts, from Its First Settlement in 1657 to 1861* (Boston: Press of T.R. Marvia and Son, 1862), 24.

40. Allen Thorndike Rice, "Theory of American Government" The North American Review, January, 1888, Vol. 145, July to December, 1887, 542-546.

41. See *City of Lynn, Massachusetts. Semi-Centennial of Incorporation. Events and Exercises of the 50th Anniversary Celebration Held May 13th, 14th and 15th, 1900* (Lynn, MA: Whitten & Case, Printers, 1900), 167-167.

42. "The Connecticut Intestacy Law" The Yale Review. A Quarterly Journal of History and Political Science, vol. iii. May, 1894, to February, 1895 (New Haven, CT.: Tuttle, Morehouse & Taylor, 1895), 261-263.

43. Alexis De Tocqueville and Henry Reeve, *Democracy in America* (London: Longmans, Green, and Co., 1875), 26-28.

44. Charles de Secondat Baron de Montesquieu, *Montesquieu's Considerations on the Cause of the Grandeur and Decadence of the Romans: A New Translation, together with an Introduction, Critical and Illustrative Notes, and Analytical Index* (New York: D. Appleton and Company, 1894), 70.

45. William Smith, *A History of Greece, from the Earliest Times to the Roman Conquest. With Supplementary Chapters on the History of Literature and Art* (New York: Harper & Brothers, Publishers, 1869), 53.

46. Ibid.

47. Richard Frothingham, Jr., *History of Charlestown, Massachusetts* (Boston: Charles C. Little and James Brown, 1845), 55-56.

48. William B. Weeden, *Economic and Social History of New England, 1620-1789, Vol.1* (Boston and New York: Houghton, Mifflin and Company, 1896), 54, 56, 61.

49. See *Records of Plymouth Colony* (Boston: William White, 1861), 9, 13.

50. Francis C. Gray, *Remarks on the Early Laws of Massachusetts Bay; With the Code Adopted in the Year 1641, And Called the Body of Liberties, Now Printed* (Boston: Charles C. Little and James Brown, 1843), 30.

51. See *The Eleventh Part of the Reports of Sir Edward Coke, Kt.*, 85-88.

52. See *Records of the Colony of Rhode Island and Providence Plantations, in New England, 1636 to 1663, vol.1* (Providence, RI: A Crawford Greene and Brothers, State Printers, 1856), 256).

53. See *The Charters and General Laws of the Colony and Province of Massachusetts Bay* (Boston: T. E. Wait and Company, 1814), 186-187.

54. See "Report of the Commissioner of the School fund, May 1822, to the honorable general assembly of the state of Connecticut, holden at New Haven on the first Wednesday of May 1822. Signed James Hillhouse, Commissioner of the School Fund. The North American Review, vol. xvi. April., 1823), 380-381. The school law of New Haven declared that "it is ordered that the deputies for the particular court, in each plantation within this jurisdiction, for the time being, or were there are no such deputies, the constable or other officers in public trust, shall from time to time have a vigilant eye over their brethren and neighbors within the limits of the said plantation, that all parents and masters do duly endeavor, either by their own ability and labor, or by improving such schoolmaster or other helps and means as the plantation do afford, or the family may conveniently provide, that all their children and apprentices, as they grow capable, may, through God's blessing, obtain at least so much as to be able to read the scriptures and other good and profitable printed books in the English language being their native language, &c."

55. See *Fourth Report of the Record Commissioners of the City of Boston. Dorchester Town Records. Second Edition, vol.4* (Boston: Rockwell and Churchill, 1883), 55.

56. Ibid., 54-55.

Notes to Chapter 6

1. William R. Staples, *Annals of the Town of Providence, from Its First Settlement, to the Organization of the City Government, in June, 1832* (Providence: Knowles and Vose, 1843), 12-13.

2. John Winthrop and James Savage, ed., *The History of New England from 1630 to 1649, vol.1* (Boston: Phelps and Farnham, 1825), 158.

3. Ibid., 170-171, 175.

4. Samuel Greene Arnold, *History of the State of Rhode Island and Providence Plantations, Vol.1* (New York: S. Appleton & Company, 1859), 20-22.

5. Charles Francis Adams, *Antinomianism in the Colony of Massachusetts Bay, 1636-1638, including the Short Story and other Documents* (Boston: The Prince Society, 1894), 14.

6. Oscar S. Straus, *Roger Williams. The Pioneer of Religious* (New York: The Century Co., 1894), xi-xii.

7. Richard P. Hallowell, *The Quaker Invasion of Massachusetts* (Boston: Houghton, Mifflin and Company, 1883), 33.

8. See *Records of the Colony of Rhode Island and Providence Plantations, in New England, 1636 to 1663, vol.1* (Providence, R.I.: A. Crawford Greene and Brothers, 1856), 351-352.

9. Winthrop and Savage, ed., 50.

10. Ibid., 62.

11. John Callender "An Historical Discourse, on the Civil and Religious Affairs of the Colony of Rhode-Island" Collections of the Rhode Island Historical Society, Vol.1 (Providence: Knowles, Vose & Company, 1838), 210-211.

12. John Hayward, *The Book of Religious: Comprised the Views, Creeds, Sentiments, or Opinions, of all the Principal Religious Sects in the World, Particularly of All Christian Denomination in Europe and America; to Which are added Church and Missionary Statistics, Together with Biographical Sketches* (Boston: John Hayward, 1843), 387.

13. Edward Peterson, *History of Rhode Island* (New York: John S. Taylor, 1853), 53.

14. William Ives Budington, *The History of the First Church, Charlestown, in Nine Lecture, With Notes* (Boston: Charles Tappan, 1845), 56-58.

15. See *The Charters and General Laws of the Colony and Providence of Massachusetts Bay* (Boston: T.B. Wait and Co., 1814), 88.

16. William R. Staples, *Annals of the Town of Providence from its First Settlement, to the Organization of the City Government, in June, 1832* (Providence, RI: Knowles and Vose, 1843), 23.

17. See *Records of the Colony of Rhode Island and Providence Plantations, in New England, 1636 to 1663, vol.1* (Providence, R.I.: A. Crawford Greene and Brothers, States Printers, 1856), 16.

18. Staples, 41. See also the *Records of the Colony of Rhode Island and Providence Plantations, in New England, 1636 to 1663, vol.1* (Providence, R.I.: A. Crawford Greene and Brothers, 1856), 28.

19. William B. Weeden, *Early Rhode Island. A Social History of the People* (New York: The Grafton Press Publishers, 1910), 174.

20. See *The Proceedings of the First General Assembly of "the Incorporation of Providence Plantation." And the Code of Laws Adopted by that Assembly in 1647. With Notes Historical and Explanatory* (Providence: Charles Burnett, Jr., 1847), 50.

21. Hallowell, 34-46.

22. See *The Proceedings of the First General Assembly of "The Incorporation of Providence." And the Code of Laws adopted by that Assembly in 1647. With Notes Historical and Explanatory* (Providence: Charles Burnett, Jr., 1847), x. The response of the Rhode Island officials to the United Colony requests regarding the Quakers was as follows: "whereas freedom of conscience to be protected from enforcement was the principal cause of our charter, both with respect to our humble suit for it, as also the true intent of the honored and renowned parliament of England, in granting the same to us."

23. See *Records of the Colony of Rhode Island and Providence Plantations, in New England, 1636 to 1663, Vol.1* (Providence, R.I.: A. Crawford Greene and Brothers, State Printers, 1856), 378-380.

24. Thomas Williams Bicknell, *The History of the State of Rhode Island and Providence Plantations, vol.1* (New York: The American Historical Society Inc., 1920), 138.

25. Winthrop and Savage, ed., 272-273.

26. Ibid., 38.

27. Ibid., 40.

28. Ibid.

29. *The Famous Old Charter of Rhode Island, Granted By King Charles II., in 1663. Also, the Rhode-Island Bill of Rights, and the Declaration of Religious Freedom* (Providence: I. H. Cody, 1842), 1-2.

30. See *The Constitution of the State of Rhode Island and Providence Plantations Adopted by the Convention, Assembled at Newport, September, 1842* (Providence: Knowles and Vose, 1842), 3.

31. Ibid.

32. See *The Constitution of Massachusetts. Constitution of the United States. Rules and Orders of the House of Representatives, 1853* (Boston: White & Potter, Printers of the State, 1853), 5.

33. See *The Constitution of New Hampshire, as Altered and Amended by a Convention of Delegates, Held at Concord, in Said State, approved by the People, and Established by the Convention on the first Wednesday of September 1792* (Concord: George Hough, 1792), 8.

34. See *The Constitution of the State of Connecticut, together with the Amendments Printed by the Order of the Legislature* (Hartford: Printed by C. Babcock, 1829).

35. See *The Constitution of the United States of America, with the Several Amendments. Printed from the Official Records, in Conformity with the Original Orthography, for the use of the Senior Class in Yale New Haven, 1881.*

36. See *Laws of New Hampshire. Including Public and Private Acts and Resolves and the Royal Commissions and Instructions, and with Historical and Descriptive Notes, and Appendix, Vol.1. Provincial Period* (Manchester, NH: The John B. Clarke Company, 1904), xxvi.

37. Jeremy Belknap, *The History of New Hampshire, Vol.1* (Dover: SC Stevens and Ela & Wadleigh, 1831), 19.

38. *Laws of New Hampshire. Including Public and Private Acts and Resolves and the Royal Commissions and Instructions, with Historical and Descriptive Notes, an Appendix, Vol.1. Provincial Period* (Manchester, N.H.: The John B. Clarke Company, 1904), xxxiii.

Notes to Chapter 7

1. William Chauncey Fowler, *Local Law in Massachusetts and Connecticut. Historically Considered; and the Historical Status of the Negro, in Connecticut; Also; A Speech delivered in the Senate of Connecticut June 22, 1864* (Albany: Joel Munsell, 1872), 13.

2. Charles Henry Bell, *History of the Town of Exeter, New Hampshire* (Exeter: The Quarter- Millennial Year, 1888), 3.

3. Richard Frothingham, Jr., *The History of Charlestown, Massachusetts* (Boston: Charles C. Little & James Brown, 1845), 49-50.

4. William Bradford, History of Plymouth Plantation (Boston: Privately Printed, 1856), 89. Bradford notes that the Pilgrims had to use their own liberty to form the government and select the location where to plant their plantation. He went on that they did not have any power to command them as they

traveled to America under the paten of the Virginia company, but the New England was out of that company's jurisdiction. The New England region was under the jurisdiction of the Plymouth company. As a result, they were obligated to self-govern by using their own conscience or liberty.

5. Ibid.

6. William Douglass, *A Summary, Historical and Political, of the First Planting, Progressive Improvements, and Present State of the British Settlements in North-America, Vol.1* (Boston, New England, printed: London, re-printed for R. Baldwin in 1755), 372.

7. Bradford, 89-90.

8. See *Records of the Company of the Massachusetts Bay in New England from 1628 to 1641* (Cambridge: Bolles and Houghton, 1850), 30.

9. Dorchester Antiquarian and Historical Society, *History of the Town of Dorchester, Massachusetts* (Boston: Ebenezer Clapp, Jr., 1859), 22.

10. Winthrop, 28.

11. Francis S. Drake, *The Tour of Roxbury. Its Memorable Persons and Places. Its History and Antiquities, with Numerous Illustrations of Its Old Landmarks and Notes, Personages* (Boston: Principal Printing Office, 1908), 10.

12. Ibid., 12 William Pynchon came to New England in the same ship with governor John Winthrop. In the colony, he was one of the assistants.

13. Alexander Young, *Chronicles of the First Planters of the Colony of Massachusetts Bay, from 1623 to 1636. Now First Collected from Original Records and Contemporaneous Manuscripts, and Illustrated with Notes* (Boston: Charles C. Little and James Brown, 1846), 380-381.

14. Joseph B. Felt, *The Annals of Salem from Its First Settlement* (Salem: W. & S. B. Ives, 1827), 6.

15. Ibid., 5.

16. Young, 259.

17. Felt, 33.

18. Frothingham, Jr, 11.

19. Alonzon Lewis, *The History of Lynn, Including Nahant* (Boston: Samuel N. Dickinson, 1844), 60-61.

20. Ibid., 11.

21. Edward R. Lamber, *History of the Colony of New Haven, before and after the Union with Connecticut. Containing a Particular Description of the Towns which Composed that Government, VIZ., New Haven, Milford, Guilford, Branford, Stamford, & Southold, L.I., With a Notice of the Towns which has been set off from: The Original Six."* (New Haven: Hitchcock & Stafford, 1838), 25.

22. Daniel Denton, *Brief Description of New York: Formerly called New-Netherlands. With the Places Thereunto Adjoyning* (London: John Hancock and William Bradley, 1670). 57.

23. Edwin F. Hatfield, *History of Elizabeth, New Jersey; Including the Early History of Union County* (New York: Carlton & Lanahan, 1868), 60.

24. Ibid.

25. See *Records of the Town of Jamaica, Long Island, New York,1656-1751, Vol.1* (Brooklyn: The Long Island Historical Society, 1914), 1-2.

26. E. B. Huntington, *History of Stamford, Connecticut, From Its Settlement in 1641, to the Present Time, Including Darien, which was one of its Parishes until 1820* (Stamford: Gillespie & Co., 1868), 14.

27. See *The Public Records of the Colony of Connecticut 1636-1665. Prior to the Union with New Haven Colony, May 1665* (Hartford: Brown & Parsons, 1850), 7.

28. George Rogers Howell, *The Early History of Southampton, L.I., New York, with Genealogies. Revised, Corrected and Enlarged* (Albany: Weed, Parsons and Company, 1887), 20, 50.

29. Daniel M. Mead, *A History of the Town of Greenwich, Fairfield County, Conn., with Many Important Statistics* (New York: Baker & Godwin, Printers, 1857), 26.

30. Huntington, 14.

31. Benjamin Trumbull, *Complete History of Connecticut, Civil and Ecclesiastical, from the Emigration of Its First Planters, from England, in the Year 1630, to the Year 1764; and to the close of the Indian Wars, Vol.1* (New-Haven: Moltby, Goldsmith and Co., and Samuel Wadsworth, 1818), 121.

32. Benjamin F. Thompson, *The History of Long Island; from its Discovery and Settlement, to the Present Time. With many Important and Interesting Matters, Including Notices of Numerous Individual and Families. Also a Particular Account of the Different Churches and Ministers, vol.2* (New York: Gould, Banks & Co., 1843), 3, 19-20.

33. Silas Wood, *A Sketch of the First Settlement of the Several Towns of Long Island: with their Political Condition to the end of the American Revolution* (Brooklyn, N.Y.: Alden Spooner, 1828), 19-21.

34. Hugh Hastings, *Ecclesiastical Records State of New York, Vol.2.* (Albany: J. B. Lyon Company, State Printers, 1902), 1464.

35. Thompson, 97.

36. Ibid.

37. James Riker, Jr., *The Annals of Newton, in Queens County, New York: Containing its History from its First Settlement, together with many Interesting*

Facts concerning the Adjacent Towns; Also, a Particular Account of Numerous Long Island Families now Spread over this and Various other States of the Union (New York: D. Fanshaw, 1852), 26-28.

38. J. Gardner Bartlett, *Robert Coe, Puritan. His Ancestors and Descendants, 1340-1910. With Notices of other Coe Families* (Boston, Mass: Published for Private Circulation by the Author, 1911), 67-72.

39. Joseph Atkinson, *The History of Newark, New Jersey, being a Narrative of Its Rise and Progress, from the Settlement in May, 1666, by Emigrants from Connecticut, to the Present Time, including a Sketch of the Press of Newark, from 1791 to 1878* (Newark, NJ: William B. Guild, 1878), 10-17.

40. Ibid., 14-18, 29.

41. Ibid.,18.

42. Ibid., 7.

43. See *Records of the First Church at Dorchester in New England, 1636-1734* (Boston, MA: George H. Ellis, 1891), 13.

44. William H. Sumner, *Memoir of Increase, Governor of Massachusetts. By His Son. Together with a Genealogy of the Sumner Family. Prepared for the New England Historical and Genealogical Register* (Boston: G. Drake, Publisher, 1854), 43.

45. William Sumner Appleton, *Records of the Descendants of William Sumner, of Dorchester, Massa., 1636* (Boston: David Clapp & Son, Printers, 1879), 3-7.

46. Georgia Howe, *History of the Presbyterian Church in South Carolina, Vol.1* (Columbia: Duffie & Chapman, 1870), 268.

47. Charles C. Jones, Jr., *The Dead Towns of Georgia* (Savannah: Morning News Stearn Printing House, 1878), 149.

48. Ibid., 173-178.

49. See Dorchester Antiquarian and Historical Society, *History of the Town of Dorchester, Massachusetts* (Boston: Ebenezer Clapp, Jr., 1859), 31.

50. Ibid.

51. Ibid., 33.

52. See *The Records of the Town of Cambridge (Formerly Newtown) Massachusetts, 1630-1703* (Cambridge: Printed by Order of the City Council under the Direction of the City Clerk, 1901), 11-13.

53. See *The Charters and General Laws of the Colony and Province of Massachusetts* Bay (Boston: T.B. Wait and Company, 1814), 195.

54. See *The Public Records of the Colony of Connecticut, 1636-1663. Prior to the Union with New Haven Colony, May, 1665* (Hartford: Brown & Parson, 1850), 1-2.

55. Ibid., 36.
56. Ibid.
57. See *Records of the Colony of Rhode Island and Providence Plantation, in New England, 1636 to 1663, Vol.1.* (Providence, RI: A. Crawford Greene and Brothers, State Printers, 1856), 107.
58. Ibid., 43.
59. Ibid., 212.
60. See *The Compact with the Charter and Laws of the Colony of New Plymouth: Together with the Charter of the Council at Plymouth, and an Appendix, Containing the Articles of Confederation of the United Colonies of New England, and other Valuable Documents* (Boston: Dutton and Wentworth, Printers to the State, 1836), 47,57.
61. Ibid., 64.
62. Francis C. Gray, *Remarks on the Early Laws of Massachusetts Bay; with the code Adopted in the Year 1641, and Called the Body of Liberties. Now First Printed* (Boston: Charles C. Little and Jones Brown, 1843), 40.
63. See *Laws of New Hampshire, including Public and Private Acts and Resolves and the Royal Commissioners and Instructions, with Historical and Descriptive Notes, and an Appendix, Vol.1* (Manchester, N.H.: The John B. Clarke Company, 1904), xxxiii.
64. Ibid., 32.

Notes to Chapter 8

1. See *The Charters and General Laws of the Colony and Province of Massachusetts Bay* (Boston: T. E. Wait and Co., 1814), 97.
2. John Winthrop and James Savage, ed., *The History of New England from 1630 to 1649, Vol.1* (Boston: Phelps and Farnham, 1825), 70.
3. Ibid., 76.
4. Joseph B. Felt, *The Annals of Salem, from Its First Settlement* (Salem: W. & S. B. Ives, 1827), 56.
5. Francis Bayles, *Historical Memoir of the Colony of New Plymouth, from the Flight of the Pilgrims into Holland in the Year 1608, to the Union of that Colony with Massachusetts in 1692, vol.1* (Boston: Wiggin & Lunt, 1866), 127.
6. Samuel G. Drake, *The History and Antiquities of Boston, the Capital of Massachusetts and Metropolis of New England, from Its Settlement in 1630, to the Year 1770. Also Introductory History of the Discovery and Settlement of New England* (Boston: Luther Stevens, 1856), 139.

7. See Thomas Prince, *A Chronological History of Hew-England in the Form of Annals* (Boston: Cumming, Hillard, and Company, 1826), 394. see also Lucius Paige, *History of Cambridge, Massachusetts, 1630 -1877. With A Genealogical Register* (Boston: H. O. Houghton and Company, 1877), 599. For the information regarding Abraham Palmer, See Richard Frothingham, Jr. *The History of Charlestown, Massachusetts* (Boston: Charles C. Little and James Brown, 1845), 22.

8. Prince, 394.

9. Drake, 139.

10. See "A Letter of Israel Stoughton to John Stoughton written in 1635" in *Proceedings of the Massachusetts Historical Society, October, 1924-June 1925, Vol.3* (Norwood, MA.: The Plimpton Press, 1925), 450-452.

11. Ibid.

12. Winthrop and Savage, ed., 132.

13. Ibid., 128.

14. Ibid., 128-129.

15. Richard Frothingham, Jr., *The History of Charlestown, Massachusetts* (Boston: Charles C. Little and James Brown, 1845), 22.

16. For the deputies elected in Boston in 1634, see *Collections of the Massachusetts Historical Society, Vol.x. of the Second Series* (Boston, 1823), 23. In this document, the names of the Boston freemen who served as representatives of the people are listed.

17. See Andrew T. Servin, *The Phelps Family of America, and their English Ancestors, with Copies of Wills, Deeds, Letters, and other Interesting Papers, Coats of Arms and Valuable Records, Vol.1* (Pittsfield, MA: Eagle Publishing Company, 1899), 73.

18. Drake, 439.

19. See *The Charters and General Laws of the Colony and Province of Massachusetts Bay* (Boston: T. E. Wait and Co., 1814), 97-98.

20. See *Secord Report of the Record Commissioners, of the City of Boston. 1877* (Boston: Rockwell and Churchill, 1877, City Printers, 1877), 10. In 1637, Harry Vane, William Coddington and Atherton Haulgh were chosen as deputies for the General Court (18).

21. See "The names of Deputies from towns in New Hampshire to the General Court of Massachusetts, in Boston from 1641 to 1679. Provincial Papers" in *Documents and Records Relating to the Province of New Hampshire, from the Earliest Period of Its Settlement: 1623-1686, Vol.1* (Concord: George E. Jenks, State Printer, 1867), 369-429.

22. William D. Williamson, *The History of State of Maine, from Its First Discovery, A.D. 1602, to the Separation, A.D. 1820, Inclusive with an Appendix and General Index, Vol.1* (Ralomell: Glazer, Masters & Smith, 1839), 346-352.

23. Winthrop and Savage, ed., 160.

24. Tomas Hutchinson, *The History of the Colony of Massachusetts Bay, from the First Settlement thereof in 1628, until Its Incorporation with the Colony of Plimouth, Province of Main, &C. by the Charter of King William and Queen Mary, in 1691* (London: M. Richardson, 1760), 449.

25. Ibid.

26. William Stith, *History of the First Discovery and Settlement of Virginia: Being an Essay towards a General History of this Colony* (Williamsburg: William Parvis, 1747), 160.

27. Charles Campbell, *History of the Colony and Ancient Dominion of Virginia* (Philadelphia: J. B. Lippincott and Co., 1860), 138-139.

28. Ibid.

29. Winthrop and Savage, ed., 141.

30. Ibid., 160.

31. Ibid., 322.

32. Ibid., 245.

33. *The Compact, Charter and Laws of the Colony of New Plymouth* (Boston: Dutton and Wentworth, Printers to the State, 1836), 63.

34. Ibid.

35. Francis Baylies, *Historical Memoir of the Colony of New Plymouth, from the Flight of the Pilgrims into Holland in the Year 1608, to the Union of that Colony with Massachusetts in 1692, Vol.1* (Boston: Wiggin & Lunt, 1866), 304.

36. See *The Compact with the Charter and Laws of the Colony of New Plymouth: Together with the Charter of the Council at Plymouth, and an Appendix, Containing the Articles of Confederation of the United Colonies in New England, and Other Valuable Documents* (Boston: Dutton and Wentworth, Printers to the State, 1836), 91.

37. For the information regarding John Alden, see *Register of the Society of Colonial Wars in the District of Columbia, 1897* (Washington City: The Law Reporter Company, 1897), 12.

38. Justin Winsor, *A History of the Town of Duxbury, Massachusetts, with Genealogical Registers* (Boston: Crosby & Nichols, 1849), 48, 55, 58.

39. Augustus E. Alden, *Pilgrim Alden. The Story of the Life of the First Alden in America. With the Interwoven Story of the Life & Doing of the Pilgrim Colony, an Some Account of Later Aldens* (Boston: James H. Earle & Company, 1902), 71, 85-86.

40. See *Register of the National Society of Colonial Dames of America in the State of New York, 1893-1926* (New York: Tobias A. Wright, Inc. Printers and Publishers, 1926), 459.

41. Henry R. Howland "A Biographical Sketch of John Howland", in *John Howland A Mayflower Pilgrim edited by William Howland* (Detroit, Michigan: Saturday Night Press, 1926), 3-25.

42. Baylies, 2.

43. See *The Public Records of the Colony of Connecticut [1636-1665] Prior to the Union with New Haven Colony, May, 1665* (Hartford: Brown & Parsons, 1850), 21.

44. Ibid., 23.

45. Ibid.

46. Ibid.

47. Ibid., 24.

48. Ibid.

49. See *Register of the Connecticut Society of the Colonial Dames of America* (Published by the Connecticut Society, 1907), 296.

50. Ibid., 292-296.

51. Ibid., 290.

52. Ibid. 241-256.

53. Ibid., 239, 276.

54. See *Register of the Society of Colonial Wars in the District of Columbia, 1904* (Washington City, 1904), 43.

55. Ibid., 51.

56. Forrest Morgan, *Connecticut as a Colony and as State, or One the Original Thirteen, Vol.1* (Hartford: The Publishing Society of Connecticut, 1904), 146.

57. Roger Welles "Constitutional History of Connecticut", The Connecticut Magazine, Vol. 5. no.2, Feb., 1899.

58. See *Records of the Colony and Plantation of New Haven from 1638 to 1649* (Hartford: Case, Tiffany and Company, 1857), 114.

59. Ibid., 73.

60. Edward R. Lamberton, *History of the Colony of New Haven before and after the Union with Connecticut* (New Haven: Hitchicock & Stafford, 1838), 22.

61. Ibid., 24.

62. Ibid.

63. See *Records of the Colony of Rhode Island and Providence Plantations, in New England, 1636 to 1663, vol.1* (Providence, R.I.: A. Crawford Greene and Brother, State Printers, 1856, 209. See also William R. Staples, *Annals of the*

Town of Providence, from Its First Settlement, to the Organization of the City Government, in June, 1832 (Providence: Knowles and Vose, 1843), 71.

64. Ibid., 210. The names of the deputies who served in the general assembly was as follows: Providence: Thomas Olney, Thomas Harris, William Withenden, Hugh Benett, Robert Williams, Gregory Dexter. For Warwick: John Smith, Ezek. Holyman, John Warner, Robert Potter, Christopher Helmes, and Peter Green. For Newport: Nicholas Easton, Moderator, Wm Dyere, Clerk, James Weeden, James Barker, and Joseph Clarke. From Portsmouth: Capt. Richard Morris, John Tripp, George Layton, William Almy, John Briggs, and Sam'l Wilbor, Jr.

65. Ibid., 228. The Records of Rhode Island writes that "an act was then established that the representatives committee should have the full power of the General Assembly."

66. Ibid., 229. This order was passed in 1650.

67. Ibid., 228.

68. Ibid., 228-229.

69. Ibid.

70. John M. Shirley "The Early Jurisprudence of New Hampshire" Proceedings of the New Hampshire Historical Society, 1872-3; including Semicentennial Exercises, May 22. 1873, Vol.1. The Annual Address, June 13, 1883.

71. Charles W. Brewster, *Rambles About Portsmouth. Sketches of Persons, Localities, and Incidents of two centuries: Principality from tradition and Unpublished Documents* ([Portsmouth]: C. W. Brewster & Son, 1859), 28.

72. For the laws respecting the representative system in New Hampshire, see the *Provincial Papers. Documents and Records Relating to the Province of New Hampshire, from the Earliest period of its settlement: 1623-1686, Vol.1.* (Concord: George E. Jenks, State Printer, 1861), 408.

73. Jeremy Belknap and John Farmer, *The History of New Hampshire, vol.1* (Dover: S C Stevens and Ela & Wadleigh, 1831), 91.

74. Charles H. Bell, *History of the Town of Exeter, New Hampshire* (Exeter: The Quarter-Millennial Year, 1888), 151.

Bibliography

Primary Sources

Data on the emergence of Democracy, Theocracy, Aristocracy, and Rules of Law in the New England colonies were collected from various public documents and records from the colonies of Massachusetts Bay, Plymouth, Connecticut, Rhode Island, and New Hampshire. In addition, town records from municipalities in Massachusetts Bay were also consulted for the same purpose. Furthermore, charters and laws of the colonies under investigation were also explored for the same purpose.

Public Records, Papers and Charters

Charter of the Connecticut 1662, Hartford: The Case, Lockwood & Brainard Company, 1900.
Provincial Papers. Documents and Records Relating to the Province of New-Hampshire, from the Earliest Period of Its Settlement, 1623-1686, Concord: George E. Jenks, State Printer, 1867.
Papers of the New Haven Colony, Vol.7 (New Haven: Printed for the Society, 1908).
Records of the Colony of Rhode Island and Providence Plantations, in New England, vol.1, 1636 to 1663, Providence, RI: A. Crawford Greene and Brothers, State Printers, 1856.
The Charter Granted by His Majesty King Charles the Second, to the Colony of Rhode Island, and Providence Plantations in America, Boston in New England, Printed by John Allen, for Nicholas Boone, 1719.
The Public Records of the Colony of Connecticut [1636-1665] prior to the Union with New Haven Colony, May, 1655, Hartford: Brown & Parsons, 1850.
Records of the Company of the Massachusetts, in New England, from 1628 to 1641, Cambridge: Bolles and Houghton, 1850, Vol. 1.
Records of the Governor and Company of the Massachusetts Bay, in New England, 1644-1657, Vol.3, Boston: William White, 1854.

Records of the Governor and Company of the Massachusetts Bay in New England, Vol. 4-Part II. 1661-1674, Boston: William White, Printer to the Commonwealth, 1854.

Records of the Colony and Plantation of New Haven, from 1638 to 1649, Hartford: Case, Tiffany and Company, 1857.

Records of the Court of Assistants of the Colony of the Massachusetts Bay, 1630-1692, Vol.1, Boston: Publish by the County of Suffolk, 1904.

Records of Plymouth Colony in New England, Laws, 1623-1632, Boston: William White, 1861.

Town Records

Fourth Report of the Record Commissioners of the City of Boston. 1880. Dorchester Town Records. Second Edition. 1888, Boston: Rockwell and Churchill, 1883, Vol.4.

The Early Records, of the Town of Dedham, Massachusetts, 1636-1650, Dedham, Transcript. 1892.

Records of the Town of Jamaica, Long Island, New York, Vol.1, Brooklyn: The Long Historical Society, 1914.

Second Report of the Record Commissioners of the City of Boston. 1877, Boston: Rockwell and Churchill, City Printers, 1877.

The Records of the Town Cambridge (Formerly Newtown) Massachusetts 1630-1703, Printed by Order of the City Council under the Direction of the City Clerk, Cambridge, [MA], 1901.

Watertown Records prepared for Publication by the Historical Society, Watertown, MA, 1894.

Primary Source on the Laws of the Colonies

The Charters and General Laws of the Colony and Province of Massachusetts Bay, Boston: T. E. Wait and Co., 1814.

The Compact with the Charter and Laws of the Colony of New Plymouth: Together with the Charter of the Council at Plymouth, and an Appendix, Containing the Articles of the Confederation of the United Colonies of New England, and other Valuable Documents, Boston: Dutton and Wentworth, Printers to the State, 1836.

Laws and Acts of Her Majesties Colony of Rhode Island, and Providence Plantation Made from the First Settlement in 1636 to 1705. With Historical Introduction by Sidney S. Rider, Providence, RI: Sidney S. Rider and Burnett Ridder, 1896.

Laws of New Hampshire Including Public and Private Acts and Resolves and the Royal Commissions and Instruments, with Historical and descriptive Notes, and an Appendix, Vol.1, Manchester, NH: The John B. Clarke Company, 1904.
The Code of 1650, Being a Compilation of the Earliest Laws and Orders of the General Court of Connecticut, Hartford, CT: Andrus & Judd, 1833.
The Famous Old Charter of Rhode Island, Granted by King Charles II., in 1663. Also, the Rhode Island Bill of Rights, and the Declaration of Religious Freedom, Providence: I. H. Cady, 1842.
The Statutes at Large; Being A Collection of all the Laws of Virginia, from the First Session of Legislature, in the Year 1619, Vol.1, New York: R. &. W. G. Barton, 1823.

Constitutions

Constitution of Massachusetts. Constitution of the United States. Rule and Orders of the House of Representatives 1853, Boston: White & Potter, Printers of the State, 1853.
The Constitution of the United States pf America. Literal Print, Washington: Government Printing Office, 1933.
The Constitution of the State of Connecticut, together with the Amendments, Hartford: C. Babcock, 1829.
The Constitution of the United States of America: With the Latest Amendments: Also the Declaration of Independence, Articles of Confederation, with the Federal Constitution, New York: Evert Duyakinck, 1820.
The Constitution of the State of Vermont: Established by Convention July 9, 1793; And Amended by Convention, in 1828, 1836, 1850, and 1870, and by the People in 1883, Brottleboro: C. H. Davenport & Co., 18891.
The Constitution of New Hampshire, as Altered and Amended by a Convention of Delegates, Held at Concord, in Said State, Approved by the People, and Established by the Convention, on the First Wednesday of September 1792, Concord: George House, 1792.
The Constitution of the State of Rhode Island and Providence Plantations. As Adopted by the Convention, Assembled at Newport, September, 1842, Providence: Knowles and Vose, 1842.
Constitution of the State of Maine, Formed in Convention at Portland, October Twenty-Ninth, and Adopted by the People in Town Meetings, on the Sixth Day of December A.D. 1819, and of the Independence of the United States the Forty-Fourth. Together with Amendments Subsequently made thereto, and Arranged, as Amended, in Pursuance of a Resolve of the Legislature approved

February twenty-Fourth A.D. 1875, with Amendments Adopted since the last named date, Augusta: Burleigh & Flynt, Printers to the State, 1893.

Printed Books on the Laws of the Colonies

Bacon, Leonard. *A Discourse on the Early Constitutional History of Connecticut, delivered before the Connecticut Historical Society, Hartford, May 17, 1843*, Hartford: Case, Tiffany & Burnham, Printers, 1843.

Clarke, J. B. *The Government and Laws of New Hampshire before the Establishment of the Province, 1623-1679*, Manchester, NH: The John B. Clarke Company, 1904.

Fowler, William Chauncey. *Local Law on Massachusetts and Connecticut. Historically Considered; and The Historical Statues of the Negro, in Connecticut; Also; A Speech Delivered in the Senate of Connecticut June 22, 1864*, Albany: Joel Munsell, 1872.

Gray, Francis C. *Remarks on the Early Laws of Massachusetts Bay: With the Code Adopted in the Year 1641, and Called The Body of Liberties, Now First Printed*, Boston: Charles C. Little and James Brown, 1843.

Loomis, Dwight and Calhoun, Gilbert J. *The Judicial and Civil History of Connecticut*, Boston, MA: The Boston History Company, Publishers, 1895.

Story, Joseph. *Commentaries of the Constitution of the United States: With a Preliminary Review of the Constitutional History of the Colonies and Sates, Before the Adoption of the Constitution, Vol.1*, Boston: Little, Brown, and Company, 1873.

The Earliest New England Code of Laws, 1641, New York: A. Lovell & Company, 1896.

Washburn, Emory. *Sketches of the Judicial History of Massachusetts from 1630 to the Revolution in 1775*, Boston: Charles C. Little and James Brown, 1840.

Willard, Joseph. *Address to the Members of the Bar of Worcester County, Massachusetts, October 2, 1829*, Lancaster: Carter, Andrews, and Company, Printers, 1830.

Whitmore, William H. *The Colonial Laws of Massachusetts. Reprinted from the Edition of 1660, with the Supplements to 1672. Containing also, the Body of Liberties of 1641*, Boston: Rockwell and Churchill, City Printers, 1889.

Documentations on the Laws of England

Care, Henry. *English Liberties: Or, the Free-Born Subject's Inheritance, Containing I. Magna Carta, the Petition of Right, the Habeas Corpus Act; and Divers other most useful Statutes: With Large Comments upon each of them*, London: G. Larkin, 1680.

Crabb, George. *A History of English Law; Or An Attempt to Trace the Rise, Progress and Successive Changes, of the Common Law, from the Earliest Period to the Present Time*, Burlington: Chaucey Goodrich, 1831.

Coke, Edward. *The Eleventh Part of the reports of Sir Edward Coke, Kt. Chief Justice of England, of Pleas to be held before the King himself assign'd, and of the Privy Council of State: of divers Resolutions and Judgements given on Solemn Arguments, and with great Deliberation and Conference of the most Reverent Judges and Sages of the Law, of Cases in Law, which were never Resolved or Adjudged before: And the reasons and Causes of the said Resolutions and Judgements*, In the Savor: Printed by E. and Nutt, and R. Gosling, 1727.

Creasy, E.S. *The Text-Book of the Constitution: Magna Carta, the Petition of Right, and the Bill of Rights*, London: Richard Bentley, 1848.

Fortescue, John. *The Governance of England: Otherwise Called the Difference between an Absolute and a Limited Monarchy. A Revised text edited with introduction, notes, and appendices by Charles Plummer*, Oxford: The Clarendon Press, 1885.

Hales, Matthew. *The History of the Common Law of England and Analyses of the Civil Part of the Law*, London: Printed for henry Butterworth, Law-Book Seller, 1820.

Giles, J. A. *William of Malmesbury's Chronicle of the Kings of England from the Earliest Period to the Reign of King Stephen. With Notes and Illustration*, London: George bell and Sons, 1895.

Johnson, Samuel. *A History and Difference of Magna Carta*, Dublin: Printed for James Williams, 1769.

The Golden Passage in the Great Charter of England, called Magna Carta. Or the Charter of Britain Liberties, Granted by King John to His Subjects, in the 17th Year of His Reign, in Running-Mead, between Stains and Windsor, June 15, in the Year 1215, and 560 Years Ago. With Lord Coke's Remarks and Explanations, London: Printed for the use of the London Association in 1776.

Thomson, Richard. *An Historical Essay of the Magna Carta of King John: To Which are added, the Great Charter in Latin and English: The Charters of Liberties and Confirmations, Granted by Henry III. And Edward I*, London: Printed for John Major, and Robert Jennings, 1826.

Turner, Sharon. *The History of the Anglo-Saxons from the earliest Period to the Norman Conquest, Vol.3*, London: Longman, Brown, Green, and Longmans, 1852.

Blackstone, William. *Commentary on the Laws of England*, Dublin: Printed for the Booksellers, 1775.

Printed Books with accounts on New England Democracy, Theocracy, and Aristocracy

Andrews, Charles M. *The River Towns of Connecticut. A Study of Wethersfield, Hartford, and Windsor*, Baltimore: Johns Hopkins University Press, 1889.

Boregeaud, Charles and Birkbeck Hill. *The Rise of Modern Democracy in Old and New England*, New York: Charles Scribner's Sons, 1894.

Camp, George Sidney. *Democracy*, New York: Harper and Brothers, 1841.

Capen, Nahum. *The History of Democracy; Or, Political Progress, Historically Illustrated, from the Earliest to the Latest Periods, Vol.1*, Hartford: American Publishing Company, 1875.

Cobb, Sanford H. *The Rise of Religious Liberty in America*, New York: Macmillan Company, 1902.

Fiske, John. *The Beginnings of New England or the Puritan Theocracy in Its Relation to Civil and Religious Liberty*, Boston: Houghton, Mifflin and Co., 1889.

Frothingham, Jr. *Richard, History of Charlestown, Massachusetts*, Boston: Charles C. Little and James Brown, 1845.

Johnson, Alexander. *American Commonwealths. Connecticut: A Study of A Commonwealth Democracy*, Boston: Houghton, Mifflin and Company, 1896.

Hattersley, Alan F. *A Short History of Democracy*, Cambridge: The University Press, 1930.

Hays, Bridget T. *American Democracy. Its History and Problems*, New York: Henry Holt and Company, 1921.

Sanborn, Frank B. *New Hampshire: An Epitome of Popular Government*, Boston: Houghton, Mifflin and Company, 1904.

Stearns, Jonathan F. *First Church in Newark. Historical Discourses Relating to the First Presbyterian Church in Newark; Originally Delivered to the Congregation of the Church during the Month of January, 1851*, Newark: Printed at The Duly Advertiser Office, 1853.

Uhden, H. F. *The New England Theocracy. A History of the Congregationalists in New England to the Revivals of 1740*, Boston: Gould and Lincoln, 1858.

Walker, George Leon. *Thomas Hooker, Preacher, Founder, Democrat*, New York: Dodd, Mead, and Company Publishers, 1891.

Weeden, William B. *Early Rhode Island: A Social History of the People*, New York: The Grafton Press Publishers, 1910.

West, Willis M. *The History of American Democracy Political and Industrial*, Boston: Allyn and Bacon, 1922.

Further Readings

Adams, Nathaniel. *Annals of Portsmouth*, Portsmouth: Published by the Author, 1825.

Baylies, Francis. *An Historical Memoir of the Colony of New Plymouth, Vol.2*, Boston: Hilliard, Gray, Little and Wilkins, 1830.

Belknap, Jeremy. *The History of New Hampshire, Vol.1*, Dover: S. C. Stevens and Ela & Wadleigh, 1831.

Bicknell, Thomas W. *The History of the State of Rhode Island and Providence Plantations, Vol.1*, New York: The American Historical Society, Inc., 1920.

Brewster, Charles. *Rambles About Portsmouth. Sketches of Persons, Localities, and Incidents of tow Centuries: Principally from Tradition and Unpublished Documents*, Portsmouth, N.H.: C. W. Brewster & Son, 1859.

Brooks, Charles. *History of the Town of Medford, Middlesex County, Massachusetts: From Its First Settlement in 1630 to 1855*, Boston: Rand, Avery, 1886.

Caulkins, F. M. History of Norwich, *Connecticut, from Its Settlement in 1660, to January 1845*, Norwich: Thomas Robinson, 1845.

Corey, Deloraine P. *The History of Malden, Massachusetts, 1633-1785*, Malden: Published by the Author, 1899.

Currier, John J. *History of Newbury, Massachusetts, 1635-1902*, Newbury, MA, Damrell and Upham, 1902.

Deane, Samuel. *History of Scituate, Massachusetts, from its First Settlement to 1831*, Boston: James Loring, 1831.

Douglass, William. *A Summary, Historical and Political, of the First Planting, Progressive Improvements, and Present State of the British Settlements in North-America, Vol.1*, Boston, New England, Printed, London, Re-printed for R. Baldwin, 1755.

Emery, Geo. Alex. *Ancient City of Gorgeana and Modern Town of York (Maine) from Its Earliest Settlement to the Present Time*, Boston: G. Alex Amery, 1874.

Felt, Joseph B. *The Annals of Salem, from Its First Settlement*, Salem: W. & S. B. Ives, 1827.

Howard, George E. *An Introduction to the Local Constitutional History of the United States, Vol.1*, Baltimore: Johns Hopkins University Press, 1889.

Hubbard, William. *General History of New England from the Discovery to MDCCXXX*, Boston: Charles C. Little and James Brown, 1848.

Hutchinson, Thomas. *The History of the Colony of Massachusetts Bay, from the First Settlement thereof in 1628, until Its Incorporation with the Colony of Plimouth, Province of Maine, &c. By the Charter of King William and Queen Mary, in 1691*, London: M. Richardson, 1760.

MacDonald, William. *The Government of Maine. Its History and Administration*, New York: The MacMillan Company, 1902.

Prince, Thomas. *A Chronological History of New England, in the Form of Annals*, Boston, N.E. Kneeland & Green, Cummings, Hillard, and Company, 1826.

Roads, Jr., Samuel. *The History and Traditions of Marblehead*, Boston: Osgood and Company, 1880.

Stuart, Isaac W. and W.M.B., Hartley. *Hartford in the Olden Time. First Thirty Years*, Hartford: F. A. Brown, 1853.

Trumbull, Benjamin. *Complete History of Connecticut, Civil and Ecclesiastical from the Emigration of Its First Planters, from England, in the Year 1630 to the Year 1764; and to the Close of the Indian Wars, Vol.1*, New Haven: Moltby, Goldsmith and Co., and Samuel Wadsworth, 1818.

Williamson, William. *The History of the State of Maine; from Its First Discovery, A.D. 1602, to the Separation, A.D. 1820, Inclusive, Vol.1*, Hallowell: Glazier, Master & Company, 1832.

Willis, William. *The History of Portland, from Its First Settlement: with Notes of the Neighbouring Towns, and of the Changes of Government in Maine. In Two Parts*, Portland: Printed by Day, Fraser & Company, 1831.

Winthrop, John. *The History of New England from 1630 to 1649. From His Original Manuscripts, Vol.1*, Boston: Phelps and Farham, 1825.

Young, Alexander. *Chronicles of the First Planters of the Colony of Massachusetts Bay, from 1623 to 1636. Now First Collected from Original Records and Contemporaneous Manuscripts, and Illustrated with Notes*, Boston: Charles C. Little and James Brown, 1846.

Index

Abraham, 67–68
Abuse of power, 22–23
Act of 1632, 10
Agamenticus, 69
Allen, John, 71
American liberties, as inviolable, 85
Andrews, Charles M., 34
Andros, Edmund, as governor, 71–72
Antinomian controversy, 37
Aristocracy in Massachusetts Bay, 34–35
Artillery Garden, perfection of company of, 62
Australia
   prohibition of excessive bail in, 94

Bacon, Leonard, 48–49
Bail, prohibition of excessive, 93–94
Baker, John, 69
Bancroft, George, 5–6
Barnet, Barh, 71
Barnett, Bartholomen, 67
Barry, John, 14
Batchellor, Albert Stillman, 29–30, 60
Baxter, James Phinney, 61
Beccaria, Caesar, 92
The Beginnings of New England Or the Puritan Theocracy in Its Relations to the Civil and Religious Liberty (Fiske), 48
Belknap, Jeremy, 62
Bell, Charles H., 29, 60, 63, 64
Bellingham, Richard, 15, 17
   election of, 27
   as governor, 34
Bentham, Jeremy, 92–93

Berwick, tax assessment for, 68
The Bill of Rights and the State, 75–76
Black Point, 66
Blackstone, Sir William, 3, 77, 78–80, 84
Body of Liberties of Massachusetts Bay, 81–83, 86–87, 88–89, 91, 93, 94–95
Bonighton, Richard, 67–69, 70, 71
Borgeaud, Charles, 5, 34
Boston, 87
   challenge of authority of chief men in, 33–34
   freemen in, 15, 19, 25
Boyse (or Boyes), Matthew, 64
Bradford, William
   as author of *History of Plymouth Plantation*, 8–9
   as governor of Plymouth, 21
Bragdon, Arthur, 67
Branford, unification of, 58
Brinley, George, formation of town government in Connecticut, 44
Brockholls, Anthony, as governor, 71–72
Brooke, Lord, 61
Brown, Richard, election as selectman, 28
Bullen, Robert, 93
Burdett, George, 61–62
   disenfranchisement of, 61
   as governor, 62
Burnet, Bishop, 95

Caesar's Communtaties of the Gallic Wars (Harkness), 77–78
Calendar of State Papers, 62–63
Calhoun, Gilbert J., 44
   form of government in Connecticut, 44

Cambridge, as advocate of democratic
    principles, 36
Cammock, Thomas, 67
Camp, George Sidney, 50
Canada, prohibition of excessive bail in,
    94
Canute, King, liberties under, 85
Cape Elizabeth, 69
Cape Porpus, 69–70
    inhabitants of, 70
Care, Henry, 77
Casco, 68
    tax assessment for, 68
Caulkins, Frances Manwaring
    formation of town government in
        Connecticut, 44
Charles II, King, 71, 76
    charter of 1662 under, 44, 60
    formation of government in
        accordance with the charter of
        Charles II, 44
    granting of New Netherlands to James,
        the Duke of York, 72–74
    reign of, 20
    restoration of, 72
    surrender of Pemaquid to Massachsetts
        Bay, 71
Charlestown, 87
    free elections in, 20
Charter of 1643, 38, 39
*The Charter of British Liberties, Granted
    by King John to His Subjects in the
    17th Year of His Reign, in Running-
    Mead*, 79
*The Charters and the Laws of the Colony
    and Province of Massachusetts Bay*,
    xii, 86
Children, Vines, Richard selling of
    patents to, 71–72
Church and State in New England
    (Lauer), 9
Church of England, 6
Clarke, John, introduction of religious
    liberties, 75
Cleeves, George, 69–71

Coddington, William, 25
    support for democratic principles, 36
Coke, Sir Edward, 78, 80, 83, 94
*The Collections of the Maine Historical
    Society*, 71–72
Collier, Christopher, 75–76
Colonies, value of personal security in,
    81–85
Commentaries on the Laws of England
    (Blackstone), 78
*The Compact, Charter and Laws of the
    Colony of New Plymouth*, xii, 11
Conley, Patrick T., 75–76
Connecticut
    as architect of democracy in New
        England colonies, 36
    democratic form of government in, 6,
        44–48
    differences of Winthrop with, 25
    evidence of democratic norms and
        principles in, 48–50
    freemen in, xi, 25
    liberties of Puritans in, 85
    Quakers in, 9
    recording laws in, xiii
    vote by proxy in, 43
Connecticut Charter of 1662, 76–77
Connecticut Fundamental Orders (1639),
    50–51, 75, 82
Conscience, liberty of, 77
Consensual system in Rhode Island, 43
Constitutional liberty
    birth of, 7
Constitution of the United States, 80
    Amendment XIV, 85
Cotton, John, 16, 18, 24
    influence of, 18
    invocation of scripture, 33–34
    support for aristocratic form of
        government, 35
    on type of government, 32–33
Council of Plymouth, 67
Court of Assistants, 17
Cradock, Matthew, 23
Criminal code, 5

Criminals, German punishment of, 94
Cutt, John, 65
    Code of, 80

Davenport, John, 54–56
    support for aristocratic form of government, 54
Deane, Samuel, 13–14
Declaration of Rights, 75
De Laudibus Legum Angliae (Fortescue), 94
Democracy
    description of, 5
    principles of, 5–7
    pure, 6
Democracy (Camp), 50
Democratic elections, 27–29
Democratic form of government
    in Connecticut, 44–50
    under Endicott, John, 20–21
    in Massachusetts Bay, 22–23
    in Plymouth, 7–11
    in Rhode Island, 6, 36, 37–40
Dennis, Lawrence, 71
A Discourse on the Early Constitutional History of Connecticut (Bacon), 48–49
Dixon, Jerimy [Jeremy], 55
Dollin, John, 71
Donforth, Thomas, 74
Dongan, Thomas, 73
    as deputy-governor, 74
Dorchester, democratic government in, 36, 44
Dover, 62, 66, 67
    freemen of, 64
    power to self-govern, 64
    unification with Massachusetts Bay, 29, 64
    union with Massachusetts Bay, 65
Dover Neck, Puritans in, 61
Dow, Joseph, 63
Dudley, Thomas, 16–17, 22
    championing of free speech by, 16
    as Deputy-Governor, 24–26
    as executive officer, 34
    policies of, 15
    power struggle with Winthrop, John, 24
    resignation attempt by, 24
    supporters of, 25
    use of pacific resistance by, 22
Dy, John, 60

Eaton, Nicholas, 42
Eaton, Theophilus, 54–55
    support for aristocratic form of government, 54
Edward I, 78, 87
    charter of, 80
Edward III, granting of liberties to English, 84
Elbridge, Thomas, 67
Elections
    democratic, in Massachusetts Bay, 27–29
    democratic principles during, 74
Electors, power of, 26–27
Endicott, John, 26
    democratic form of government under, 20–21
    loss of election, 26
England
    as constitutional monarchy, 20
    government in, 11
English children, rights and immunities of, 78
English Liberties: Or, the Freeborn Subject's inheritance (Care), 77
Essex County, 66
Exeter, 66, 67
    democracy in, 64–65
    founding and settlement of, 64
    freemen in, 65

Fiske, John, 48
    link of Hooker d=sermons to the writing of the Constitution, 52
Folsom, George, 66
Fortescue, John, 10, 20, 96

Franchise system, 50
  existence of democratic principle and, 13
  in Rhode Island, 40–41
Free Mans Charge, 55–56
Freemen
  in Boston, 19, 26
  in Connecticut, 28
  desire or positive laws, 79–80
  of Dover, 66
  in Exeter, 65
  historical development of liberties of, in New England, 74
  importance of, in New England colonies, xi
  legal power to make laws, 10
  liberties of, 83
  in Maine, xi, 66
  in Marblehead, 19
  in Massachusetts Bay, xi, 14–15, 18–19
  in New Hampshire, xi, 62
  in New Plymouth, 43
  in Plymouth, xi, 5, 7, 10–11, 13
  political spirits of, 18
  of Portsmouth, 66
  in Rhode Island, xi, 17
  rights of franchised, 18
  in Saco, 28
  in Salem, 19
  in Watertown, 19, 27
  in Wells, 28
Frothingham, Richard, Jr., 28
  on freemen's liberties, 75
Fuggill, Thomas, 55
Fundamental Orders, 59
  amendment of the, in 1654, 47–48
  language of, 45–47

Garde, Roger, 69, 70
Gardiner, Sir Christopher, 61
General Court, 35
Georges, Sir Ferdinando, control of Maine by, 60
Georges, William, 67–69

Germans
  belief in freemen's liberties, 77–78
  punishment of criminals by, 92
Gibbons, Ambrose, 62
Gilbert, Mathew, 55
Goddard, William G., narrative on democracy, 37–38
Godfred, Richard, 93
Godfrey, Edward, 67, 69, 71
  as governor of Maine, 68
  western Maine under, 68–69
The Golden Passage in the Great Charter of England, called Magna Charta, 78
Gordon, Samuel, 76
Gorgeana, 68, 69, 70
  administration of Gorges in, 69
  tax assessment for, 68
Gorges, Sir Ferdinando, 29, 67, 68, 69, 75
  administration of, in Gorgeana, 67–68
  issuance of charter by Charles II, 71
  land claims of, 74
  oath prescribed by, 69
  opening of office at Saco, 69
Gorges, Thomas, 73
  government of, 67
Gorton, Samuel
  as advocate of liberties, 37
  political and religious spirit of, 37
Government
  mixed forms of, in Massachusetts Bay Colony, 14–20
  pacific resistance against arbitrarily policies, 23–24
The Government and Laws of New Hampshire before the Establishment of the Province, 1623-1679 (Clarke), 60
Governor and Company of the English Colony of Connecticut, 77
Gray, Francis C., xii, 3, 17, 79
Griffis, William Elliot, 5, 7–8
Gross, Isaac, as first ruler of Exeter, 63–64
Guilford, unification of, 59
Gyles, Thomas, 71

Hale, Sir Matthew, 79, 81
  as source of English rights, 80
Hampton, 64–65
  settlement of, 70
Harkness, Albert, 77
Hartford, 87
  town government in, 45
  town meetings in, 45
  unification of, 58
Hass, James D., 77
Hattersley, Alan F., 50
Haverhill, 65
Haynes, John, 15, 17
  as architect of the Connecticut
    Fundamental Orders, 54
  as governor, 17, 54
Henry I, King
  charter of, 78
  granting of liberties under, 86–87
Henry III, 87
Henry VI, torture and forcible confession
  under, 94
Higginson, Francis, election of, 21
Hilton, Edward, 65
*Historical Notes on the Constitution of
  Connecticut, 1639-1818* (Trumbull), 48
*The History of Ancient Windsor,
  Connecticut* (Stiles), 50
The History of Charlestown, Massachusetts
  (Frothingham), 28, 74
The History of New England (Winthrop),
  xii, 25, 87
*The History of New England from 1630 to
  1649* (Winthrop), 61
History of Plymouth Plantation (Bradford),
  8–9
History of Scituate, Massachusetts, 14
*History of the Town of Exetor, New
  Hampshire* (Bell), 29, 60
Holland, tolerance in, 9
Hooke, William, 68
Hooker, Thomas, 18, 48
  principles advocated by, for the
    formation of the government,
    52–54

sermons delivered by, 51–52
support for democratic principles, 36
Hopkins, Edward, as architect of the
  Connecticut Fundamental Orders, 53
Howard, A. E. Dick, 75–76
Hull, Parson, 73
Hussey, Christopher, 28, 63
  election as selectman, 28
Hutchinson, Anne, 17
  religious views of, 36–37
Hutchinson, Thomas, 17
  settlement of civil and ecclesiastical
    policy, 32

*An Introduction to the Principle of Morals
  and Legislation* (Bentham), 93
Ipswich, 65, 79

James, the Duke of York
  granting of New Netherland to, 72–74
James I, King, 77
Jardine, David, 94
Jocelyn, Henry, 69, 71
Jocelyn, John, 71
John, King, 80
  granting of liberties to the English, 87
  signing of Magna Charter under, 80,
    85, 89
Johnson, Edward, 69, 71
Johnston, Alexander, 45, 49–50, 53
  link of Hooker, sermons to the writing
    of the Constitution, 51
Josseline, Henry, 71
Josselyn, John, 66
Jourdaine, John, 71
Judicial proceeding liberties, 85–95
*The Judiciary and Civil History of
  Connecticut*, 44–45
Jurors, impaneling of, 35
Jury system, 7
  in Plymouth, 14
  power of, 5

Kelsey, Rayner Wickersham, 42
Kenebeck, 66

Kent, Rchard, election as selectman, 28
Kittery, 66
   tax assessment for, 68
Knight, Richard, election as selectman, 28
Kohlrausch, Frederick, 77

Lamber, Edward R., 58, 136
Land, division of, 74
Lauer, Paul E., 6, 9, 11
Laws
   establishment of laws, 76
   repeal of unnecessary, 74
Lewis, Thomas, 67–68
Liberties
   American, 72
   body of, for Massachusetts Bay, 82–83
   English, 82
   judicial proceeding, 89–97
   personal, 88–89
   Saxons, 80
Little Harbor, 62
Logan, Walter Seth, 52
Loomis, Dwight, 44
   form of government in Connecticut, 43
Lothrop, John, 14
Ludlow, Roger, as architect of the Connecticut Fundamental Orders, 53
Lyconia, Rigby purchase of, 69–70

Mackworth, Arthur, 69
Magna Carta, 75, 78, 79–80, 83–84, 87
   excessive amercement in, 94
   invocation of, 16
Maine
   death of proprietor of, 60
   early government in, 67–69
   freemen in, xi, 62
   Gorges, Sir Ferdinando, control of, 60
   under Massachusetts government, 64–65
   new settlements in, 61
   under the Royal Government, 65–66
   under Vines, Richard, 68
   vote by proxy in, 43
   western, under Godfrey, Edward, 64–65
Marblehead
   drinking of liquor in, 30
   freemen in, 19
   violations of colonial laws in, 30
Mary I, Queen
   torture and forcible confession under, 94
Mason, John
   management of Strawberry Bank, 62
Mason, Sir John
   control of New Hampshire by, 60
Massachusetts Bay
   aristocratic form of government in, 20
   Article xxiii of the Constitution in, 10
   banishment of Puritans from, 37
   banishment of Underhill from, 61–62
   Body of Liberties of, 81–83, 87, 88–89, 91, 93, 94–95
   capitalistic and restricted liberties in, 6–7
   civil political dialogues in, 24–26
   court of Assistants in, 87
   decriminalization of the election crimes by, 28
   democratic elections in, 27–29
   democratic principles in, 5, 22–23, 62
   founders of, 6–7, 19
   freemen in, xi, 14–15, 18–19, 23
   illegal voting in, 28
   impact of assistants in forming of government in, 17
   laws of, xii
   liberal approach for the union of New Hampshire with, 29–30
   Maine under, 68–71
   mixed forms of government in, 14–20
   New Hampshire under, 65–66
   organization of government, 17
   perceptions of officials on the forms of government, 32–33
   power of electors in, 26–27
   religious ministers in, 35
   representative government in, 31–32

rule of law in, 92
surrender of Pemaquid to, 71
theocracy government in, 17, 33–34
towns or plantations in, 91
use of illegal proceeding against
  suspects in, 89
vote by proxy in, 43
Massachusetts Body of Liberties, xiii, 85
Masson, John, 29
Maverick, Samuel, 68
Mayflower Compact, 10, 12, 76
  language of, 7
Mayflower Compact, signers of, xi
Medford, 87
*The Memorial History of Hartford County
  Connecticut* (Trumbull), 45
Middlesex County, 109
Milford
  unification of, 58
  union with New Haven, 6, 56, 58
Mixed forms of government
  in Massachusetts Bay Colony, 14–20
  rule of law in, xii–xiii, 14, 21
Montesquieu, Baron de, 53
Moulton, John, as deputy, 63

Neal, Walter
  as governor of Piscataqua, 62
  management of Strawberry Bank, 62
  as member of king's expedition, 62
New England colonies. *See also specific
  colonies*
  civil liberties in, 6
  cruel and unusual punishment in,
    92–93
  democratic towns in, 5–6
  importance of freeman in, xi
  liberties of settlers in, 74–81
  voting by proxy in, 42
The New England Theocracy (Uhden), 33
New Hampshire
  Code of Governor Cutt in, 65, 80
  death of proprietor of, 60
  democratic principles in, 65
  freemen in, xi, 62

government of, under the royal
  province, 66–67
government under proprietors in,
  61–64
lack of government in, 60
liberal approach for the union of, with
  Massachusetts Bay, 29–30
under Massachusetts Bay, 61–64
mixed form of government in, 60
new settlements in, 61
vote by proxy in, 42
New Haven, 89
  democratic principles in, 39–40, 44, 48
  recording laws in, xiii
  theocracy, aristocracy and democracy
    in, 55–59
  unification of, 58
  union of Milford with, 56
  vote by proxy in, 42
Newman, Robert, 55
New Netherlands, Charles II granting of,
  to James the Duke of York, 71–73
New Plymouth
  consensual system in, 43
  freemen in, 43
  vote by proxy in, 42
Newport, 89
  democratic government in, 37
  settlement of, 78
  unification under Charter of 1643, 38
Newtown, democratic government in, 43
New York, Pemaquid under, 71–72
New Zealand
  prohibition of excessive bail in, 95
Nicholls, Richard, 71
Norfolk County, 65
Northam, settlement of, 61

An Old Mountaineer, 62

Pacific resistance, against arbitrarily
  government policies, 23–24
Paine, William, 64
Palfrey, John G., 75
Palmer, Willi, 63

Pemaquid, 67
   under New York government, 71–72
   surrender to Massachusetts Bay, 73
Personal liberty, 88–89
Personal security, 83–87
Petition of Right, 80
Pettishall, Richard, 71
Pilgrims
   as English citizens, 10
   founding of government by, 5
   identification of James as sovereign Lord, 76
   tolerance of, 8–9
The Pilgrims in their Three Homes England, Holland, America (Griffis), 5
Piscataqua, 29, 65, 66
   Neal, Walter, as governor of, 61
"Plantation Covenant," 54
Plough patent, Rigby's purchase of, 68
Plymouth
   democratic form of government in, 5, 7–11
   differences of Winthrop with, 25
   founders of, as separatists, 6
   franchise system in, 13
   freemen in, 6, 7, 13
   governing of affairs through consensus, 9–10
   judges in civil cases in, 88–89
   jury system in, 14
   observation of the Rule of Law in, 14
   patriarchal government in, 10
   Pilgrims in, 7, 9
   recording laws in, xiii
   religious freedom in, 4, 75
   representative government in, 11
   signers of May Flower Compact in, xi
   submission to colonial laws in, 12
   Williams, Roger, in, 8–9
Ponderson, John, 55
Portsmouth, 66, 67
   democratic government in, 37
   formation of government in, 41
   freemen of, 64
   power to self-govern, 64
   settlement of, 70–71
   unification under Charter of 1643, 38
   unification with Massachusetts Bay, 29–30, 65
   weakness of settlements of, 64
Pound, Roscoe, 84
Preble, Abraham, 68
Proprietors, government under, in New Hampshire, 60–63
Providence, 77, 87
   formation of, 30
   unification under Charter of 1643, 38
Providence Plantations, incorporation of, 39, 77
The Provincial Papers, Documents and Records relating to the Province of New Hampshire, 61
Public Record of Connecticut, 82
The Public Records of the Colony of Connecticut, 47
Puddington, George, 69
Purchase, Thomas, 67
Pure democracy, 6
Puritans
   banishment from Massachusetts Bay, 37
   in Dover Neck, 61

Quakers
   in Connecticut, 9
   elections of, to the executive office in Rhode Island, 42
   mistreatment of, in Plymouth, 9
Quorum, 71

Ratcliff, Philip, 23
A Reading of the Use of Torture in the Criminal Laws of England (Jardine), 94
Records of the Colony of Connecticut, 50
Records of the Colony of Rhode Island and Providence Plantations in New England, 38
Records of the Colony of Rhode Island and Providence Plantations in Rhode Island, 42–43

Records of the Company of the Massachusetts Bay in New England, 19
Records of the Governor and Company of the Massachusetts Bay in New England, 1642-1649, 65
Records of the New Haven Plantation, 55
Religious freedom
    emergence of, 74–75
    Williams, Roger, and, 37
Religious ministers in Massachusetts Bay, 35
Remarks on the Early Laws of Massachusetts Bay (Gray), xii, 17, 79
Representative government, emergence of, in Massachusetts Bay, 31–32
Rhode Island
    as architect of democracy in New England colonies, 36
    charters of, 76, 78
    codification of English liberties, 84
    consensual system in, 43
    democracy in, 5, 37–40
    elections in, 42–43
    engagement of inhabitants in, 41
    franchise system in, 41–42
    freemen in, xi, 17
    law against double jeopardy in, 89
    opposition to theocratic government, 36
    recording laws in, xiii
Richard I, King, 78
Rigby, Alexander
    death of, 70
    purchase of Lyconia, 69
    purchase of Plough patent, 70
Rigby, Alexander (check Rigby), 70
The Rise of Modern Democracy in Old and New England (Borgeaud), 5, 34
The River Towns of Connecticut: A Study of Wethersfield, Hartford, and Windsor (Andrews), 34
Roads, Samuel, Jr., 30
Roberts, Thomas, as governor, 62
Rogers, John, 67
Roxbury, as advocate of democratic principles, 36, 43
Royal government, Maine under, 72–73
Rudlow, Roger, loss of re-election, 26
Rule of law, xi, xi–xiii, 12, 17
    in New England colonies, 74
    in Plymouth, 14

Saco, 68
    freemen as eligible voters in, 27
    inhabitants of, 71
    opening of office at, 67
    tax assessment for, 68
Sagadebock, 66
Salem, 30
    consensual government in, 21
    free election for selection of town officers in, 20
    freemen in, 19
    Williams, Roger, as pastor in, 37
Sales
    migration of women and children to, 62
Salisbury, 65
Saunders, John, 64
Saxons, freedrom of, 78, 80
Say, Lord, 32–33, 62
Schools, establishment of, 74
Scituate, 13, 14
Security, personal, 83–87
Seely, Robert, as plantation marshal, 56
Selden, 94
Separatists, founders of Plymouth as, 6
Settlers, liberties of, in the New England colonies, 76–97
Sharpe, Thomas, 71
Short, Henry, election as selectman, 28
A Short History of Democracy (Hattersley), 49
Simpson, Henry, 67
Skelton, Samuel, election of, 21
Sketches of the Judicial History of Massachusetts from 1630 to the Revolution (Whitmore), xii
Small, Edward, 69

Southhold, unification of, 58
Stackpole, 63
Stamford, unification of, 58
Stephen, King, 82, 87
Stiles, Henry R., 50, 53
    formation of town government in Connecticut, 45
Story, Joseph, 34
Stow, John, 78
Strawberry Bank, 65, 73
    settlement of, 62, 63
Suffolk County, 65
Survey of London (Stow), 78
Swain, Richard, 63

Tacitus, 98
Theocracy government, in Massachusetts Bay, 33–34
Tolerance of Pilgrims, 8–9
Town meetings, xi, 7
Trial by jury, 7
Trumbull, Hammond, 49, 53
    formation of town government in Connecticut, 45, 49
    link of Hooker d=sermons to the writing of the Constitution, 51
Turner, Nathaniel, 56

Uhden, H. F., 33
Underhill, John
    as deputy from Boston to General Court, 63
    disenfranchisement of, 61–62
United Colonies, 9
United States, prohibition of excessive bail in, 93
U.S. Constitution
    Admendment VIII, 95
    Article VI of, 95
Utility, principle of, 92

Vane, Henry, 15, 24, 39
    democratic principles under, 16–17
    leadership of, 25
    loss of election by, 26

Vines, Richard, 68–69
    Maine under, 70
    selling of patent to Child, 69
Vote by proxy in New England colonies, 43

Wakefield, William, as town clerk, 63
Walderne, WilliM, 65
Walker, George Leon, 52–53
Ward, Nathaniel, xiii, 18
Warwick, 76
    unification under Charter of 1643, 38
Warwick, Sir Robert, Earl of, 76–77
Washburn, Emory, xii
Watertown
    as advocate of democratic principles, 36
    democratic government in, 43
    electors in, 26
    freemen in, 19, 25
    paying of taxes and, 36
    refusal to pay taxes, 23
Wells, 68, 70
    freemen as eligible voters in, 27
West, Willis Mason, 34, 36
Wethersfield
    town government in, 45
    unification of, 47
Wheelwright, John, 17, 18
    banishment from Massachusetts, 63
    founding of Exeter by, 63
    religious views of, 36–37
Wiggin, Thomas, 62, 65
    as governor of Dover, 61
Wilcott, Henry, as architect of the Connecticut Fundamental Orders, 53
William, Francis, as governor of Strawberry Bank, 62
Williams, Roger, 18
    as advocate of democratic principles, 37, 38–39
    formation of Providence, 38, 39
    introduction of religious liberties, 75
    as minister, 37

religious liberty and, 36
tolerance and, 8–9
Williams, Thomas, 68
Williamson, William D., 68
Willis, William, 67–68
Wilson, John, 24
Windsor
  town government in, 44
  unification of, 47
Winnacunnet, establishment of
  plantation at, 63
Winter Harbor, 66
Winthrop, John, 17
  abuse of power and, 15–16, 22
  as architect of Massachusetts Bay
    Colony, xii
  codification of Body of Liberties, 80–83
  differences with Connecticut and
    Plymouth, 25
  election as governor, 28
  as executive officer, 34
  favoring of aristocratic form of
    government, 15
  as governor, 61
  policy regarding form of government
    in, 15
  power struggle with Dudley, Thomas,
    24
  supporters of, 25
  support for aristocratic government,
    32–33
Winthrop, John (son)
  power to execute justice under, 91
Winthrop, John, Jr.
  return to England as colony agent, 44
Woldrop, Alexander, 71
Woodbridge, John, election as selectman,
  28
Woodman, Edward, election as
  selectman, 28